THE LAST EMPEROR

THE LAST EMPEROR

by Arnold C. Brackman

Charles Scribner's Sons, New York

PHOTOGRAPH CREDITS

Wide World Photos, Inc.: 1, 9, 11, 12, 13, 14

From *Emperor to Citizen: The Autobiography of Aisin-Gioro Pu Yi* (Peking: Foreign Language Press, 1964): 2, 3, 7, 10, 19, 20, 21, 22

Courtesy of the Smithsonian Institution, Freer Gallery of Art, Washington, D. C.: 4

From *Twilight in the Forbidden City* by Sir Reginald Johnston (New York: Appleton-Century, 1934): 5, 6, 8

Sovfoto: 15

United States Army Photograph: 16

International Military Tribunal for the Far East, Tokyo: 17, 18

Copyright © 1975 Arnold C. Brackman

LIBRARY OF CONGRESS CATALOGING IN PUBLICATION DATA

Brackman, Arnold C
  The last emperor.

  Bibliography: p.
  Includes index.
  1. Ch'ing Hsüan-t'ung, Emperor of China, 1906–1967.
I. Title.
DS773.C518B7   951'.03'0924 [B]   75–1427
ISBN 0–684–14233–3

1 3 5 7 9 11 13 15 17 19 C/C 20 18 16 14 12 10 8 6 4 2

Printed in the United States of America

Voor mams en paps

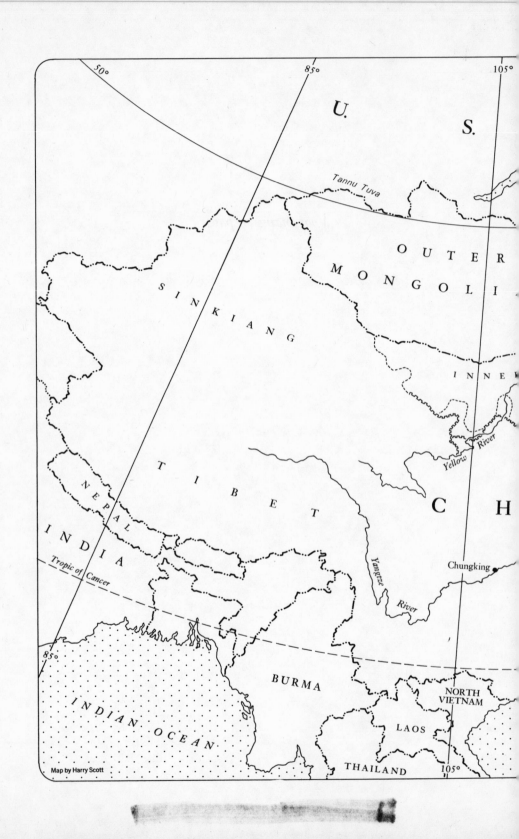

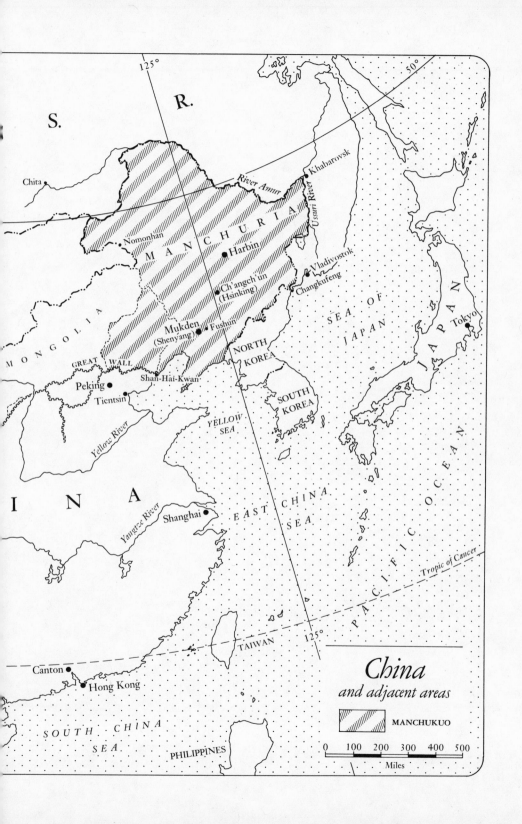

S. R.

S.

Chita

River Amur

Khabarovsk

Nomonhan

M A N C H U R I A

Ussuri River

Harbin

Vladivostok

Ch'angch'un
(Hsinking)

Changkufeng

M O N G O L I A

Mukden
(Shenyang)

Fushun

NORTH
KOREA

GREAT   WALL

Shan-Hai-Kwan

SOUTH
KOREA

SEA OF

JAPAN

Peking

Tientsin

YELLOW
SEA

J A P A N

Tokyo

Yellow River

I N A

Yangtze River

Shanghai

E A S T   C H I N A

S E A

P A C I F I C   O C E A N

Tropic of Cancer

TAIWAN

125°

China
and adjacent areas

Canton

Hong Kong

MANCHUKUO

SOUTH   CHINA

SEA

0   100   200   300   400   500

PHILIPPINES

Miles

Contents

CONTENTS

Preface: The Celestial Prisoner

In 1945, as summer waned, the Soviet armored vehicles bearing the last emperor of China raced across the barren Siberian landscape, which stretched out flat and immense on both sides of the convoy. As the vehicles approached a wood, the road narrowed. The last of the Celestial Emperors was overcome by fear.

"I was terrified," P'u Yi said later.

Stalin was already demanding that Hirohito, the emperor of Japan, be tried as a war criminal. The murder of the Russian royal family during the Bolshevik Revolution twenty-eight years earlier was still fresh in P'u Yi's memory, and in the memory of other monarchs. What kind of treatment could he expect in the hands of Stalin, the architect of what Robert Conquest called "the great terror"?

Suddenly, the convoy rolled to a halt at the edge of the wood.

Through the limousine's mud-streaked windows, P'u Yi saw Red army soldiers, armed with submachine guns, drop to the ground from their trucks. A Soviet officer, in black boots and field grey tunic, approached the emperor's car. The moment of truth neared.

PREFACE

The Red army officer flung open the door of the limousine and pointed to the wood.

"Get out!" he shouted in fluent Chinese, "Get out if you want to take a leak." *

How did the winds of history sweep P'u Yi into such a humiliating situation, he who had twice sat on the Dragon Throne, the Son of Heaven, He Who Is Above, the Enthroned One, the Lord of Ten Thousand Years, The Lord of Myriad Years, the One Who Faces South, the Celestial Emperor, the last Emperor of Cathay, of the Middle Kingdom, of China, of a land which embraces a fourth of mankind?

Bewildered, puzzled, a captive of the foreign devils after a storybook career that had carried him from the Dragon Throne to these Siberian wastes, he probably would have been astounded to learn that he was embarking on still another odyssey. This time he would find himself a prisoner not only of Stalin, but also of MacArthur and Mao Tse-tung. And then at the crest of the Great Proletarian Cultural Revolution he would be swept from the stage of history and mount the dragon to ascend at last to heaven.

* One year after this incident occurred, in 1946, I spent two weeks in the emperor's presence. See "Author's Note," p. 342.

PART I

PRELUDE

CHAPTER 1

The Enthronement

In the winter of 1908 the Austro-Hungarian Empire annexed
Bosnia-Herzegovina and set in motion the train of events which
culminated in World War I. In Peking as that formative year drew
to a close on December 2, an exceptionally cold day, the princes,
mandarins, young noblemen, governors, viceroys, generals, and
other officials of the Celestial Empire gathered at the Hall of
Supreme Harmony in the center of the Violet Enclosure, the sacred
precinct which foreigners called the Forbidden City. This sacred
precinct, "The Great Within," has often been described as the
kernel of a nut protected by a triple shell of walls. The Manchu
Emperor Ch'ien Lung, at the time of the American Revolution,
eloquently called it "the hub and center about which all the quarters
of the globe revolve."

That December the occasion was the ascension to the Dragon
Throne of a new emperor in a line of sovereigns receding to the
very dawn of recorded history and beyond, to the legendary Yellow
Emperor who reigned in 2698 B.C.

Throughout the night and into early morning a stream of

3

fur-lined horse carts, sedan chairs borne by coolie runners, and riders astride muscular Mongolian ponies flowed in a seemingly endless procession through the Gate of Spiritual Valor and into the Violet Enclosure. In the great Heavenly Peace Square in front of the Forbidden City rows of Manchu bannermen stood at parade rest against a field of yellow, white, red, and blue standards, each color denoting a Manchu clan. Peking itself, the seat of the Manchu Empire, was dressed for the investiture. From the rooftops of public and private buildings yellow dynastic streamers flew in the brisk, icy wind as swirls of yellow dust from the Gobi desert wheeled along the city's streets.

The focus of attention was on "the stage of emperors," the Hall of Supreme Harmony, where "all great diplomatic measures and dark deeds are transacted by the Emperor between midnight and daylight." Hastily, the chroniclers of empire add, these decisions are rendered in the middle of night "not because their deeds being evil they loved darkness rather than light but because the emperor was so eager to serve his people that he went about their business even before daybreak."

As the need arose, the hall also served as the enthronement chamber. A cavernous room two hundred feet in length and one hundred feet wide, its ceiling soared more than a hundred feet above the glistening yellow-tiled floor. Painted bright vermillion, the ceiling was adorned with five-clawed golden dragons, symbols of the emperor's power and virility. The great doors to the hall were fashioned from exquisitely carved teak. The eaves were painted red, gold, and green, and five tiers of polished marble terraces girdled the structure. The serpentine, burnished-yellow roof was easily visible to the horizon. From this hall the Son of Heaven ruled over his terrestrial subjects and was accountable alone to heaven for his mandate. Today the building is still in use as the Great Ceremonial Hall to which all roads lead and where the chiefs of state and heads of government of the greater and lesser powers are entertained on their pilgrimages to Peking.

Almost seventy years ago as midnight, the hour selected by the board of astronomers, neared for the grand entrance of the heir to the throne, the hall fell silent. Only the crackling of charcoal braziers violated the stillness of the setting. The princes, viceroys, generals, mandarins, and other military and civilian officials, attired in richly brocaded ceremonial robes with white cranes and yellow pheasants on the front of their coats, their official hats adorned with peacock feathers, red ruby buttons, and other badges of office, quietly assumed their designated places.

As a huge gong was struck, those present bent their knees three times and kowtowed nine times. The new Lord of Myriad Years was being borne into the hall astride a blinding yellow satin chair embroidered with fire-spitting dragons. The ritual of the Great Ceremony of Enthronement commenced. Its highest point came when, in the presence of the assembly, the imperial seal of office, borne by a bodyguard from the Hall of Fusion and Permeation, was handed over to the new emperor. Inscribed in Manchu and Chinese, the seal consisted of eight interlocking pieces of jade of extraordinary luster and purity. According to legend, the jade originally had been found by a peasant who, recognizing its rarity and magical powers, rushed to the Forbidden City to present it to the emperor. The peasant was roughly turned back at the gate. The second time he attempted to gain entrance, his two legs were cut off by the imperial executioner as a lesson to him. Yet the man persisted and, on bloody stumps, dragged himself back to the front gate. When the stone was finally accepted and tested, it broke into three perfect pieces. One was fashioned into the imperial seal, another was presented to Lao Tse, the mystic, who preached the Heavenly Way, and the third piece was given to the venerable sage, Confucius, whose political theory explained the recurring periods of chaos in China out of which a new dynasty always emerged with "a mandate from heaven." As long as a sovereign retained the imperial seal in his possession, he was the undisputed emperor of China.

Once again a signal was given and this time the great hall reverberated to the shout of "*Wan wan sui!* Ten thousand years! *Wan wan sui!*"—the Chinese equivalent of "forever." Outside the

Hall of Supreme Harmony, along the crenelated walls of the Violet Enclosure, the imperial bodyguard, under a cloud of yellow and white banners, raised their halberds and swords in confirmation of the investiture of a new vicar on earth for the Supreme Being, *Shang Ti*. Within the hall, the assembled multitude in unison again bent their knees three times and kowtowed nine times as an act of fealty. By performing this ritual, they pledged their lives, their loyalty, and their fortunes to the new Lord of Ten Thousand Years. In this manner, the tenth Manchu emperor of the Great Pure *(Ta Ch'ing)* Dynasty ascended the golden Dragon Throne.

The gravity, the color and the import of the occasion notwithstanding, the emperor ruined the ceremony by crying. "I found the ceremony long and tiresome," he later explained. "Moreover, it was a very cold day, so that when I was carried into the Hall of Supreme Harmony and placed on the high and enormous Dragon Throne, I could bear it no longer."

During the ceremony, the new emperor was accompanied by his father, the second Prince Ch'un, who kneeled beside the throne and, through his teeth, pleaded with his son not to cry. Among the Manchu there was no law of primogeniture and an emperor chose a successor as he saw fit, sometimes his eldest son or as in this instance the son of a brother. But the newly enthroned emperor struggled for his freedom. "I want to go home," he cried out. "I want to go home."

As the emperor's cries grew louder, Prince Ch'un soothed him. "Soon all will be over," he murmured. "Soon all will be over."

Why did the emperor cry and fidget like a child on receiving the Great Inheritance? The answer is manifest: he was a child. The emperor, who reigned under the title Hsüan Tung—P'u Yi was his personal name—was only three years old. The elevation of a child to the Dragon Throne was not unprecedented. The first Manchu to rule from the Violet Enclosure was placed on the throne at the age of six and his successor, the famed K'ang Hsi, was also enthroned at six and assumed personal control of the empire at the age of thirteen.

Still the court officials within hearing distance of this exchange were shaken. The story of this brief dialogue flew across the Hall of Supreme Harmony and swept through Peking's teahouses like the dust storms which periodically whirl through the streets of the capital. What did the emperor mean when he said he wanted to "go home?" What did his father mean when he replied that it will "soon be over"?

Gloomily, in hushed tones, the Manchu nobility and the Chinese and Mongolian officials who served alongside them analyzed the incident. Reluctantly, they concluded that the exchange between father and son, regent and emperor, was a bad omen. As the emperor later wrote in his memoirs, "They knew that the real premonition of impending disaster did not come from these two phrases." They knew, as did others, that the Great Pure Dynasty of the Manchu, which had ruled without interruption for almost three centuries, was no longer great nor pure. The empire was a shambles, tottering on collapse. Indeed, it was widely whispered within and without the Violet Enclosure that the dynasty was gradually losing the mandate of heaven. The rot was visible everywhere. The empire had been repeatedly humbled by the foreign devils. Worse, it had been humiliated by its smaller neighbor, Japan, the country of semibarbarians. Just as the Japanese defeat of Russia was the outward cause of the first Russian revolution in 1905, so the Japanese defeat of China in 1895 was the outward agent for spreading anti-Manchu sentiment in China. Outside the Great Within, among the revolutionary secret societies, the child's cries were greeted joyously as a good omen, as a sign that all would soon be over for the dynasty; the alien Manchu rulers of China would "go home" to their Manchurian borderlands along the Sino-Russian frontier.

CHAPTER 2

The Rise of the Manchu

When P'u Yi ascended the Dragon Throne, the Manchu had occupied the Forbidden City for 244 years. But the rise of Manchu power had its origin much earlier, as early as the close of the sixteenth century.

At that time the celebrated Ming Dynasty was in the process of disintegration. The Celestial Empire was racked by the telltale signs of a dynasty in decline—brigandage and warlordism, that periodic Chinese phenomenon in which a general, bandit or landowner establishes a private army and proclaims a slice of territory his own. Drought parched the millet and rice fields. The peasants scratched the earth for subsistence. Tribute from Thailand, Burma, Malacca, and other vassal states evaporated. South Vietnam shed Peking's domination and declared its independence. The Ming armies were scattered. In the north, they successfully repelled an invasion of their lands in Korea by the upstart Japanese. In the south, they struggled incessantly to stamp out insurgency. Though harvests were poor, the Ming raised taxes to finance their military operations, generating a new current of unrest. Rapidly, the Ming lost the respect, confidence, and support of the countryside. In the teahouses and marketplaces, it was said that the dynasty was losing the mandate of heaven. Nobody could rule China without it.

Decadence at the imperial court hastened the Ming decline. Within the sacred Inner City of Peking the emperor was the only normal male in residence—the obverse of a beehive. Surrounded solely by drones—women and eunuchs—the emperor exhausted his vitality. The women ran the gamut from wives, consorts, concubines, and widows of former emperors to 2,000 female servants, including housekeepers, cooks, *amahs* (nursemaids) and seductive sing-song girls in brocaded gowns. As for the eunuchs, these "rats and foxes" of the Forbidden City numbered 3,000. They bore the emperor's sedan chair, served as bodyguards, worked as custodians, ran the imperial household, played the role of royal procurers, and held numerous official positions within the administration.

At different periods in Chinese history, the "fawning sycophants," as they were also called with both contempt and envy, accumulated only slightly less power than the emperor. This was particularly true of the chief eunuch.

If an emperor mounted the Dragon Throne in childhood, as was often the case, he was raised in a suffocating environment of women, eunuchs, and tutors. Frequently, the impact on his psyche was devastating. In the isolation of the Violet Enclosure, where his every whim was a command from heaven, the emperor's moral fiber, manliness and strength of character were drained. The imperial life-style was self-destructive. Rarely was an emperor strong enough to rise above the debauchery of the court; in the Manchu era only two did so, Ch'ien Lung and K'ang Hsi. The latter's effort was no mean feat: with his active harem life, he produced thirty-five sons.

In many respects, Chinese imperial history is a register in which the rising influence of the eunuchs coincided with the declining fortunes of a dynasty. Decadence was the death mask of every dynasty.

As the decline of the Ming unfolded, a new and formidable

military power emerged among the Tartar or "dog" people of the north, as the Chinese called them. These people lived in garrison towns hewn from the forests along the Black Dragon River, or Amur River, which today partly serves as a boundary line between China and the Soviet Union. Seminomadic, they farmed virgin land for six or seven years and then moved on to plow new fields. They raised wheat, millet, and barley; cooked their food in sesame oil; and lighted their thatched homes with flax candles. Their horses, oxen, cattle, and chickens shared their living room. They kept slaves and were polygamous, some men possessing as many as ten wives. Coarse and earthy, they were destined to inherit and rule over the most complex and refined civilization of its day.

The Chinese sought to keep them at bay and built the Great Wall for that purpose. According to Chinese poets, that stupendous feat of engineering was the only work of man clearly visible on earth from the moon. The Wall commenced at Shan Hai Kwan (Mountain Sea Gate), a port on the Yellow Sea, and stretched inland like a dragon's tail for almost 2,000 miles into the wasteland of the Gobi desert. Built in the course of centuries, by forced laborers, prisoners of war and common criminals, the foundation stone was laid in 221 B.C. at a time when Hannibal crossed the Alps. The Wall took 700-million man-days to complete. Forty-foot towers lined it every two hundred yards. "The Great Wall," an imperial soothsayer forecast, "will not be completed until 10,000 men are buried beneath it." His estimate was on the conservative side.

In strategic terms, the Wall was an equestrian trap. Tartar military strength lay in the saddle. The Wall effectively limited the maneuverability of cavalry. Only once did the Tartars succeed in outflanking it and, as a consequence, Genghis Khan conquered China. But the Khans' rule was short-lived and the Ming who displaced them promptly extended the Wall deeper into the desert and then at right angles to preclude it ever again being outflanked. In total length, under the Ming, the Wall stretched 3,000 miles. Even in the twilight years of Ming power, the Great Wall admirably served its purpose and held the Mongols and their Tartar cousins, the Manchu, in check.

For more than two centuries the Ming emperors played the game of divide and rule north of the Wall with devastating results. They pitted one Tartar clan against another. A few taels of silver, a tandem of ponies, a dozen brocaded dragon robes, a few pieces of jade, were usually enough to retain the loyalty of a clan or to turn one clan against another. But as the sixteenth century ended, a solitary figure emerged out of the welter of warring tribal leaders and earned the name of "The Dragon and Tiger General."

A member of the Aisin-Gioro (gold) clan of the Ju-chen Tartars, he pulled the warring factions together, and welded the clans into the most powerful military machine in Asia since the days of Genghis Khan. Under the leadership of Nurhachu (variously spelled Nurhachi, Nurhacha), the 5-million Tungusic-speaking people along the Amur River extended their realm from the Yellow Sea in the east to the Gobi in the west. In effect, Nurhachu overran the area north of China's Great Wall. Korea and Mongolia recognized him as their suzerain, and his tribal banners flew the length and breadth of the Manchurian plain. But the Great Wall blocked Nurhachu's southward expansion, although on occasion a war party breeched the Chinese line. Once the Manchu horsemen even poured south to gaze on the shimmering golden rooftops of the Forbidden City, in the heart of Peking, before retreating to their sanctuary north of the Wall.

Nurhachu's strength lay in a disciplined military organization, a dedicated feudal administration, and a devoted entourage. Following a Mongol precedent, he organized the clans into eight "banners." Each banner, headed by a prince directly responsible to Nurhachu, raised its own army of 7,200 men. Each banner was a highly mobile, armored striking force composed of lancers and archers, supported by its own supply train, administrative units, engineering companies (to man scaling ladders and catapults), and other auxiliary forces. At each level of command, the men fought with a sense of unity, purpose, and invincibility. Individualism was discouraged; initiative

11

ignored; valor scorned. The bannermen fought set-piece battles, and won every battle they fought. On three occasions north of the Great Wall they defeated Ming armies which outnumbered them as much as ten to one.

Astride their Mongolian ponies, wrapped in seal-lined mail, with streamers adorning their lances, broad-edged swords dangling from their camel-hide saddles, endlessly drilled, the bannermen struck terror into the hearts of their adversaries. The three superior banners, which fought under Nurhachu's personal direction, flew standards of yellow, white, and yellow with white trim. The five inferior banners flew standards of red, red trimmed with white, white trimmed with red, blue, and blue trimmed with white.

As Nurhachu's control spread, he adopted for himself and his clansmen the name *Manchu*, the Masters. And as far as the eye could see, in every direction except southward, where the rising watch-towers of the Great Wall blocked their vision, the Manchu lived up to their name. They were the masters.

In 1616 Nurhachu proclaimed himself *T'ien Ming*, the Heavenly Appointed Emperor. "I announced to heaven and earth," he solemnly declared at a conference of the Manchu Grand Council, "that we have assumed the dynastic title of *Ta Ch'ing*, the Great Pure Dynasty." In this manner, the Ch'ing—or as it is popularly called in the West, the Manchu—dynasty was born. Nurhachu's 365,000 square mile domain was called Manchuria, the land of the Manchu. For political reasons, to this very day, the Chinese assiduously avoid using the term; to do so implies that Manchuria is not Chinese but Manchu. Instead, the Chinese insist on calling Manchuria the "three eastern provinces" (Kirin, Fengtien, and Heilungkiang).

The news was spread by swift couriers. In the hamlets from Mongolia to Korea, and in the tents of the bannermen, there was great feasting and love-making to celebrate the founding of a new dynasty. As the Heavenly Appointed Emperor reviewed his army, his troops cheered him as *T'ai Tsung*, the Exalted Founder.

Shortly thereafter, the new emperor established his capital of

Mukden, in the Manchurian heartland. With an eye to the future, the Exalted Founder dryly observed that Mukden "is a position from which the Chinese frontier can be readily reached in the event of trouble; it lies on the road to Korea; and Mongolia is within two days striking distance." Mukden became the strategic center of Manchu power.

With the consolidation of his empire, the new emperor offered the Ming a liberal arrangement, China's partition. He proposed the creation of "two nations so that we can dwell side by side in peace for ten thousand years." But Nurhachu wanted peace on his terms. He proposed dividing China at the Yellow River, which is located south of the Great Wall. He made no effort at subtlety. The Manchu wanted to control both sides of the Great Wall, the Wall itself. "All northern Manchuria has submitted to me," the Exalted Founder wrote to the Ming emperor on a silk scroll. "Even the descendents of your Mongol emperors and the sovereign of the Hermit Kingdom have recognized my supremacy in the north." In effect, he told the Ming: "Be reasonable, do it my way." Of course, it is possible that Nurhachu, negotiating from strength, made the offer as a bargaining counter and may have settled for the Wall itself as a man-made demarcation line between the two empires.

Yet as long as the Wall held the Manchu at arm's length, the Ming emperors could afford the luxury of ignoring Nurhachu's proposal. If the status quo had remained, it is very likely that two separate and powerful states would have emerged along the East Asian rimland, China and Manchuria. But rising brigandage within China proper took its toll. "The passing of each day," Nurhachu's counselors observed, "lessens the power of the Ming and increases the power of the Manchu."

The crunch came in 1644 in a manner neither side foresaw. In a brazen assault that memorable year in China's history, one of the warlords stormed Peking. The debilitated Ming emperor, deserted by his myrmidons, hanged himself in the classic tradition with a silken yellow cord. The rebels overran the Forbidden City and turned Peking into an abattoir. Mandarins were tortured into surrendering their hidden valuables and then beheaded, their wives and daughters were gang-raped and their small children hurled down wells. For a time Peking's wells were so stuffed with bodies that the capital suffered a water shortage.

The Ming emperor's suicide stunned the commander-in-chief of the imperial armies who was then in the south putting down yet another warlord. "The sad tidings of the death of my Lord of Ten Thousand Years reached me at camp while I was hurrying north," he wrote. "Heaven was rent and the earth shaken by this catastrophic event. The waves of the sea wept in unison. The trees withered on the hill."

These sentiments were echoed by the veteran commander of the Ming garrison at Shan Hai Kwan, the critical Mountain Sea Gate at the eastern end of the Great Wall. In an act of desperation and anguish, he invited the Manchu bannermen into China to liberate Peking from the bandit horde, to avenge the death of the emperor, and, at a more personal level, to assist him in recovering his favorite concubine, who was held captive in the capital. The bannermen streamed unopposed into China, drove rapidly on Peking and routed the rebels. The commander recovered his mistress, was rewarded with a hereditary title and rich lands.

The Manchu were certain that the mandate of heaven had slipped from Ming hands. They ordered the Ming nobles to repair to Peking and do obeisance before the Manchu throne. The Manchu had come to stay.

With Peking firmly under their control, the bannermen moved south. "Take no innocent life, carry off no man's wife and family, nor any wearing apparel, and loot not to excess nor plunder stores of grain except when required," the bannermen were admonished. Atrocities, they were told, violated the humane principles which inspired the creation of the new Ch'ing Dynasty.

"Loot not to excess and plunder only as required" was a phrase which pointedly exposed the hollowness of this memorial from the Dragon Throne. Like so many edicts, it was propaganda in an age before the word was invented. In truth, the bannermen cut a swath of terror on their march south with the deliberate purpose of instilling fear and respect into the hearts of their new subjects. Outnumbered as they were by more than one hundred to one, they made terror an integral element in their strategy of conquest. Tens of thousands of persons were murdered pitilessly. Nanking fell. Wuchang, Hangchow, and Hankow, the so-called Wuhan cities. Then the coastal ports. Finally, Canton, the home of the traditionally independent-minded Cantonese. Six years after they drove the rebels from the Violet Enclosure, the Manchu, "The Masters," were the masters of China.

The Manchu were as adept at administration as at war. In China, they retained the Confucian concept of government almost intact. Their code of laws was largely a reissue of the Ming code. The Chinese system of official examinations was not only maintained but also strengthened. The highest officials of the Ming regime were retained in office.

Confucius wrote that when barbarians enter China they become Chinese. Superficially, the Manchu adopted Chinese customs and mores. To the outsider—to the Chinese—they became more Chinese than the Chinese, more Confucian than the Confucianists. Shrewdly, they encouraged the study of the Chinese sages and thereby strengthened their hold on the bureaucracy which they inherited.

"The wheel of the world has turned," the Manchu proclaimed. "The decline and fall of the Ming has opened the way for a new dynasty. The Ming have lost the mandate of heaven. By heaven's design, a new emperor has conquered China." This was the Confucian language their new subjects could appreciate.

But the Manchu became Chinese by cold calculation. In matters of raw power, they remained aloof, privileged, and distinct from the people they ruled. Elitists, they became, to use Milovan Djilas's expression in another context, China's "new class." Their subjects were aware of it. Until the last day of the Manchu Dynasty, the Chinese considered them, for all their Chinese veneer, alien rulers.

The Manchu preserved their elitist rule in a variety of ways. Intermarriage between Manchu and Chinese was barred. Manchu were raised bilingually, retaining their clan language while outrivaling native Chinese in their command of the Chinese language. Manchu women retained their mode of dress; they did not bind their feet as Chinese women did. For a time the Manchu princes debated whether or not to retain the unique Manchu headdress, the queue. Finally, by imperial edict, the Manchu demanded that Chinese males, as a symbol of loyalty and allegiance to the new dynasty, shave part of their head and grow the queue or pigtail, as it was later derisively called by foreigners.

The Manchu recognized that power grew from the tips of their lances and the strings of their bows. Bannermen were stationed at strategic locations throughout the empire. Manchu cantonments were established in large cities with special sections walled off as their private preserve, a self-created ghetto. Thus, even today, a walled area in Peking is still known as the Tartar City.

Although the Manchu raised eight new banners, recruiting Mongolian and Chinese subjects to fill the ranks, the Manchu did not integrate their banners with those of their subjects. The Manchu troops were admonished "never to forget the art of mounted archery," a lesson, they learned so well that they continued to practice archery into the nineteenth century when it was already apparent that power, as Mao Tse-tung would later put it, grew out of the barrel of a gun. By then, however, the bannermen were reduced largely to ceremonial functions like the Beefeaters on guard today at the Tower of London.

Thus, in matters of marriage, language, and military affairs, the Manchu remained by choice a separate and distinct group. Until the end of their Ch'ing or Great Pure Dynasty, the Manchu considered themselves alien conquerors, despite their boast of being more Chinese than the Chinese.

Even before their conquest of China, the Manchu attributed the Ming decline to debauchery, especially to the corrupting influence of the eunuchs. "The Ming lost their empire," a Manchu chronicler wrote, "because of wine and women." Thus the abolition of the eunuch system was among the first measures adopted by the Manchu on ascending the Dragon Throne. The eunuchs, 100,000 in number at the time of the Ming collapse, were summarily restored to their original role as court menials. Under penalty of the bamboo lash and the executioner's ax, they were barred from holding official positions, engaging in public matters, or exercising authority in any way.

But the reform was short-lived. The eunuchs offered too many pleasures as procurers. Life within the Forbidden City was too enticing. The eunuch system was gradually restored. By the nineteenth century, the eunuchs had regained the formidable power they had exercised under the Ming Dynasty. Although there were limits set to their numbers and functions during the late years of the Manchu Dynasty, by the early twentieth century their number had risen to more than 3,000.

The duties of the eunuchs were extensive. In addition to being in attendance at all hours, according to the Book of Palace Regulations, their tasks included the transmission of imperial edicts, receiving memorials to the throne, and arranging for audiences with the Son of Heaven. They handled official documents, and received money and grain sent by treasuries in the provinces. They maintained a fire watch within the Forbidden City; operated the imperial library; performed custodial duties; maintained the palace guard; policed the imperial art collection, which included not only masterpieces but all *vertu*; kept the court records; burned incense before portraits of the deceased and the tutelary gods; guarded the imperial seal; recorded the history of the dynasty; maintained the gardens of the Forbidden City; performed housekeeping chores; cut the emperor's hair; prepared medicinal remedies; flogged offending eunuchs and dealt out punishments with bamboo rods to serving women; recited the classics and put on entertainments for the emperor; and performed Chinese classical operas, which required a falsetto voice that was ostensibly enhanced by castration. And when a child ascended the Dragon Throne, as the young P'u Yi did in 1908, his upbringing was almost completely in their charge.

Despite the removal of their testicles, some eunuchs retained their sexual desire; others sublimated their frustration with careers as torturers or executioners. Some of the chief eunuchs to the emperors lived outside the Forbidden City in magnificent mansions in the style of a warlord with several concubines and a host of female servants. For pleasure, they were known on occasion to beat their concubines or servants to death. But they were beyond the authority of the law.

Palace eunuchs fell into two principal categories: first those in direct attendance on the empress dowager, the emperor, and the empress and the imperial consorts; and second, all the others, the "eunuchs of the presence." Eunuchs were strictly graded and were divided roughly into chief eunuchs, head eunuchs, and ordinary eunuchs. In the Manchu court, there were nine grades of officials. Each wore a "button" denoting rank. Officials of the highest grade, the first rank, wore a red button, an egg-shaped ruby. They were never eunuchs; the highest rank ever accorded a eunuch was the second grade.

The official salaries of the eunuchs were low, with the very highest being 8 taels of silver, 8 catties of rice, and one string of 300 copper coins a month. With various legal and illegal "extras," however, their actual incomes were far higher, particularly for eunuchs of the senior grade. "Squeeze" or corruption was organized. Requests for an audience with the emperor passed through the eunuchs and many a viceroy or governor paid heavily to "bask in the glory of the Son of Heaven." But the life of the ordinary, ungraded, humbler eunuchs was hard. They ate poorly and were regularly beaten. In old age they lived on a meager imperial bounty, and if they were driven out of the Forbidden City as a punishment, they looked forward to a future of begging and starvation.

Princess Der Ling, a member of the Manchu nobility who lived for two years within the Forbidden City between 1903 and

of Divine Repose. She was deposited, naked, at the foot of the emperor's bed. The following morning, the eunuch reentered the bedchamber and made a notation of the name of the girl and the hour of sexual intercourse as best as could be determined. Then the eunuch whisked the girl, draped in her red cloak, back to her apartment.

This *Penthouse-Playboy* fantasy scene had political overtones. The custom of depositing a naked woman at the imperial bedside was inaugurated during the Ming Dynasty after a concubine, summoned to the emperor's suite, secreted beneath her brocaded gown a silken yellow cord. During the night, she tried to strangle the Son of Heaven, unsuccessfully, as it turned out. Similarly, the chronicle of the emperor's love-life was maintained in case a pregnancy ensued. Presumably the authenticity of the child's blood line could then be easily proven.

In 1852, for the first time a girl from the Yhe branch of the Aisin-Gioro clan was introduced into the Violet Enclosure among the concubines, a girl named Yehnola. She scarcely made it, receiving the rank of concubine third-grade. Earlier, the sixteen-year-old girl had fallen in love with a Manchu garrison commander, Jung Lu, and looked forward to marrying him. But the summons to the Chamber of the Divine Repose preempted all other possibilities. Yehnola felt honored, if not preordained, and entered the Forbidden City that summer in a spirit of great expectation. She had cause for optimism. Her jade tablet was turned over more often than those of the other concubines.

Of all his wives, consorts, and concubines, Yehnola alone bore the emperor a son. In China, the birth of a boy is proclaimed by sending relatives, friends, and associates red-colored eggs. This was to be the last time the eggs were colored red during the reign of a Manchu monarch.

With the emergence of an heir apparent, Yehnola, or Tzu Hsi (Kindly and Virtuous) to use her court name, was promptly raised to concubine first-grade. Twelve months later, after the boy survived his first year, she was elevated to the rank of secondary consort and awarded the title of Empress of the Western Palace. In this role, she won the emperor's confidence and soon became expert in proffering advice on affairs of state. Before his death, the emperor had come to rely on her judgment in important official matters. He had also come to fear her. She was, he felt, too ambitious, too aggressive, too shrewd, too domineering. He was also mindful of a curse that had been pronounced on the house of Aisin-Gioro, a curse that reads like something drawn from the libretto of a Verdi opera. At the time Nurhachu founded the Manchu Empire, an oracle which few took seriously, had proclaimed that a female of the Yhe clan—which Nurhachu subdued—would bring about the fall of the Manchu. She would rise to power at the Manchu court and, so the tale went, lead the Manchu to their doom. Tzu Hsi was the first Yhe woman admitted to the court. She prepared for the day she would assume control of the empire as empress dowager. Of that event she never doubted. Nor did she have long to wait. Dissipated, Hsien Feng soon died. He "mounted the dragon and ascended to heaven" at the age of thirty-four.

Tzu Hsi was ready to shoulder the affairs of state, but she came perilously close to losing the game on the first roll. Just before his death, the emperor, in accordance with dynastic law, openly designated his son as heir apparent and named eight regents to act on the child's behalf until he reached a majority. Secretly, he prepared an edict which authorized the regents to eliminate Tzu Hsi, as necessary, if she interfered in the conduct of state affairs. In death he assumed the courage he lacked in life.

Through the eunuchs, whom she assiduously cultivated as her influence broadened within the Violet Enclosure, Tzu Hsi learned of the secret decree, and, in a maneuver which was a measure of the risk she was prepared to accept in pursuit of absolute power, she contrived to destroy it. During the elaborate arrangements for Hsien Feng's funeral, Tzu Hsi and the regents engaged in an intense struggle for power. With Jung Lu, her childhood sweetheart and his bannermen at her side, she won the day. On gaining control of the throne, her first decree was to order the arrest and decapitation of all her opponents. As the heads rolled, one of the most remarkable women in history moved onto center stage.

Autocratic, cunning, ruthless, superstitious, ignorant, opportunistic and, above all, ambitious, she lusted for ever greater power. Within and outside the Forbidden City, she was feared. "Hear and obey!" she hissed or snarled as the occasion demanded. And the empire trembled. Of all the dynastic rulers of China, she is perhaps the best known in the West. Her career was more or less contemporary with that of another great empress, Victoria, whom Tzu Hsi frequently boasted she would outlive—and she did. Victoria died in 1901 at the age of eighty-five; Tzu Hsi died seven years later at the age of seventy-three.

Tzu Hsi's reign encompassed the most humiliating period of China's modern history, including the empire's critical, agonizing confrontation with the West. This confrontation ran far deeper than a political struggle. It was a clash between China and the pitiless actuality of the industrial revolution, between Cathay's dream world and the real world.

In the West, the empress dowager was alternately compared to Cleopatra, Elizabeth, Catherine, and Victoria. A better comparison would be with Clytemnestra, Lucrezia Borgia, or Lady Macbeth. From the crown to the toe, Tzu Hsi was top-full of the direst cruelty, unsexed, remorseless. Her milk was gall.

As empress dowager, she was the power behind the throne for three emperors: her son, her nephew, and her grand-nephew, P'u Yi, dominating the regents who ostensibly held power. Each regency was manipulated with a view to maintaining her absolute control. Her achievement was remarkable, given the nature of male-dominated Chinese society. A woman ruling China, in the words of a Chinese writer, is as absurd as a hen crowing at dawn. Yet there was precedent; indeed, in China, the oldest self-governing state in the world, there is always a precedent, or so it seems. During the T'ang Dynasty, during Europe's Dark Ages, an empress dowager assumed control of the government, staged a coup d'etat and usurped the throne. She proclaimed herself empress and ruled for fifteen years. Although Tzu Hsi reinterpreted many of the dynastic laws of the Manchu to suit her own purposes, she was never able to short-circuit the house law that only a male, a prince of the blood, could rule the clans.

For all her vaunted ambition, Tzu Hsi climbed to the apex of a crumbling pyramid. By now the Manchu Dynasty had acquired the characteristics of the Ming in the last years of their decline. Once again the eunuchs were in ascendancy, and their influence expanded under the empress dowager who possessed no trustworthy ally in the empire except for them and Jung Lu, her lover, whom she had conveniently appointed a grand councillor shortly after her son's enthronement. In this guise, and as viceroy and commander of the North Army, which later became the core of China's modern military machine, Jung Lu remained at her side through the years, a source of immeasurable personal and political strength, the foremost commander of the bannermen. To squelch rumors, she selected a wife for him; but even this gesture did not still the gossip of the court.

The ascendancy of the eunuchs signaled the revival of corruption and graft on the massive scale. Tzu Hsi squandered the treasury on the frills of power—jewelry, brocades, lavish banquets, and palaces. Funds set aside to build a modern navy of iron-clad, steam-driven warships, so desperately needed to repel foreign encroachment, were rechanneled into building a new summer palace, a Disneyland of artificial lakes and marble boats.

The rot within China surfaced with internal rebellions and external pressures. As Tzu Hsi matured, the empire was rocked by revolt: the Tai Ping (Great Peace) Rebellion, which belied its name, once claimed millions of lives; and the Boxer Rebellion at the turn of the century, which was encouraged by the empress in an insane attempt to drive the foreign devils into the sea and return China to the splendor and seclusion it had once enjoyed. The Western European nations continually wrested rights of extraterritoriality from the Celestial Empire. Legalisms aside, extraterritoriality meant that China lost a degree of sovereignty. Ultimately, whole sections of Chinese cities were transformed into "international settlements" on a pattern similar to the Allied occupation of Berlin after World War II.

But the Western encroachment paled by comparison to the grand designs of the Russians and Japanese. For them, history had come full circle.

When the Manchu conquered China, the Japanese had been confined to their home islands, after having failed to conquer Korea and Manchuria. The Russians, similarly humiliated, were forced to retreat north of the Amur River. But in the nineteenth century the humbling of China by Britain and France convinced the Russians and the Japanese that the dragon no longer breathed fire. St. Petersburg and Tokyo returned to the carving table.

The Russians resumed their southward push from Siberia toward the Manchurian plain and the warm water ports of the Pacific Ocean. In 1858, as Tzu Hsi consolidated her position within the Forbidden City, the Manchu bowed to Russian pressure and by the terms of the Treaty of Aigun handed over to the Czar all the territory north of the Amur. The Russians also won joint control over the region east of the Ussuri, a strategic area bordering the Pacific. Two years later their appetites whetted, the Russians returned and asked for more. The condominium was dissolved and Russia gained control over the lands east of the Ussuri, including the site of the present-day Vladivostok, the capital of the Soviet Union's maritime province, the site of the Ford-Brezhnev summit talks in 1974.

Adopting Western technology, imitating the political style of her Western mentors, the Japanese joined the game. In 1895 Japan stunned Asia and the West by declaring war on China and routing the Chinese on the land and the sea. In a struggle between the elephant and the flea, the flea won. As a result, the Celestial Empire lost first Korea and then Taiwan. China had acquired Taiwan with the rise of the Manchu; now with their decline, Taiwan was lost.

But Korea and Taiwan were only appetizers. Above all, Japan coveted the main course—Manchuria, with its surplus food production, underpopulated areas, and huge storehouses of industrial raw materials. The Japanese demanded a sphere of influence in the region. But Japan was still a newcomer to the great power pack. Russia, France, and Germany interceded on behalf of China and the Japanese retreated. As it developed, the European powers were more interested in disciplining upstart Japan and filling their own platters, than in befriending China. If anything, the Japanese triumph of arms exposed China's weakness as never before.

With Japan on probation, the Great Powers once again turned their attention to China. As compensation for protecting China from the rapacious Japanese, the French demanded and received additional territory in Vietnam. Vietnam had been a protectorate of China, beginning around 1860. The French systematically lopped off piece after piece, consolidating Cochin, Annam, Tonkin, Cambodia, and Laos into French Indochina. Britain demanded and received additional Burmese territory. The Russians demanded and received permission to build a railroad, the Chinese Eastern, across Manchuria and, better still, the right to exercise extraterritoriality in the corridor over which the line passed. The Russians also secured a twenty-five year lease on a Manchurian harbor, Port Arthur, and the strategic Liaotung peninsula, as well as the right to build another railroad linking Port Arthur with their Manchurian line. Both lines, of course, were tied into the newly opened Trans-Siberian, which stretched from St. Petersburg on the Gulf of Finland to Vladivostok on the Sea of Japan, an accomplishment in that era no less awesome than the building of the Great Wall in a previous one. Patently, the Russians were in a race with Japan for control of Manchuria. Like Nurhachu before them, they recognized it as a strategic heartland that could dominate Korea, Mongolia, and China.

The Germans, belatedly emerging in search of a place in the sun, also made demands on the demoralized Manchu. Berlin acquired the Chinese port of Tsingtao and 200 square miles of adjacent territory, in addition to railroad and mining rights. On this note, the British returned to the carving table and acquired a lease on 375 square miles of territory on the Chinese mainland opposite

Hong Kong, which they had acquired in the 1840s. This in turn prompted France to refill its platter and the French carved out 200 square miles of territory in Kwangtung Province, also on the South China coast. During these open territorial raids, the Americans were conspicuously absent.

By the turn of the nineteenth century, as the power of the Manchu ebbed, China was in the process of being partitioned. Tzu Hsi, the ruler of the empire, was unable to stem the tide. Fulfilling the ancient prophecy, she was leading the Manchu to their doom.

CHAPTER 4

In the Wings

From the outset of Tzu Hsi's first regency, there was little doubt who governed the Celestial Empire. Her young son, Tung Chih was trained to parrot his mother's words. A bamboo screen was erected behind the throne. The child was placed on the throne to conduct official business. An official, bending the knee three times and kowtowing nine times, delivered his report. From behind the screen, Tzu Hsi rendered a decision and the child, trained to repeat her words, recited his lines, a member of the court recalled, "with all the accuracy of the thoroughly trained parrot."

Tzu Hsi also prepared for the day her son reached his majority at seventeen. She personally selected a wife and four concubines for him. With his marriage, of course, the regency ended, but in China, under the Confucian code of filial piety, blending respect for elders with ancestor worship, a son, no matter his rank, had to honor his mother. Although he was emperor in name, Tung Chih deferred to his mother in important matters. She chose to exercise her prerogatives.

With five wives, the young emperor was far too preoccupied

30

with the ecstasies of life to devote more than casual attention to state affairs. Dissipated, ravaged by venereal disease, he died at the age of nineteen, two years after he mounted the Dragon Throne.

Tung Chih's favorite concubine was pregnant at the time. If she gave birth to a male, the child would inherit the throne as emperor-designate and the concubine would displace Tzu Hsi as empress dowager.

Determined to maintain her authority, Tzu Hsi plotted several moves ahead, like a chess master. She suggested to the distraught girl that she follow her husband. "Your husband loved you," the mother-in-law said. "He would wish you to be with him. So completely did Tzu Hsi dominate the people around her that her lightest verbal aside was tantamount to an imperial command. The young girl took the hint and committed suicide.

With the concubine's body still warm, the empress dowager selected the four-year-old son of her own sister, who had married a brother of Hsien Feng as heir apparent. The Manchu nobles recognized this deft maneuver as a power play but were unable to stop her. Shortly after the boy was enthroned under the reign title of Kuang Hsu (Bright Order), his mother conveniently died. Thus, Tzu Hsi successfully bridged the gap from one reign to another, retaining the power and rank of dowager empress.

With a grotesque sense of planning, the new emperor Kuang Hsu was raised solely by eunuchs and, as a result of their ministrations, he developed strong homosexual tendencies. Nor did this set a precedent. At various periods in Chinese court history, homosexuality was not uncommon.

Tzu Hsi dominated the boy personally. As he matured, the emperor so feared his aunt that he always stammered in her presence. Before he reached his majority he developed a permanent stutter. When the emperor turned seventeen, the dowager empress again played the role of marriage broker. She chose a wife and two concubines for him. Impotent or disinterested, or both, he remained childless.

With Kuang Hsu's enthronement in 1888, the empress

dowager's second regency ended. Officially, she retired and withdrew to the summer palace, situated about six miles west of the Forbidden City. But the emperor was so indecisive, weak, and sickly that he constantly turned to her for advice, and, in effect, Tzu Hsi continued to govern the empire. Though the foreign devils were at the gate, the empress dowager was preoccupied with the never-ending consolidation of her personal power.

In the first years of his reign, Kuang Hsu regularly visited the summer palace for instructions. But seven years later, China's defeat at the hands of the inferior Japanese in the war of 1895 was so shattering an experience that it shook even Kuang Hsu from submissiveness, lethargy, and torpor. He responded to the humiliation as an emperor, in a manner which surprised his aunt and almost every observer of the China scene. The pathetic, plastic figure was suddenly transformed into a daring, imaginative, and articulate ruler. He shed the make-believe wonderland of the Forbidden City for the reality of the world outside, and he read the future.

"We are in a crisis," he declared in a memorial from the throne, "where we are beset on all sides by powerful neighbors who craftily seek advantage from us and who are trying to combine their strength in overpowering us. Our neighbors see our defensive preparations in a state of neglect and decay and our fleet small and insignificant. In our opinion, therefore, the need of the day is that we begin reforming ourselves and diligently reorganize our defenses."

His words jolted the empire. Like his predecessors, he breathed "the dragon's fire."

The Celestial Empire, he declared, must abandon "bigoted conservatism and obsolete and unpractical customs." In terms astonishing for a Son of Heaven, the emperor declared: "We must select subjects of Western knowledge that will keep us in touch with the times and diligently study them and practice them in order to place our country abreast of other countries."

Influenced largely by a small group of reformers from southern

China, the emperor launched his Hundred Days of Reform. "Hear and obey!" he admonished his subjects. Unless China reforms, adapts to the industrial revolution, adopts the methods of the Japanese in copying the foreigners, the Celestial Empire will fade into a song for future generations to sing.

For centuries, China had been the arrogant, Asian colossus, humbling her weaker neighbors—Burma, Tibet, Sikkim, Nepal, Bhutan, Thailand, Vietnam, Mongolia, and Korea. She demanded tribute, and received it. Now China was humbled. "If we talk of peace to other countries, without the force to back up our words, we will be the laughing stock of the world," an imperial counselor advised Kuang Hsu. "If countries are evenly matched, international law is enforced; otherwise, the law is inoperative." For the first time in her history, China recognized herself as but one star in the constellation of nations and not as the sun around which other nations revolved. She had been taught this historical truth by Japan and the West.

One after another, like leaves in autumn, the reforms showered down from the Dragon Throne. "Hear and obey: Purchase models of various kinds of machinery. Hear and obey: Educate the masses. Hear and obey: Invent articles of practical use. Hear and obey: Write useful books. Hear and obey: Give up part of your time and train as soldiers. Hear and obey: Create a university and put our country on a level with the West."

The courts were instructed to make a clean sweep of their docket. Plans were formulated for reform of the legal system. In fiscal affairs, officials were ordered to adopt a Western device known as the "budget." The bureaucracy was overhauled. Indolent Manchu officials were cashiered, patronage slashed, superfluous posts dissolved.

Initially, the emperor's edicts drew accolades from the viceroys, the generals, and mandarins, all of whom had also been shaken by Japan's triumph of arms. Tokyo jarred China like no European power ever did. Japan was a country the Chinese could understand;

the Japanese "are our kind," their culture was largely of Chinese origin. Europeans might be superhuman but the Japanese were human. Anything Japan did, China could do better.

But as the imperial rescripts rolled off the emperor's tongue, the reforms gradually came to be viewed in another light. If they were implemented, the empire would undergo a radical social, political and economic reorganization. The princes suddenly realized that the emperor was undercutting their traditional sources of wealth and power—official squeeze and the bureaucracy. The emperor had mounted an attack on the establishment.

The mandarins trekked to the summer palace and complained to the empress dowager. They appealed to her to save the empire from the emperor's "reform madness." Thus, inexorably, the lines were drawn between two factions, the emperor and the reformists on the one hand and the empress dowager and the traditionalists on the other.

The Emperor Kuang Hsu recognized the built-in danger in the situation. He defied his aunt. The success of the reform movement, the emperor knew, depended on keeping Tzu Hsi in retirement even against her will.

In what later developed as the first overt move in the internal struggle, the emperor appointed Yuan Shih-k'ai, a Chinese general of reformist sympathies who especially favored a radical overhaul of the armed forces, as inspector general of the Northern Army commanded by Viceroy Jung Lu, the empress dowager's faithful companion. The imperial edict which announced Yuan's appointment tipped the emperor's strategy. "We are now passing through a crisis," the decree read. "Yuan Shih-k'ai's promotion is a token of the great trust and confidence we intend to repose in him."

At a secret audience in the Hall of Supreme Harmony, the emperor instructed Yuan to proceed to Tientsin, the headquarters of the Northern Army, and dispose of Jung Lu. This would destroy the empress dowager's military power base. At the same time, he authorized Yuan to surround the summer palace and keep the Old

Buddha, as Tzu Hsi was affectionately called, under palace guard and out of harm's way.

During the cabal, Yuan's thoughts momentarily wandered. He was Chinese, and steeped in Confucian concepts. As he gazed on the Dragon Throne he sensed that the dynasty was in the process of gradually losing the mandate of heaven and that eventually, in the age-honored tradition, a new dynasty would replace it. What would prevent him from founding the new dynasty? Such things had happened before in China's history.

After the audience, Yuan Shih-k'ai went straight to Tientsin, betrayed the content of the emperor's strategy to Jung Lu and, embellishing on it, confided, "I am to surround the summer palace by surprise and assassinate Old Buddha." Alerted, the Manchu commander rushed to Tzu Hsi's side. In fury, Tzu Hsi descended on the Forbidden City.

At three in the morning, a eunuch stationed in the watchtower overlooking the western gate reported a burst of rockets from the direction of the summer palace, the customary signal that an imperial procession was en route from the summer palace. The flares were reported to the emperor. Recounting the episode later, the emperor recalled: "I knew instantly that I was lost."

Engulfed by the fear instilled into him since childhood, Kuang Hsu trembled uncontrollably. His newly acquired manliness evaporated and he reverted to character. When the imperial retinue arrived at the main gate, the emperor rushed out and flung himself on the ground in front of his aunt's sedan chair. She glared at him and said nothing, until they entered the Hall of Supreme Harmony. There she turned on him with unbridled wrath. "Ingrate," she screamed. "I raised you like a son and this is how you repay me."

The chief eunuch, Li Lien Ying, witnessed the scene with smug satisfaction. "I am a weakling," the emperor stammered. "I am unworthy to rule. Punish me as I deserve."

"Make a decree here and now," she rasped, "and abdicate the throne."

"There was nothing I could say," the emperor later explained. "I had ordered Yuan Shih-k'ai to throw soldiers about the summer palace to prevent Old Buddha leaving until I could put my decrees into effect. This, and this act alone, merited punishment in itself."

Tzu Hsi's first impulse was to have her nephew beheaded but the decapitation of an emperor would set a dangerous precedent. She could publish his abdication edict and raise a new child-emperor. But there was no assurance that the new emperor would not develop a will independent of her own as Kuang Hsu had. Exile was the answer. Let Kuang Hsu retain the title and be confined to the Chinese version of The Tower. A Manchu official recorded her decision: "Imprison the emperor on Ying Tai—the Ocean Terrace," she thundered. "Give him only the barest necessities in the way of food. See that he is never unguarded. Assign a eunuch to be at his side perpetually. Hear and obey!"

Banishment to the Ocean Terrace truly meant exile. No more than a fifteen minute walk from the Dragon Throne, the Ocean Terrace was an artificial island in an artificial lake within the Forbidden City. But it might as well have been 15,000 miles away, in the South Seas. To characterize the emperor's detention on that make-believe island in the center of a make-believe sea as exile may seem an exaggeration. But within the compass of the Forbidden City, make-believe was reality.

Some of the emperor's reformist advisers fled to Japan to join other Chinese revolutionaries in refuge there—among them, Sun Yat-sen, the Cantonese revolutionary who was destined to found the Chinese Republic. Those not fortunate enough to escape were arrested, tortured, and beheaded. The families of the executed were not permitted the traditional decency of sewing back onto their bodies the severed heads of their loved ones. They were executed in the public square with Peking in the gallery; the city's mangy alley curs lapped the pools of blood that spurted from headless trunks of the reformers. The Hundred Days of Reform ended in a nightmare.

The emperor's abortive coup d'etat and the empress dowager's successful counter coup occurred in the summer following Japan's humiliation of the Celestial Empire. On September 21, 1895, in the name of the imprisoned emperor, Tzu Hsi proclaimed that, with the nation in crisis, "wise guidance was necessary," and that the emperor implored the empress dowager, who on two previous occasions had performed the functions of regent "to perfection," once more to administer the government. The rescript, dictated by the empress dowager and bearing the seal of the emperor, concluded: "The empress dowager has answered our prayer." The following day the emperor-in-name-only led the princes and ministers of the government to perform obeisance before the empress dowager in the Hall of Diligent Government.

Tzu Hsi embarked on her third regency. Once again she alone guided the destiny of the dynasty, a dynasty in decline, an empire in decay.

With the forces of tradition gathered around her, Old Buddha took a personal hand in trying to drive foreigners from the empire. The result was the Boxer Rebellion. It was not a "rebellion" against the establishment; it was a rebellion against foreign domination, against the forces of change. Throughout China Europeans were attacked and slaughtered. The only effect was an invasion by the European powers. The rebellion collapsed. With its collapse, Tzu Hsi demonstrated a resiliency and flexibility which touched on statesmanship. She, too, recognized the irresistibility of the industrial revolution. In an astonishing about-face, she instituted her own program of reform in an effort to save the dynasty and the empire.

By imperial decree, the penal code was modified. "Slicing," the death of a thousand cuts, was outlawed. An intensive and remarkably successful campaign was launched against the opium habit. The opium habit had always been pernicious in China. But in the nineteenth century, encouraged by European and Japanese opium traders backed by their own governments, narcotic addiction engulfed China, sapping the nation of its energy and vitality. Tzu Hsi's Anti-Opium Edict, issued in 1906, directed that the growth, sale and consumption of poppy should end within a decade. This was not a paper decree. Army officers and men were beheaded if they smoked opium. For many, the decree was a death warrant.

A series of edicts was also issued aimed at obliterating the distinction between the Manchu and the Chinese, the master race and the subject race. Intermarriage was permitted, but the Manchu nobility were still barred from acquiring Chinese wives. The empress abolished the Manchu quota system, under which the Manchu had held half the important official posts though they numbered less than one percent of the population. Sparsely populated Manchuria, "the Forbidden Country," preserved by the dynasty as a Manchu reservation, was opened to Chinese settlers to flood the territory with Chinese subjects and thwart the imperialist designs of Russia and Japan. Soon thereafter Manchuria became known as "the granary of China."

New technical schools were opened, patterned on European and Japanese models. Chinese women were encouraged to abandon foot-binding, but, liberal as the reform appeared, many Chinese women preferred to retain the custom of crippling their daughters as a badge of political honor to retain the distinction between the women of China and the alien Manchu.

Observing her seventy-first birthday in 1906, the dowager empress promised the nation a constitution and outlined a Nine-Year Plan for preparing for representative government. A decade earlier, anyone who merely suggested such a reform would have been decapitated.

While the empress was ruling as official regent, the daughter of her lover Jung Lu married the second Prince Ch'un, the empress's nephew and the brother of the deposed emperor, who was now imprisoned on the island deep within the Forbidden City. In 1906 the young couple gave birth to a son. As their lives drew to a close, Tzu Hsi and Jung Lu gazed fondly on the boy as the grandson they would have had if she had not been drawn into the Chamber of Divine Repose more than half a century earlier. Tzu Hsi took unusual maternal interest in her nephew and named him herself. "P'u Yi," she called him, "Ceremony of Tribute."

Craftily, the Old Buddha planned a fourth regency. The next puppet emperor was in the wings.

PART II

THE MANDATE
OF HEAVEN

CHAPTER 5

Journey into History

During the summer of 1908 the dowager empress suffered a mild stroke, and, as the natural accompaniment to a serious illness, her thoughts turned to the hereafter. Politics dominated her life and characteristically dominated her thoughts about the future. Of one thing she was determined: The imprisoned ex-emperor must not outlive her.

In autumn, while celebrating her seventy-third birthday, Tzu Hsi took ill for the second time that year. She contracted dysentery. After lying ill for ten days, she made preparations for the imperial succession.

On November 13, in the middle of a starless night, couriers were dispatched to the Peking mansion of Prince Ch'un. His son, the three-year-old P'u Yi, was summoned to the palace. The imperial command, written in vermillion ink on a yellow scroll, threw the Ch'un mansion into disorder. The child's grandmother fainted before hearing the end of the empress dowager's order. Servants poured ginger tea for the imperial emissary and for the eunuchs who had come with him from the Forbidden City. Prince

Ch'un was overwhelmed and wandered about the mansion in a daze. The child, awakened in the middle of the night, howled and struggled against the efforts of his nurse and the eunuchs to dress him for his journey into history. As the official chroniclers of the dynasty later quaintly interpreted it, "He resisted the edict."

The child did not realize it, of course, but his nighttime tantrum was the beginning of a futile life-long struggle against the fortunes of destiny.

Later he recalled that historic midnight meeting with the aged, emaciated and sickly Tzu Hsi. "The shock of the meeting left a deep impression on my memory," he wrote.

"I remembered suddenly finding myself surrounded by strangers, while before me was hung a drab curtain through which I could see an emaciated and terrifyingly hideous face," he said.

"I burst into loud howls," he continued. The empress dowager, in a placating mood, ordered a eunuch to give him a string of candied *haws*. But to the displeasure of his benefactor, the boy threw the candy on the yellow-tiled floor. "What a naughty child," the empress dowager said with fatigue. "Take him away," she said, and quickly added as an afterthought, "to play."

Turning to the distraught Prince Ch'un, Tzu Hsi made known her plan for the imperial succession.

Conveniently, on the following day, the imprisoned ex-emperor on the enchanted isle of the Ocean Terrace succumbed to a mysterious ailment.

The grotesque timing of his death was the sensation of the day and led to speculation within the Forbidden City and outside it. The consensus was that he had been poisoned. This view was substantiated by P'u Yi. "I was later told by a descendant of one of the imperial household department officials that before his death the Emperor Kuang Hsu was only suffering from an ordinary case of flu, P'u Yi said. The servant had seen the diagnosis himself; it had described Kuang Hsu's pulse as normal. Moreover, the ex-emperor was seen in his room standing and talking as if he were in good health, so that people were very shocked to hear that he was seriously ill. What was even stranger was that within four hours of this came the news of his death."

"All in all," P'u Yi concluded laconically, with a touch of understatement, "Kuang Hsu's death was very suspicious."

Two hours after the ex-emperor's death, Tzu Hsi busied herself with preparations for her fourth regency. Her brush moved deftly as she wrote out a series of edicts in vermillion ink.

Designating P'u Yi emperor, she appointed Prince Ch'un the prince regent and accorded herself the title of grand empress dowager. Tzu Hsi left little doubt that she had every intention of continuing to direct the empire's destiny until she adorned the Robes of Longevity. "You shall administer all affairs of state," she informed the prince, "in accordance with *my* instructions." The emphasis, as usual, was on the empress dowager herself.

That night, perhaps as a result of the stress of her recent illnesses—stroke and dysentery—compounded by the excitement and strain accompanying her complicity in the murder of the former emperor, Tzu Hsi suffered a relapse. "My condition is critical," she remarked. "I fear I may never recover."

In this situation, the strong-willed grand empress dowager ordered the preparation of her last edict. "Looking back upon the memories of the last fifty years," she dictated, "I perceive how calamities from within and aggression from without have come upon us in relentless succession. The new emperor is an infant . . . at the age where wise instruction is of the highest order. . . . It is my prayer that he diligently pursue his studies and add fresh luster to the glorious achievements of his ancestors." In a no-nonsense manner, she scratched at the bottom of the edict, "Mourning to be worn for twenty-seven days only."

The eunuchs now dressed her in the ceremonial robes of burial, and, as the prince regent and court officials gathered around her deathbed, she delivered her last instructions.

"Never again," she said, "allow a woman to hold the supreme power in the state. It is against the house law of our dynasty and should be forbidden. Be careful not to allow the eunuchs to meddle in government matters. The eunuchs brought the Ming Dynasty to ruin and its fate should serve as a warning to my [Manchu?] people." Thus, as she completed her journey through history, she learned the lesson her forebears had learned almost three centuries earlier when they first occupied the Forbidden City. But Tzu Hsi learned too late. The dynasty was in decline, and she knew it.

Yet so political was her nature that even at the end she could not resist the temptation of engaging in ambiguity, the tactic of divide and rule. "In the future, all affairs of state are to be decided by the regent," she whispered. But she promptly and inexplicably contradicted herself and added: "When there are important matters on which he requires direction from the empress dowager, the prince regent shall appear before her and ask her instructions before dealing with them."

In the last analysis, she left the prince regent, weak and ill-fitted for the task as he was, even weaker in authority. Then dark death and the strong hand of fate gripped her and closed her eyes. With her death, it can be seen in restrospect, the Celestial Empire died.

An Italian diplomat, who attended the funeral of the grand empress dowager, described the occasion as a memorable pageant. "Tzu Hsi's funeral offered a gorgeous spectacle," Danielle Varé recorded. "Red robes of bearers, yellow robes of Lamaist priests, silver and gold rich embroideries. The Chinese bring to a funeral the colors of a sunset."

Her mausoleum was more than a tomb; it was a treasure trove. Her body was wrapped nine times by a single strand of matched pearls; her death robe was embroidered with gold thread and studded with gems; images of Lord Buddha, carved from jade, rose quartz, green quartz, amethyst, carnelian, and agate, lined her coffin; her tomb was filled with exquisite porcelains, bronzes, silver ornaments, and gold ingots. On her coverlet was a peony fashioned from gems, and on her arm was a bracelet of dazzling brilliance in the form of a large chrysanthemum and six small plum blossoms set with diamonds. In her hand was a wand made of emeralds. Her feet were encased in pearl shoes. She was buried in a manner befitting the ruler of one-fourth of mankind.

With the funeral completed, talk in the tea houses turned to why Tzu Hsi selected P'u Yi as heir to the throne. In his memoirs, published in Peking in 1964, the last emperor of China entertained no illusions. "The reason why she chose such a regent as my father and such a successor to the throne as myself was that she was going to die as soon as she in fact did," he said. "As Grand Empress Dowager, she would not have been able to rule on the emperor's behalf, but with a docile prince regent between herself and the child emperor, she could still have had everything her own way."

At the same time, of course, by naming his grandson emperor, she repaid in part the boundless debt she owed Jung Lu, her faithful counselor; without his assistance she would have been liquidated a half century earlier before she consolidated her power within the Violet Enclosure. She also protected the throne for the Aisin-Gioro clan to which she, Jung Lu, Prince Ch'un, and P'u Yi belonged. She may have thought her choice also absolved her of a blood debt because the prince regent whom she selected was a brother of the emperor she had murdered.

Whatever her motivations, there is evidence that Tzu Hsi decided on P'u Yi as the next in the imperial succession even before he was born. In 1905 Katharine Carl, an American painter, was commissioned by the empress dowager to paint her portrait for the Chinese pavilion at the St. Louis Exposition. In an account of her adventures within the Forbidden City, written that year, Miss Carl, with an insight into Chinese affairs which would make contemporary intelligence services and pompous scholars blush, forecast the empress dowager's choice. Among the most frequent visitors to the palace, Miss Carl observed, was Prince Ch'un and his wife, the daughter of Jung Lu. "Should they have a son," she surmised, "he will probably be the next heir to the throne."

When P'u Yi ascended the Dragon Throne a few years later, there was still hope for the survival of both his dynasty and his empire. Tzu Hsi's death coincided with the launching of her

47

revolutionary Nine-Year Plan aimed at harnessing the industrial revolution and propelling China into the twentieth century. The program was finely detailed, like a religious ritual: 1908–1909, the organization of provincial assemblies; 1909–1910, the opening of elementary schools; 1910–1911, inauguration of a national assembly; 1911–1912, a national census and the introduction of a system for auditing government accounts; 1912–1913, elections to parliament; 1913–1914, comprehensive law reforms and preparation of a national budget; 1915–1916, complete abolition of distinctions between Manchu and Chinese; 1916–1917, the national literacy rate to be raised to 5 percent.

Evolution, the Manchu hoped, would avert revolution. With a view to the independence and integrity of China, the massive reorganization of the government would, above all, stiffen the empire's defenses against foreign encroachment.

Implemented, the grand strategy might have led China through the difficult period of transition from an absolute to a constitutional monarchy, from the illusions of past grandeur to the realities of the contemporary scene. In time, conceivably, government for the people and by consent of the people, as preached by Mencius centuries earlier, might have evolved, and the misery and agony of warlordism, civil war, and a return to absolute rule avoided.

To save the dynasty, to guide the empire through the period of transition, the kingdom required a strong and vigorous hand on the tiller. For all her political wiles, Tzu Hsi's choice for a great helmsman was a miserable one. The prince regent was prone to panic and indecision. Unimaginative and unambitious, he was inexperienced in statecraft. Prince Ch'un was cast in the mold of the Chinese squire and dilettante. He was at a loss assaying the role of prince regent. He was disinterested in politics and court intrigue, and he sorely lacked background on the nature of the international power rivalries which swirled around China.

Worse, the prince regent was badgered by two forceful women—the new empress dowager, the widow of Kuang Hsu, a carbon copy of the Old Buddha, whom Tzu Hsi had personally selected and whom Kuang Hsu had feared and despised, and Prince Ch'un's wife, who inherited from her father, Jung Lu, a high spirit and penchant for high living. Hovering behind the silk screen were the great powers, Britain, Russia, Japan, France and Germany, ready to pounce on the prince regent and carve out still larger spheres of influence within the decaying empire.

As if this were not enough for the pusillanimous prince regent, Tzu Hsi's program for political reform was interpreted by the anti-monarchist, anti-Manchu secret societies as evidence of dynastic weakness. Revolutionary sentiment spread in the provinces. In Chinese, the world revolution, *keh ming,* is a combination of two characters which mean "to change the mandate." Clearly, insofar as the people embody the will of heaven, the Great Pure dynasty was losing the mandate to govern.

Oblivious to these historical forces, the three-year-old boy emperor ascended the Dragon Throne, the last of the Manchu emperors.

CHAPTER 6

The Change of Mandate

When the empress dowager died and a child in the custody of a feeble and irresolute regent ascended the throne, the deterioration of the Celestial Empire gained irreversible momentum.

In the provinces, antiforeign and anti-Manchu sentiment spread. The secret societies held the dynasty responsible for China's decline. The movement's anti-Manchu and antiforeign tone attracted widespread popular support, especially in urban centers, among students, the military, and the intellectuals. When the revolution came, the cities would go first, then the rural areas.

But the revolutionary movement lacked unity. The various factions agreed on the need to modernize China, resist foreign encroachment, secure greater provincial autonomy, and win greater representation at Peking. But they could not agree on how to achieve these objectives. Some favored the creation of a limited constitutional monarchy, which would keep P'u Yi on the Dragon Throne. Others preached the overthrow of the dynastic system in its entirety, an end to Manchu rule, and the proclamation of a republic. Among those pressing for a break with the past, one man soared over the others like an eagle, Sun Yat-sen, a Cantonese revolutionary who became the father of the Chinese republic and creator of modern China. Sun Yat-sen argued that under the inept Manchu, China had been reduced to semicolonial status, a thinly disguised vassal of the foreign devils, the "sick man of Asia," and the world's laughing stock.

In the face of these assaults, the decline of Manchu authority was hastened by the empire's financial plight. In the aftermath of the 1895 war with Japan and the subsequent reaction against the industrial revolution, the Boxer Rebellion, China's treasury was largely depleted. By 1908 the country was on the verge of bankruptcy and at the mercy of her foreign creditors. The grand dowager empress's program for constitutional reform was in financial trouble. Her currency, educational, and legal reforms were overly ambitious. Peking sought to implement, by edict, basic reforms that would take generations to accomplish. The Western world's industrial revolution had been the by-product of centuries of learning and experimentation. Under the Manchu and later under the Nationalists and then the Communists, China desperately searched for a short passage. In one great leap forward, China hoped to attain an equal footing in the modern world. But as Peking's authority weakened, the viceroys and governors in the provinces passively resisted the reforms, preferring chaos in the capital so that they could consolidate their own position in the provinces. This situation presaged a return to warlordism, the chronic disease that accompanied the collapse of a dynasty in China.

In the border areas, Manchu authority had virtually disappeared. The Tibetans, sensing the weakness of the dynasty, seized on the situation to free themselves from Peking's domination. The Mongolians, foreseeing the departure of the Manchu and the probable emergence of a native Chinese dynasty, also moved to free themselves from Peking's control. Revolt seared the Gobi desert. Naturally, it attracted interest in Moscow.

Britain and Russia moved for strategic advantage. The British recognized an opportunity to turn Tibet into a buffer between

China and India, the crown jewel of their empire. The Russians possessed an even stronger motivation to do the same in Mongolia, the fear that one day the Chinese would explode by sheer numbers into Russia's virgin lands in Central Asia. Better still, Mongolia was situated only 600 miles from Peking, within striking distance of the Chinese heartland.

While Britain and Russia maneuvered along China's frontiers, the Japanese were far from idle. Openly forecasting "revolution in China in three years," Tokyo developed contingency plans. Japan's great desire was to detach underdeveloped, underpopulated Manchuria, the ancestral home of the Manchu. In a subplot, the Russians developed similar plans for Manchuria with a view to keeping Japan at bay. Thus, within two years of entering the Cloudless Heaven Palace, P'u Yi's reign was in a condition of deepening peril. The core of the Manchu problem was that there was no great helmsman at the tiller in Peking.

P'u Yi, of course, was a child only five years old and oblivious to the politics which whirled around the Forbidden City. His father, Prince Ch'un, was indecisive. The only strong personality on the scene, other than Sun Yat-sen, in the republican camp, was General Yuan Shih-k'ai, who held the powerful position of grand councillor to the dynasty, as a reward from the dowager empress for his betrayal of P'u Yi's uncle, the Emperor Kuang Hsu. More important, he also commanded the loyalty of the Northern Army, the most disciplined, best equipped and most experienced military force in China. But Yuan had been summarily dismissed from office after Prince Ch'un became regent. This had been the prince's only display of initiative and even this action was not of his own making. It was directed from the grave.

On his deathbed, the Emperor Kuang Hsu, Prince Ch'un's brother, in indescribable agony as arsenic seeped through his body, wrote on a piece of silk in a barely legible hand that Yuan Shih-k'ai, the general who had betrayed him to the empress dowager, was responsible for his plight. "When my time comes," the dying emperor wrote, "behead him!" Then, in his last minutes, writhing in pain, the emperor moved the first finger of his right hand, repeating over and over again the Chinese character meaning "round" or "circle," and pronounced, *ÿuan*.

Lacking the courage to order Yuan Shih-k'ai's decapitation, the prince dismissed him from office by edict on January 2, 1909, a month to the day after P'u Yi's ascension to the Dragon Throne. The announcement of Yuan's dismissal is a model of double-talk. The regent's edict, issued in P'u Yi's name, read: "We have on our ascension to the throne [learned] unexpectedly that he [Yuan] is suffering from leg disease. . . . Therefore, let him vacate his post and return to his native place for treatment. This is to show our compassion and our consideration of him."

Yuan Shih-k'ai's dismissal was inopportune. Outside Peking, the wily, dissipated, and ambitious Yuan was a more dangerous adversary to the throne than he would be as a member of the Manchu court, where an eye could be kept on him.

Under pressure from the nobility, Prince Ch'un refused to accelerate the empress dowager's reform program and convene a parliament immediately. But this action served only to intensify the clamor for representative government and for an end to the absolute monarchy. Buckling to the ground swell, the prince retreated and agreed on November 4, 1910, to telescope the reform plan and summon a parliament in 1913, four years ahead of schedule. He explained his about-face by declaring that his only desire was the creation of a strong and unified China. Once again the dissidents interpreted concession as a sign of weakness. They demanded that the dynasty dissolve the Manchu Grand Council and replace it with a cabinet, and called on Peking not to accept any more foreign loans, in effect, to stand up to the foreign devils.

Within the Grand Council, as the child P'u Yi, perched on the Dragon Throne, looked on uncomprehendingly, the Manchu nobles debated the situation. The traditionalists won the day and forced Prince Ch'un to announce that no further political concessions would be granted before parliament met in 1913. Troops would be employed to put down any student-organized demonstrations against the monarchy.

As the political crisis matured, there was an outbreak of plague in the central provinces. Worse, perhaps, the mighty Yangtze, the Son of Oceans, the world's fourth largest river, crested her banks. Floods endangered the rice crop. As famine spread through the country, the suspicion deepened in the marketplaces and tea houses that the dynasty was losing the mandate of heaven. The Chinese traditionally considered the Dragon Throne responsible for nature's bounties, and for nature's calamities too.

At this juncture Czarist Russia seized on the plague as a pretext for issuing an ultimatum aimed at consolidating the Russian handhold on Manchuria. Employing "germ diplomacy," a forerunner to the charges of "germ warfare" Peking raised during the Korean War some half century later, the Russians claimed that Chinese refugees, seeking to escape the plague, had crossed into Czarist territory. Lacking sufficient border guards, the Russians requested permission to place troops inside Manchuria to check the flow of refugees across the frontier. The Russians stressed that their request was motivated on "humanitarian, not political, grounds."

As the situation disintegrated, signs of the old-line Manchu courage and valor emerged. The Manchu war minister, General Yin Ch'ang, accused the regime of folly, cowardice, selfishness, and indecisiveness in developing a modern army. Given the choice between death with honor or humiliation, he opted for death. "Conditions are so insane," he said, "I should much prefer to start fighting, happen what may."

But the Grand Council argued that a war against Russia to save Manchuria might lead to a collapse of the dynasty. This conclusion prompted the Manchu war minister to reply, "That cannot be helped."

Other voices prevailed, however. China was in no position to wage war. War would only increase the treasury's financial burden. The empire was likely to go down to defeat, losing territories irrevocably. Patience. As it developed, the other great powers were fearful of upsetting the delicate balance of power in Manchuria. They pressured the Russians to modify their demands.

But after three years of instability, the prince regent's position collapsed. Open revolts against the Manchu flared in the west, notably in Szechwan province. Meanwhile, Sun Yat-sen, encouraged by events, staged a coup d'etat at Canton in the south which the Manchu were barely able to crush. These revolts were forerunners of things to come.

P'u Yi was five years old. In the Violet Enclosure, he spent his time playing hide and seek with the eunuchs.

When the real revolution in 1911 came, it came in a way no one expected.

The military garrison at Wuchang revolted at 10:00 P.M. on October 10, the tenth day of the tenth month, a date thenceforth designated in Chinese history as Double Ten. Their commander proclaimed a republic and the revolt spread rapidly to the nearby cities of Hanyang and Hankow. As Sun Yat-sen later acknowledged, "the sudden success at Wuchang was accidental." The revolutionaries succeeded because of the cowardice and incompetence of the provincial governor who fled at the first shot.

The rebels were surprised by the ease with which they secured the three neighboring cities. The Manchu and the foreigners were equally surprised. Clearly, each of the protagonists on the Chinese scene misjudged the true situation. So did Sun Yat-sen, who was then touring the United States, cultivating American public opinion and raising funds from the Chinese-American community, which is largely Cantonese in origin.

Within two months, thirteen of China's eighteen provinces had joined the rebellion, as army units defected to the "republican wave of the future." In the accepted manner, according to Chinese historians, the peasants sanctioned the change of mandate by standing idly by as spectators and refusing to give Peking support.

Three days after the republic was proclaimed, Prince Ch'un recognized that the moment of truth was at hand for the Manchu, for the dynastic system, for China's future. Only one royalist commanded sufficient loyalty within the army to check the defections and put down the revolt, Yuan Shih-k'ai.

Putting the dynasty's survival before his personal feelings, Prince Ch'un, with the concurrence of the Manchu Grand Council, and with the child-emperor P'u Yi again looking on in bewilderment, summoned Yuan Shih-k'ai from retirement to retake command of the army. Returning a diplomatic thrust for a diplomatic thrust, the general pleaded ill-health and declined the invitation. Yuan added that he would accept, however, "if I am offered the premiership and the supreme military command." On November 1 Prince Ch'un complied. Again, however, Yuan declined to accept the invitation.

Many Manchu nobles and their families took the hint and fled Peking for Manchuria. Government departments were paralyzed, and the revolution continued to spread from city to city.

The flight of Manchu from Peking served as a signal for anti-Manchu riots. In isolated towns, the walled up bannermen, overfed, corrupt, slothful, vice-ridden, flabby, a far cry from symbols of imperial power, were attacked and butchered. "It was racist war of the most brutal kind," wrote J. C. Keyete, an American observer who witnessed the dynasty's collapse.

The Manchu quarter of Sianfu was turned into a charnel house. Men, women, and children were slaughtered, including pregnant women. In despair, some Manchu jumped from the walls encircling their section of town. Others set fire to their houses to cheat their murderers of loot. Many leaped, in traditional fashion, into the wells of the city.

Other Sianfus loomed on the horizon as Manchu were hunted down on the streets of the big seaports and inland cities. A Manchu detected on the street would be dragged off to instant execution. Hundreds, thousands, were hunted down in this fashion. "They were known by their clothing, by their cast of countenance, by their speech, their fondness for reds and yellows, their use of white linings, their high collars and narrow sleeves, their ornate belts, their shoes—all gave them away," Keyete observed. "With the women, the unbound feet were the fatal distinction. Their peculiar head-dress, their clothing they might change, but there was no disguising their natural-sized feet."

On November 15, when Prince Ch'un repeated his offer for a third time, Yuan suddenly recovered from his illness and took the first train to Peking. However tactically clever, delaying his return to the capital for a month cost him the opportunity of saving the imperial system in China and of founding his own dynasty to succeed the Manchu.

By the middle of November, only six weeks after the Double Ten revolt, the authority of the Manchu was reduced to five provinces, three of them in Manchuria. Nonetheless, confident and overbearing, Yuan Shih-k'ai took command of the powerful North-ern Army and marched south. He quickly recaptured Hanyang, one of the three cities where the revolt had erupted, and then turned on Wuchang and Hankow. But instead of moving in for the jugular, he stopped his advance, returned abruptly to Peking, and demanded an audience with Prince Ch'un and the then empress dowager, Lung Yu.

Yuan Shih-k'ai realized that he held the balance of power between P'u Yi and Sun Yat-sen, between the throne and the republican movement. He alone was in a position to avert a prolonged civil war. His first order of business was to bring the court completely under his control.

Within a month of his return to Peking, he induced the prince regent to resign. P'u Yi's father, Prince Ch'un, gladly retreated from the picture, and he was not replaced. In effect, Yuan became regent. Then he took control of the palace treasury away from the empress dowager on the ground that the money was needed to meet military expenses in suppressing the insurrection. With military, political, and financial power firmly in his hands, he arranged for China's envoys abroad to telegraph Peking and advise the court that P'u Yi should abdicate to avert civil war and the dismemberment of the empire by foreign armies.

"At the same time," P'u Yi wrote in his memoirs, "he presented the empress dowager with a secret memorial in the name of the whole cabinet saying a republic was the only solution."

The memorial came as a shock to the Manchu, for, if nothing else, Yuan was considered a staunch monarchist. Unknown to the Manchu, and the republicans, of course, Yuan Shih-k'ai nursed thoughts of establishing his own dynasty.

But if Yuan plotted to replace the Manchu with a new dynasty, why did he suddenly exhibit republican sympathies? The reason was not far to seek.

Yuan was pinned between an old dynasty, struggling against dissolution, and a new republic, fighting to be born. He could have been crushed between them. A wily strategist, he turned the situation in his favor by establishing himself as the broker between the contending parties. If he could induce the child-emperor to step aside, he could use the abdication as leverage with Sun Yat-sen, to nominate him as president to avoid a civil war. The restoration of the imperial system and the founding of his new dynasty would await developments.

P'u Yi was present when Yuan Shih-k'ai for the first time raised the subject of abdication. The emperor was then five years old, six years by Chinese reckoning since in China a child is considered one year old at birth.

"One incident of those last days stands out clearly in my memory," P'u Yi recalled.

The scene, as he described it later, took place in the Mind Nurture Palace. The Empress Dowager Lung Yu sat on a *kang* wiping tears from her eyes. The boy emperor sat on her right. Before them stood the corpulent Yuan Shih-k'ai, ribbons of fat encircling his waist, tears trickling down flabby cheeks and double chins. P'u Yi was bewildered and wondered why the two adults cried. The fat man sniffed loudly as he spoke but the boy did not have the faintest idea of what the conversation was about. "This was the only time I ever saw him," P'u Yi said many years later.

During the audience, Yuan delicately raised the question of the emperor's fate if the Manchu held on. "Delay in abdicating might lead to a fate similar to that suffered by Louis XVI and his family in the French revolution," he suggested delicately. "If the Manchu sought to retain the throne," he continued, "the evil consequences cannot be described." China, he said, would be irretrievably ruined, an allusion to foreign intervention, and there might follow mutual slaughter among the people, resulting in the horrible effects of a racial war.

The Manchu Grand Council gathered in emergency session in the Palace of Supreme Harmony. The empress dowager recounted to them Yuan Shih-k'ai's secret memorial. They were not alarmed by the reference to the French revolution, but they were badly shaken by the sudden change in Yuan's loyalties. The hard-liners balked at the suggested abdication and preferred to fight. At that very moment, the war minister reported, a unit of bannermen was attacking the republicans at Nanking (and doing surprisingly well). Another hard-liner, the interior minister, proposed that if worst came to worst, the court should withdraw to north of the Great Wall and reestablish itself in Manchuria as an independent state. He argued that, in effect, the continuity of the throne would remain intact: it would be a case of China's secession from Manchuria and not the other way around. The council rejected the plan. The bannermen were scattered south of the Wall and Manchuria was in no position to fight. Moreover, given the weakness of both China and Manchuria, the Manchu homeland would be at the mercy of the foreign powers.

As the council debated the dynasty's future, Yuan Shih-k'ai grew alarmed. Each day he delayed in obtaining the abdication of P'u Yi, Sun Yat-sen became stronger. But the general had little cause for concern. As he expected, the idealistic, self-sacrificing Sun Yat-sen, in an effort to avert bloodshed on a massive scale, offered Yuan Shih-k'ai the presidency—providing that the Manchu abdicated peacefully. Yuan was now in the position, as the Chinese say, to give the falling wall a push. He arranged for the Northern Army to telegraph the emperor that it was useless to continue the struggle against the republican upsurge. The army called on the emperor to abdicate and announced that it refused to press the offensive against the republican forces.

The dynasty was lost. On February 3, 1912, the Grand Council held its most momentous session in three centuries. Before the assembly, Yuan offered the empress dowager a tempting concession in a bid to smooth the course of the abdication: the survival of the Manchu house by a device known as the Articles of Courteous, or Favorable, Treatment. In the back of Yuan's mind was the need to forestall a "French solution" since he himself planned to restore the dynastic system with himself as emperor.

At the meeting, the hard-liners insisted that they were prepared to fight if for no other reason than to avenge the slaughter of Manchu at Sianfu and elsewhere.

"And what if we lose in battle?" the empress dowager asked. "Surely, we won't be able to fall back on the Articles of Favorable Treatment."

She won her argument, and lost her empire. The council agreed to the abdication.

The next several days were spent in preparing the abdication edicts and putting the finishing touches on the Articles of Favorable Treatment. On February 12, 1912, the abdication edict was issued. The reign of the Manchu had been terminated.

As for the great mass of the Chinese, either peasants or coolies, the dissolution of the emperor system was beyond comprehension. It was as if somebody said the sun would never again shine. Without a Son of Heaven, who ruled the world? All this talk of no emperor made no sense.

The American Legation in Peking, in a coded dispatch, cabled Washington: "The situation presents the spectacle of about one-fourth of the world's population overturning a form of government that has been the religion of the people and the supreme expression of their civilization for over four thousand years."

Within the Forbidden City, the five-year-old P'u Yi scarcely felt a ripple from the waves of revolution that were overwhelming China. For him, life went on, much as it had before.

CHAPTER 7

Articles of Favorable Treatment

History must judge that the Manchu acted wisely in voluntarily abdicating their absolute power. By doing so, they averted civil war and foreign intervention and the probable partition of China. But in a longer perspective, however, neither civil war nor foreign intervention was averted. From the downfall of the Manchu and for a generation thereafter, China was in continual turmoil, a situation which ultimately encouraged a massive foreign intervention by the Japanese first north and then south of the Great Wall.

By custom, a new dynasty often treated the survivors of the old regime with "courteous treatment." Even in 1912 a deposed emperor was so awesome that he was accorded "Articles of Favorable Treatment." Indeed, three days after the Manchu abdication, the most republican of republicans, Sun Yat-sen himself, appeared before the tomb of the first Ming emperor, made sacrificial offerings, and reported to the spirit of the deceased Son of Heaven that the Dragon Throne had been wrested from the alien Manchu and that China had been returned to the Chinese.

The presidential prayer had racist as well as nationalist overtones, perhaps understandably after almost three hundred years of alien domination. "Often in history has our noble Chinese race been enslaved by petty frontier barbarians from the north," Sun Yat-sen said. "Peking today is at last restored to the government of the Chinese people. . . . The dragon crouches in majesty as of old, and the tiger surveys his domain and his ancient capital. . . . Your people have come here today to inform your majesty of the final victory. May this lofty shrine in which you rest gain fresh luster from today's event and may your example inspire your descendants in the times which are to come. Spirit! Accept this offering!"

Such a performance by the father of the republic boggles the Western mind; yet it provides insight into why the young P'u Yi, the Son of Heaven, the One Who Is Above, the Lord of Ten Thousand Years, was treated with such deference on his abdication.

The edicts of his abdication, as they were called, were three in number and were couched in Confucian imagery. Written on yellow silk scrolls, the documents made plain that the dynasty had acted in the best interests of the people, that the state was in reality a great family in which the Son of Heaven was the father and the people children. Although they were worlds apart both literally and figuratively, the dynasties of China and the democracies of the West were both based on the idea of a broad consensus. Without that consensus, neither system functioned properly.

Philosophy aside, the abdication decree was an extraordinary political document. In it, the empress dowager in the name of the child-emperor not only abdicated the throne but proclaimed the emperor's desire to create a republic.

"As a consequence of the uprising of the republican people's army, supported by the provinces as sound is by its echo, the empire seethed and smoked and the people were plunged into misery, . . ." the document began. "As long as the form of government is undecided, the nation can have no peace. It is now evident that the hearts of the majority of the people are in favor of a

63

republican form of government—the provinces of the south were the first to espouse the cause, and the generals of the north have since pledged their support."

"From the preference of the people's hearts," the edict said, "the Will of Heaven can be discerned."

As for the Manchu and the Great Pure Dynasty, the edict spoke with dignity. "How could we bear to oppose the will of millions for the glory of one family?" "Therefore," the imperial rescript concluded, "observing the tendencies of the age on the one hand and studying the opinion of the people on the other, we and his majesty the emperor hereby vest sovereignty in the people and decide in favor of a republican form of constitutional government. Thus, we would gratify, on the one hand, the desires of the whole nation who, tired of anarchy, are desirous of peace, and, on the other hand, we would follow in the footsteps of the Ancient Sages, who regard the throne as the sacred trust of the nation."

The edict called on the nation to "form one Great Republic of China by the union of the five peoples, namely, Manchu, Chinese, Mongols, Moslems, and Tibetans together with their territory in its integrity." *

The second of the three abdication edicts referred specifically to "articles of courteous [favorable] treatment," and, in the light of the Sianfu massacre, appealed to the nation to "remove all racial differences and prejudices." It also reflected the dynasty's concern about the perturbed spirits of its ancestral founders. Thus, it held the republic responsible "for the perpetual offering of sacrifices before the imperial ancestral temples and the imperial tombs and the completion as planned of the mausoleum of his last majesty, the Emperor Kuang Hsu."

As for P'u Yi, the second edict made clear that "I, his majesty

---

* In China, inexplicably, the *hui hui* (one who turns back, i.e., makes a pilgrimage to Mecca) or Moslem is bunched together with the "races" which make up China. This is nonsense; no religion which accepts converts, as does Islam or Buddhism, Christianity or Judaism can, by any stretch of the imagination, be considered a race.

the emperor, am understood to resign only my political power, while the imperial title is not abolished." In this paragraph, the fate of the six-year-old child was shaped. Politically, he would remain suspended in animation. He would retain his title and bide his time.

"The Ta Ch'ing Emperor, having proclaimed a republican form of government," the Articles of Favorable Treatment continued, "the Republic of China will accord the following treatment to the Emperor after his resignation and retirement."

There then followed nineteen articles, the first eight dealing with the future status of P'u Yi. The emperor was permitted to retain not only his title (the republic pledged to treat him as "a foreign sovereign"), but he also received an annuity of $4 million annually, was permitted to continue to reside in the Forbidden City, and to retain his personal bodyguards. Finally, the republic pledged to "respect and protect" the emperor's private property. The republic, however, exercised one prerogative. It demanded an end to the eunuch system. "All the retinue of the imperial household shall be employed as hitherto," the articles said, "but no more eunuchs shall be appointed."

For a number of reasons, the documents are unusual.

In abdicating power, the emperor did not abandon the throne, an extraordinary, if not unique, political development. The emperor was neither murdered nor exiled. He retained his title and his inviolability. In truth, of course, the edicts served the conflicting interests of each of the principals at that time, P'u Yi, Yuan Shih-k'ai and Sun Yat-sen.

For P'u Yi, the edict left the door ajar for his return to the Dragon Throne. For Yuan, the edict kept before the public the Confucian concept of the imperial system, clearing the way for the reestablishment of a new dynasty at a later date. For Sun Yat-sen, the republic averted a civil war and foreign intervention in return for protecting the person of the emperor. Sun's basic objective, the establishment of a republic, was painlessly achieved.

The Manchu house implied in the tone and color of these documents that it felt a republican government unsuited for China and probably short-lived, that the country could be governed only by an authoritarian ruler and that in time the dynastic system would be reinstated. Little did P'u Yi's mentors, nor anyone else for that matter, realize at the time that when the dynastic system was restored, the dynasty would be founded not by a family but by a political party—the single-minded, purposeful, authoritarian Communist Party of China, still to be born.

The edicts of abdication were also highly nationalistic in content, irrespective of the transfer of power from one form of government to another. Repeatedly, throughout the documents, the Manchu called on the new republic to maintain the unity and integrity of the empire built and extended under Manchu rule which had brought about the occupation of Tibet, Mongolia, Sinkiang, and the incorporation into China of Manchuria.

Whether China was governed by a monarchy or republic (or, for that matter, a "people's" republic), Tibet and Mongolia were certainly not Chinese except by Manchu conquest. As for Manchuria, the Manchu now considered their ancestral land as part of China. If the edict is to be taken at face value, they sought to keep their countrymen north of the Great Wall from establishing a separate Manchurian state after the dynasty's collapse. Significantly, no reference was made in the documents to another great Manchu conquest, Taiwan. The reason was obvious. The Manchu had lost the island to Japan during the 1895 war; for the dynasty to allude to Taiwan as Chinese would have antagonized the Japanese who merely looked for a pretext to intervene in Chinese affairs.

On February 12, 1912, after the abdication, some of the royal family and the nobility took sanctuary in the legation quarter in Peking. Others took refuge in the foreign concession area of Tientsin, Peking's port seventy miles to the east, astride the Yellow Sea.

P'u Yi's father, Prince Ch'un, returned home and, as the Chinese put it, "hugged his children," figuratively, if not literally, i.e., drew them to his bosom in the spirit of a family reunion. The overfed, overambitious Yuan Shih-k'ai changed hats. At lunch he dined as the premier of the cabinet of the *Ta Ch'ing* or Great Pure Dynasty. At dinner time he gorged himself as provisional president of the Republic of China.

Under the articles of favorable treatment, the boy P'u Yi became the president's neighbor. Apart from three large halls in the Forbidden City which were handed over to the republic—one of them becoming the presidential suite—the rest of the enchanted Violet Enclosure, in the heart of the republican capital, remained the private preserve of the emperor, his personal domain.

Within this enclosed world P'u Yi would spend the most absurd childhood possible.

As China and mankind advanced deeper into the twentieth century, P'u Yi lived the life of an imaginary emperor and, he wrote later, "breathed the dust of the centuries."

The ironies of history are beyond rational comprehension. In 1644 the first Manchu ascended the throne at the age of six. In 1912 the last Manchu abdicated at the age of six. A novelist could hardly improve on the scenario.

CHAPTER 8

A Chinese Wonderland

"Whenever I think of my childhood," P'u Yi recalled, "my head is filled with yellow mist."

And for reason. The Violet Enclosure might be more appropriately termed the Yellow Enclosure. The tiles on the floor and roofs of the palaces were glazed yellow. P'u Yi always sat on a yellow cushion. The lining of his hats and robes were yellow, the girdle around his waist, yellow. The porcelain dishes and bowls from which the emperor ate and drank were yellow. The cloth jackets on his schoolbooks were yellow. He slept in a bed with yellow blankets and pillows. The sedan chair in which he was carried from place to place within the Forbidden City was shielded from the sun and rain by a yellow canopy. His writing brushes were wrapped in yellow silk. The imperial standard, which flew the length and breadth of empire, was a five-clawed dragon on a field of yellow.

Brilliant yellow, perhaps, is a better description of the imperial color of China, the hue reserved exclusively for the emperor. To many early Chinese the selection seemed in accordance with nature since Chinese civilization sprang up along the yellow clay banks of the Yellow River, which was thought to be the center of the world, a notion which has permeated Chinese thought and behavior ever since. Decapitation, beating by bamboo rods and other punishments were meted out to those who misappropriated the imperial color for personal use.

Not until he reached the age of seven did P'u Yi meet and play with other children for the first time; these were his brother P'u Chieh and a sister. Until then his only companions were eunuchs.

Their first visit started off drearily. While he sat on a *kang,* a low brick bench which can be filled with live coals in winter, his brother and sister stood below him and gazed at him with a fixed stare "like attendants on duty." Later in the day it occurred to P'u Yi to invite the children to visit his living quarters in the Mind Nurture Palace, and in the normal manner of a child, P'u Yi asked his brother, "What games do you play at home?" Hide-and-seek, the brother, a year younger, replied in a very respectful manner. "I was excited," P'u Yi said. "I had played it with the eunuchs but never with children." So they began to play and in the excitement of the game his brother and sister forgot their inhibitions. After running, laughing, and shouting, exhausted, the three children climbed up on a *kang* to regain their breath. P'u Chieh was thoughtful for a while and then started to gaze wordlessly at the emperor, with a smile on his face.

When P'u Yi asked his younger brother what he was grinning about, the boy laughed and said he thought the Celestial Countenance would be different from other people, that P'u Yi would, like the emperors on the stage and in the scrolls, have a long white beard. As he giggled, the boy pretended to stroke his beard and the yellow lining of his sleeve flashed in the sunlight. First P'u Yi blanched, horror-stricken, then rage swirled within him. Screaming, he demanded to know who gave his brother permission to wear that color. P'u Chieh trembled, slid off the *kang* and stood at attention. His sister slipped over to stand with him, frightened to the point of tears. "It isn't yellow, sire," P'u Chieh stammered. "It is apricot, your imperial majesty." Although P'u Chieh would stand faithfully by his imperial brother's side through the turbulent years ahead, it was an incident which set the tone of their future relationship. Clearly, P'u Yi was not an ordinary child, and he was not being raised as an ordinary child.

P'u Yi was raised to believe not only that brilliant yellow was his private color but also that he must always be addressed as "sire" and that all people must kneel and kowtow in his presence, whether they were old officials of the dynasty, elders from the Aisin-Gioro clan, members of his family, or even, after he was dethroned, republican officials in western style dress. He became accustomed to the pomp of the retinue which followed in his train wherever he went.

Contemporary readers of the *Dream of the Red Chamber*, the great epic novel of classic literature, are often puzzled by the description of the emperor surrounded by so many people that his movement from one room in the palace to another was likened to "a swarm of bees." The pomp surrounding P'u Yi, even after the revolution of 1911 that toppled him from his throne and as late as on the eve of the First World War, explains the origin of the literary allusion. For example, in the fantastic setting of the Great Within, whenever the child-emperor strolled through the precincts of the inner city, a procession was organized to accompany him.

In front, twenty or thirty yards ahead of the party, went a eunuch whose function, P'u Yi later wrote, "was roughly that of an automobile horn." He intoned the sound "chir . . . chir . . ." as a warning to anyone in the vicinity to depart immediately. Next came two chief eunuchs advancing crabwise on either side of the path. Ten paces behind them came the center of the procession—the child-emperor. If P'u Yi was carried in a sedan chair, two junior eunuchs walked beside him to attend his wants at any moment. If the boy walked, they would stand on either side and support him. Next came a yellow silk canopy followed by a large group of eunuchs, some armed with ancient halberds. They carried a change of clothing, an umbrella, in the event of rain, a parasol, in the event of brilliant sun, and other emergency supplies. After them came the "eunuchs of the imperial presence," with boxes of various cakes and delicacies and, of course, jugs of hot water and a tea service. After them, the eunuchs of the imperial dispensary took up their position in the procession, bearing cases of medicine and first-aid equipment suspended from poles slung over their shoulders. Among the medicines were Six Harmony Pills for Stabilizing the Center, Gold Coast Heat Dispersing Cinnabar, Fragrant Herb Pills and the Three Immortal Beverages to aid digestion. At the tail end of the procession came the eunuchs who carried commodes and chamber pots. If the emperor strolled, the sedan chair brought up the rear.

Fantastic as it seemed, the retinue marched ahead in complete silence.

All this just for a stroll. What kind of a man would emerge after being brought up in such a milieu? Yet the boy in P'u Yi was always there.

"I would often throw the retinue into confusion," P'u Yi later noted with pleasure. "When I was young, I liked to run around just as any child does. At first the retainers would scuttle along after me, puffing and panting with their procession reduced to chaos. When I grew a little older and I knew how to give orders, I would tell them to stand and wait for me."

The same procession followed him daily when he went to school in a classroom set up in the Palace for the Cultivation of Happiness.

In accordance with Manchu custom, the emperor started his schooling at the age of four, under the direction of a staff of tutors. The tutors were not allowed to sit in his presence. Nor were they permitted to praise their student. If P'u Yi did well, a tutor would say, "Very good Lord of the Myriad Years but Your Imperial Majesty can do much better. The Emperor Ch'ien Lung did far better at your age." The boy was always made to compete against the ghosts of the past and he was always made to feel inferior to them.

The curriculum was steeped in the classics. The boy-emperor's principal texts were the *Thirteen Classics*, including the *Three*

Character Classics and *Hundred Surname Classics*, incorporating the basic works of Confucius. He also received lessons in the Manchu and Chinese language. But he considered himself an unconscientious student and frequently faked illness as a pretext for skipping classes. Later in his early teens, he began to understand that the textbooks had something to do with him even though he had been dethroned. He grew interested in becoming a good emperor, in understanding why an emperor was an emperor, and in what heavenly significance there had been in his appointment. His very first textbook, the *Classic of Filial Piety*, laid down the moral principle that one should "start by serving one's parents and end by serving one's sovereign." He also learned that "the ruler should be a ruler, the subjects should be subjects, that fathers should be fathers and sons should be sons." But at the same time the teachings of Mencius, the great democratic philosopher of China, were also taught. "The people are important," he read, "the spirits of the land and grain come next, and the sovereign is unimportant." And: "If the sovereign regards his subjects as so much grass, the subjects will regard the monarch as their enemy."

As he matured, he was exposed to such weighty tomes as the *General Chronological History with Comments* by the Emperor Ch'ien Lung, *The Anthology of Ancient Literature*, which he enjoyed reading, and T'ang Dynasty poetry. He also discovered he had a talent for writing couplets.

To encourage his studies, the class was enlarged at the age of eight, to include his brother, P'u Chieh, and several other children. At eight each morning P'u Yi arrived at the Palace for the Cultivation of Happiness in a sedan chair with the usual retinue in his wake. At his command, a eunuch sounded a gong and summoned tutors and fellow students from the waiting room. A eunuch carried his books. As he entered the classroom, the tutor kowtowed and the students knelt. Formalities over, the students all sat down. The boy emperor sat at the north side of the table, facing south. By tradition, an emperor always faced south, and the whole of the Forbidden City was laid out with this principle in mind. The Dragon Throne faces south (as do all the palaces) and for this reason the emperor was sometimes addressed as the One Who Faces South.

The reason is lost in mysticism and antiquity. But it probably has its origin in a common astronomical phenomenon in the northern hemisphere where the sun travels in an east-south-west arc. By facing south the emperor, the representative of heaven, is in a position to observe the sun's comings and goings, and its effect on the world.

With the curriculum's emphasis on the cosmic plan of the universe, language, and the humanities, P'u Yi learned nothing of mathematics, economics, geography, or the sciences. He was ignorant of the world beyond the Violet Enclosure. "I was totally ignorant of George Washington, Napoleon, Watt's invention of the steam engine, and Newton and his apple," P'u Yi later wrote. All he knew about the universe was what the mystics of China had divined centuries before, i.e., the Great Pole produced the two forms—*yin* and *yang,* shade and sun, male and female—that the universe was a by-product of five natural forces (water, fire, wood, metal, and earth) and that the fate of people and dynasties could be explained through an analysis of the eight trigrams, a block of three figures in different combinations which were represented on the jade imperial seal that P'u Yi owned. The source of these concepts is enshrouded in the hoary past. P'u Yi also learned and practiced in later life the sort of divination practiced by all emperors. This involved the application of fire to the bones and carapace of the tortoise, the living symbol of the north, and the interpretation of the resulting cracks.

As P'u Yi complained later, if his tutors had not been prepared to chat with him about things which were not in the ancient, obscurant texts, and had he not read more widely himself, "I would not even have known where Peking was in relation to the rest of China or that rice grew in the ground."

At the age of thirteen, P'u Yi's mentors decided that he should study a foreign language. Judiciously recognizing that English was rapidly becoming the world's *lingua franca* (a phrase, interestingly enough, which cannot be expressed eloquently in English), that

Britannia ruled the waves, and that the English-speaking Americans were the only "foreign devils" who nurtured sympathy for the fate of China, whether out of naïveté, idealism, a sense of righteousness, or enlightened self-interest, English was selected as the foreign tongue P'u Yi should learn.

Apart from an English-language grammar, the only textbooks he used were an English translation of the Chinese classics and *Alice in Wonderland*. The latter choice was extraordinary given the atmosphere of the Great Within where, until only a few years earlier, the emperor (or empress dowager) commanded, "Off with his head," in the manner of Lewis Carroll's Queen of Hearts. In imperial China, of course, off came the head. The boy must have been perplexed therefore when, in response to the command, Alice retorted, "Stuff and nonsense." But for all practical purposes, living in his own wonderland as P'u Yi did, Lewis Carroll's make-believe world probably had a realistic ring to him. But very early in his life, long before he was able to read *Alice in Wonderland*, cracks began to appear in the walls of his own wonderland, cracks that were eventually to widen enough to reveal to him the real world in which the rest of mankind lived.

CHAPTER 9

Curiouser & Curiouser

As he grew older, an emperor without an empire, dazzled by the brilliant yellows of the Forbidden City, P'u Yi's wonderland became curiouser and curiouser.

Special terms were employed to describe the young emperor's food; a servant's failure to use the proper word was an invitation to a dozen or more strokes of the bamboo lash. The food P'u Yi consumed was not called "food" but "viands." The kitchen in which the viands were prepared was known as the "imperial viands room"; serving the meal was known as "transmitting the viands"; and eating the food was called "consuming the viands." The reason was manifest. By employing the code word "viand" for food destined for the emperor's table, P'u Yi's food was always identified in the chain of command from kitchen to table. As an extraprecautionary device against poisoning, every dish or bowl from which he ate contained a strip of silver. Finally, before P'u Yi consumed his viands, the food was first tasted by a eunuch, a ritual known as "appraising the viands."

The child-emperor did not eat at regular hours, but on demand to suit his mood. Whenever he ordered, "Transmit the viands!" a eunuch standing nearby repeated the command and so on down the corridor to the eunuchs on duty outside the palace. From there the word was passed to the "imperial viands room." Before the echo of the command died, a procession of eunuchs issued forth from the "viands room" with seven lacquered teak tables of varying sizes painted with gold dragons. In the main dining hall, located in the eastern room of the Hall of Supreme Harmony, a train of white-sleeved eunuchs set up the tables and laid out the meal. Usually there were two large tables of main dishes (with another table of chafing dishes added in winter), three tables of cakes and rice, and a small table of salted vegetables. All the plates and bowls, of course, were in brilliant yellow porcelain with dragon designs, and they bore the characters, "*Wan, wan sui*—Ten Thousand Years." When the bowls were laid out, a young eunuch ordered, "Remove the covers." Four or five other eunuchs would leap forward and remove the silver lids from the bowls, placing them in red lacquered boxes emblazoned with yellow dragons.

The imperial viands always appeared on command, whether at three in the afternoon or three in the morning. In the imperial viand room, food was prepared around the clock, and kept warm in the kitchen stove awaiting the emperor's command. Normally, each meal contained a minimum of 100 or more dishes. As a boy, however, P'u Yi was rationed to 25 different dishes at *each* meal. In his memoirs, he reproduced a breakfast menu for March, 1912, a month after his abdication. It would put to shame Chinese restaurants from Peking and Hong Kong to New York. The menu that morning, for a six-year-old child, was:

Spring (egg) rolls; Four Hour Steam Chicken with Mushrooms; Triple Delight Duck (duck, ham, chicken with sauce); diced chicken with vegetables; steamed ham; Yunan pot ham; simmered tripe and lungs; diced beef with cabbage; spiced lamb; sweet potatoes with cherries; lamb with green vegetables and mushrooms; steamed pork and vegetables; sea slugs in duck stock; Peking duck; spiced duck; diced pork and broccoli; cubed lamb with spicy vegetables; lamb with scallions; tripe marinated in wine and spices; bean curds with soya sauce and spices; bean curd with bean sprouts, and ginger; sauteed vegetables; spiced cabbage; spiced fowl; white rice.

Only fortune cookies were missing.

With each meal was also served a dish that was never consumed by P'u Yi. It was known as the "ancestor meat soup," and was an offering to the emperor's ancestors who were considered to be present in spirit. As a general rule, two main meals were served daily, one at ten in the morning and the other at six in the evening. Chinese guests were sometimes appalled at the lack of beef dishes and the emphasis on lamb (a Manchu custom). While dining, P'u Yi was surrounded by eight or more personal attendants, including an expert carver, who handled suckling pigs or roasted birds; a nurse, in the event the child-emperor suddenly took ill at the meal; two attendants in charge of selecting choice morsels for him from the larger platters; and four eunuchs whose function was to wave flying insects away from the imperial viands.

Whenever P'u Yi "consumed the viands," a eunuch reported directly to the empress dowager on the child's appetite. "Your slave reports to his masters: The Lord of Ten Thousand Years consumed a bowl of white rice viands, one steamed bread roll, and a bowl of congee," the eunuch said, kneeling before her. "He consumed the viands with relish."

The waste at the Forbidden City was staggering. According to court records, during the second year of the reign of P'u Yi, the young child and his relatives consumed in a typical month more than two tons of beef, lamb, and pork, 388 chickens and ducks. Obviously, waste and graft accounted for the consumption of most of the food.

In addition, there was the monthly allocation for the palace retainers: members of the Manchu Grand Council, imperial body-guards, scholars, artists, artisans, eunuchs, priests, and others. The amount of food prepared averaged eight tons monthly. On top of this, there were the "extra dishes" which the imperial viands room prepared daily, requiring an *additional* 20 tons of beef, lamb and pork, 1,000 pounds of pork fat, 4,786 extra chickens and ducks, as well as vast quantities of fish, shrimp, and eggs. The cost of maintaining the imperial viands room was enormous. In the time of the greatest famines, the palace table remained as sumptuous as ever.

"Just as food was cooked in huge quantities but not eaten," P'u Yi recalled, "so was a vast amount of clothing made which was never worn."

Every garment he wore was brand new. In an average year royal tailors made him eleven fur jackets (usually of sable), six inner and outergowns made from fur, two fur waistcoats, thirty padded waistcoats, and thirty pairs of trousers. Leaving aside the cost of cloth, furs, and labor, the annual bill for such minor items as the pockets, buttons, and thread came to more than two thousand silver dollars. The emperor was not free to select his apparel of the day. His changes of clothing were laid down in imperial regulations and were the responsibility of the eunuchs of the imperial wardrobe. Even his everyday gowns came in twenty-eight different styles, each, of course, with a touch of brilliant yellow. On festivals and ceremonial occasions, his clothes were especially ornate and complicated, with peacock feathers, black and white fur linings, richly brocaded. Like any child, P'u Yi experimented with odd attire—cowboy and Indian suits were beyond his ken but he once put on a republican general's uniform, with a plume in its cap like a feather duster, and a sword and Sam Browne belt. When a senior high consort heard of this, she was furious. An investigation was ordered and the board of inquiry discovered the boy emperor had also been wearing foreign stockings. Each of the eunuchs involved in the harmless caper was given 200 strokes of the bamboo rod and demoted to the cleaning office to work as menials. P'u Yi was lectured about his disgraceful behavior. A Manchu emperor attired in the republican army uniform and the stockings of the foreign devils!

P'u Yi was promptly ordered to put away his beloved uniform and toy sword and change back into attire befitting an emperor, a dragon robe lined with fox fur and a surcoat trimmed in sable. In this fashion, his uniqueness was impressed upon him. The incident of the uniform reinforced the lesson of the classroom: he was one of a kind, the true and only Son of Heaven. For his further education, the offending eunuchs were flogged in the boy's presence in the traditional manner. Their buttocks were bared and they were lashed with a split bamboo cane. Without realizing it, the child gradually came to derive considerable sexual gratification from watching such punishments.

His sexual excitement was compounded by the "fawning foxes," the eunuchs, who obeyed his every command, his every whim. Whenever the boy was depressed or in a bad temper, eunuchs were flogged in his presence to cheer him up. By the age of seven he was having the eunuchs flogged regularly in his presence. These scenes increased in frequency as he crossed the biological threshold of childhood and entered puberty. On one occasion he had seventeen eunuchs whipped for a minor offense. Flagellation provided more than perverse sexual excitement for him though. It taught him how wide the parameters of celestial power were, at least within the Forbidden City. Someday through force of circumstance, in the "outer world," he would learn differently.

By any measure, P'u Yi was an orphan in these early years, figuratively if not literally. His mother had not died at childbirth and his father, Prince Ch'un, was prince regent. But from the moment that the aged Tzu Hsi summoned him in the middle of the night into the Forbidden City and into history, he was raised without parents.

His mother and father were, as he characterized it, "completely different types." His father, who died in 1951, had two wives, and they bore him four sons and seven daughters, so that P'u Yi, despite his exalted position, was a member of a sizable family. In Manchu families, there was no need for a woman's liberation movement; the women dominated the household. Indeed, among the Chinese it was frequently said that Manchu women were far more capable than the men. "And this may well be true," P'u Yi conceded in his memoirs.

One explanation was that the Manchu girls were treated with deference from their birth since they all had an equal opportunity of being chosen for service in the palace as imperial consorts.

The P'u Yi household was no different from other Manchu families in this respect. P'u Yi's mother dominated the home. She was extravagant and there was nothing the weak, indecisive Prince Ch'un could do about it. Excluding his land rents, prince's stipend, and annual "money for the Nurture of incorruptibility" (a form of payment to Manchu officials designed to discourage them from accepting bribes), his father had an income of 50,000 taels a year, an amount which was paid in full by the republic even after the abdication. But the prince no sooner received his money than his wife spent it. He tried all sorts of solutions, including giving her a fixed allowance, in order to control her behavior but none of them worked. When he was angry at her he even broke vases and crockery to intimidate his wife; but it didn't work. "As he could not bear to lose all this porcelain," P'u Yi wrote, "he replaced it with unbreakable vessels of bronze and lead." Later, P'u Yi discovered that his mother put much of the money she spent not into luxuries, but into a slush fund for clandestine political activities, something along the lines of a "committee to reestablish the monarchy."

P'u Yi entered the Forbidden City at the age of three. He did not see his mother again for seven years. On that occasion his mother and grandmother visited the Violet Enclosure. When the boy met them, he felt like a stranger. His grandmother's eyes glistened with tears and his mother seemed distant. She was probably upset at the manner in which her son was being raised. After the visit she angrily protested about his style of life to the high consorts, but to no avail.

"Although I had many mothers," P'u Yi later wrote, "I never knew motherly love."

The phrase, "many mothers," meant that when he entered the palace, he was formally adopted, as the son of the deceased emperors of the Tzu Hsi period—Emperor Tung Chih and Emperor Kuang Hsu. Therefore their wives automatically became his mothers. Tung

Chih had three wives who survived him; each became a senior high consort. Kuang Hsu's empress, Lung Yu, reigned as empress dowager. The four women fought continually among themselves over the right to exercise control over the boy. P'u Yi addressed each of them as "august mother." In turn, the empress dowager and the three senior consorts addressed him as "emperor." His own mother, pushed into the background by the empress dowager and the competing consorts, committed suicide in 1921, three years after her meeting with her son as the boy-emperor. She swallowed a fatal dose of opium after another fearful row with one of the high consorts over the rearing of her child. P'u Yi later came to realize that his mother's death was part of the terrible price he paid in being an emperor.

As for his father, it was only during Prince Ch'un's last three years as prince regent, that P'u Yi got to know him. Between 1908 and 1911, Prince Ch'un periodically visited his son at school and perfunctorily inspected his copybooks. The visits were pathetically brief. His arrival was announced by a eunuch; a moment later a beardless stranger wearing a peacock feather in his hat appeared in the doorway of the study and stood stiffly before the boy.

Father and son greeted each other in a stylized manner, and P'u Yi then read a sentence or two from his primer. His father, nervous, his head bobbing up and down, usually mumbled, "*Hao, hun hao*. Good, very good. Study hard, study hard." The prince then got up and left.

He had spent only two minutes with his son. Once every two months the prince regent made a visit. He never stayed longer than two minutes. Yet P'u Yi at least came to recognize his father's appearance—a man with an unwrinkled face, no beard, and a peacock feather at the back of his head, which was always bending like a rice stalk in the wind. Later, the son discovered that his father had something of a stutter, like his brother, the previous emperor Kuang Hsu. Thinking back in later years, P'u Yi realized that the reason the peacock feather shook so much was that his father was always nodding his head.

Disinterested in power and politics, Prince Ch'un was the wrong man at the wrong place at the wrong time in China's history. His thoughts were on the future and on the marvels of the industrial revolution. But his pressure for the modernization of the Celestial Empire was ineffective. He was one of the first Manchu noblemen to drive a motorcar and to install a telephone in his mansion. He was one of the first princes to cut off his queue, and to appear publicly in western attire. He was intensely interested in astronomy; his personal diary contained detailed records of the movement of heavenly bodies and summaries of newspaper reports on developments in the field. There was a strong contrast between the jejune daily life he led and his enthusiasm for astronomy.

"Had he been born a free man," P'u Yi reflected years later, "he might have become an astronomer." Instead, he became a prince of the royal blood at the age of nine and lived and died a prisoner of the ruling house. When the revolution of 1911 swept him from power, he went straight home from the Forbidden City and in high spirits announced, "From today onward I can stay at home and embrace my children." After his death, a couplet Prince Ch'un wrote with his own brush served as an epitaph to his unhappy role as power broker in the world arena. "To have books is real wealth," he wrote, "to be at leisure is halfway to being an immortal." The three unhappiest years of his life had been his three years as prince regent.

In the absence of a mother and father, in the absence of parental love, P'u Yi was raised like his predecessor, the homosexual emperor Kuang Hsu, by the eunuchs.

They waited on him when he ate, dressed and slept; they accompanied him on his walks and to his lessons; they told him stories, and, in return, P'u Yi said, "They received rewards and beatings from me."

They never left his presence. "They were the companions of my childhood," he wrote later. "They were my slaves, and they were my earliest teachers."

He was surrounded and suffocated by eunuchs. They remained at his side until the time he was taken captive by the Russians in

1945. By then there were only seven left out of the 3,000 he inherited from Tzu Hsi's reign. Under their constant attention and fondling, P'u Yi developed strong homosexual tendencies, similar to those of his predecessor. He was destroyed by the same system that had destroyed so many of his predecessors.

Can he be faulted? From the day he entered the Violet Enclosure, he was taught that he was omnipotent, the absolute ruler of the world; even after his abdication, the Articles of Favorable Treatment made plain that he still retained his title of the Son of Heaven, He Who Is Above, the Lord of Ten Thousand Years. Once, at the age of eight, he wanted to see whether the servile eunuchs were really obedient to a Son of Heaven. He selected one of them, pointed to a piece of dirt on the floor, and said, "Eat that for me." The terrified eunuch knelt down and ate it.

His tutors constantly quoted the sages to him about the need for "compassion and benevolence"; but at the same time they kowtowed to his authority and trained him to be authoritarian. Perhaps his mother alone realized that the boy was being turned into a monster; and in this light her suicide can be interpreted as a protest against the inhumanity of the imperial system.

P'u Yi was a sickly child, weak, underweight, and constantly besieged with colds and flu. He lacked the physical stamina and strength of his forebears. Clearly, the Manchu line was dying out. The Emperor Tung Chih, Old Buddha's son, produced no successor nor did his successor Kuang Hsu. Nor, for that matter, would P'u Yi, his successor.

Early each morning, as the sun rose in the east, beyond the palace compound, the boy-emperor heard the sounds of the outside world in those childhood years: the cries of the peddlers, the rumbling of the wooden wheels of heavy carts, and, at times, the sounds of soldiers singing. The eunuchs called this phenomenon the "city of sounds" and as a child, P'u Yi clambered atop the glistening, yellow-tiled serpentine roofs of the palace and peered longingly over the wall, to view from afar the real world outside his wonderland, a world which to him was as forbidden as the

Forbidden City was to those outside it. As he grew up, the "city of sounds"—the honking of geese on the road and the honking of automobiles on the paved streets—increasingly gave way to another "city of sounds," the sounds of the political world—rumor, speculation, news reports, secret dispatches. "I grew more and more interested as I grew older in this other 'city of sounds,'" P'u Yi later said. "The rumors were about my restoration."

Gradually it dawned on the youngster that he was being painstakingly groomed for a restoration—in the language of the Forbidden City, "the recovery of the ancestral heritage," and "the glorious return of the old order."

With a world torn and preoccupied by the agonizing struggle among the great powers on the Western front, during World War I, the Manchu moved to put P'u Yi back on the Dragon Throne and restore his Great Inheritance, dominion over 400 million people.

CHAPTER 10

The Restoration

As soon as P'u Yi had abdicated in 1912, Sun Yat-sen, the man of principle, kept his word and relinquished the presidency of the republic to Yuan Shih-k'ai, the man of no principle. Once he was in office, Yuan methodically destroyed the republic and, in the bargain, Sun Yat-sen too. First the new president refused to move the national capital to Nanking, where the republic had established the seat of government. Yuan's ultimate goal was the Dragon Throne and remaining in Peking suited his ambition ideally. Within a year, on one pretext or another, he dissolved Sun's Nationalist party, the Kuomintang, and drove the father of the republic into exile, establishing himself as China's first modern dictator. Even so, he remained dissatisfied: Something still stood between him and the throne—P'u Yi.

In the first year of his administration, Yuan had dispatched a representative of the republic to convey New Year's greetings to the deposed boy-emperor. For the occasion, P'u Yi was placed on the throne in the Cloudless Heaven Palace, dressed in the full imperial regalia of golden dragon coat and gown, hat with a pearl button, and pearl necklace. A Minister of the Presence stood on either side and beside them were Companions of the Presence and sword-bearing bodyguards. Shortly thereafter, on the occasion of the boy-emperor's seventh birthday, Yuan dispatched another envoy to convey the republic's good wishes.

These attentions from Yuan encouraged the princes and former Manchu officials who had been lying low during the first year of the republic to put on once again the robes that displayed their official insignia and to wear the other symbols of high office, the red button and the peacock feather. Emboldened, some went so far as to revive the custom of having outriders clear the way before them and having a retinue crowding around their sedan chair as they passed through the streets of Peking. Court officials who had, during the first year, visited the palace in ordinary clothes, changing into court dress after their arrival, now dared to venture out on the streets in imperial costume. When the then empress dowager died in 1913, a year after the abdication, a magnificent funeral procession passed through the streets publicly displaying the imperial standard, a five-clawed dragon on a brilliant yellow field. Yuan wore a black armband and ordered the republican flags flown at half staff for twenty-seven days. The members of the royal family and nobility wore mourning for the prescribed 100 days and wore it with pleasure as a sign of their loyalty to the emperor. Even more significant, Hsu Shih-chang, a grand tutor of the emperor, who had fled to Tientsin after the abdication, returned to Peking and paid his respects to the boy-emperor. Astounding as it may seem, he emerged later as president of the republic.

By 1914, the third year of the republic, these developments gave rise to the feeling that a restoration was near at hand. By now Yuan publicly sacrificed to Confucius, reverted to using imperial titles in his administration, and ordered the worship of Confucius throughout the country. Articles appeared in the press which urged a restoration of the emperor system. "The majority of our people do not know what the republic is, nor do they know anything about a constitution nor have they any true sense of equality and freedom," one pamphlet contended. "Having overthrown the empire and established in its place a republic, they believe that from now on they are subservient to no one and they think they can do as they please. From the moment the emperor was deposed, the centralization of power in the government was destroyed and no matter who may be at the head of the country, he cannot restore peace except by the reestablishment of the throne."

Confronted by his republican colleagues, Yuan denied that he entertained any intention of restoring the monarchy. He then exploited the fact that inquiries were being made by creating a Society for the Preservation of Peace, composed largely of scholars, and asked them to ponder the pros and cons of a restoration of the monarchy. "The change of national polity should be made with extreme care," he solemnly said. He proposed a national referendum to resolve the question, but since that would take interminably long, and the country, "of course," was impatient for the answer, he leap-frogged over the problem by setting up a Union of Petitioners under the aegis of the Society for the Preservation of Peace; this was no mean feat, since the society had yet to conduct its first meeting. The petitioners voted 1,993 to 0 in favor of the imperial system. Better still, they proposed the name of a new emperor.

"Reverently representing public opinion," the petitioners said, "we request that the president, Yuan Shih-k'ai, be made emperor of the Chinese empire." Their selection was unanimous.

Obviously, the kind of restoration Yuan had in mind did not benefit the old Manchu court, and their attitude toward him changed sharply.

In China, the symbol of power is the chop, or seal of office. Yuan sent a messenger to the Violet Enclosure and demanded the emperor's seal, his most valuable possession. The nine-year-old P'u Yi was "mortified and frightened" by this development. As his tutor Chen Pao-shen taught, "there are neither two suns in the sky nor two rulers in a country." In plain talk, Yuan Shih-k'ai's accession to the throne would be a death warrant for P'u Yi.

Like the court chronicles of other monarchies, the Chinese

87

annals are filled with the murder of monarchs and pretenders to the throne, legitimate and illegitimate. In the spring and autumn period of Chinese history, between the sixth and third centuries B.C., for example, there were thirty-six cases of regicide.

The emperor-designate's pressure notwithstanding, P'u Yi was able to hold on to his coveted seal. Yuan discovered to his chagrin that it was inscribed in both the Chinese and Manchu languages. Thus it was unsuitable for Yuan Shih-k'ai, a Chinese, who sought to found a purely Chinese dynasty, recapturing the glory of the last of the Chinese emperors, the Ming.

Nevertheless, the Manchu court feared for the life of their imperial charge, and secretly negotiated a private arrangement with the would-be emperor. The Manchu house would support him as emperor, and he, in return, agreed to scrupulously observe the Articles of Favorable Treatment. He guaranteed the personal safety of P'u Yi. As an earnest pledge of his good intentions, Yuan Shih-k'ai offered P'u Yi one of his daughters in marriage. Whether Yuan Shih-k'ai, ambitious, venal, and unscrupulous as he was, given to outbursts of terrible rage, would have honored the compact is questionable. But the Manchu had no option other than to work out an arrangement with the founder of a new dynasty.

As 1915 ended, Yuan established a bureau for the preparation of his enthronement. At this stage, of course, the great European powers were preoccupied by their global war. In this situation the Japanese could move to establish a preeminent position in Asia and the Pacific. First, the Japanese declared war on Germany—as an ally of Britain, of course—and seized the German concessions and leased territory in China. Then they delivered to the Chinese republic the infamous "twenty-one demands," whose acceptance would turn China into a Japanese vassal. Only the Americans were in a position to protest against the Japanese machinations. They did, but despite all their bluster, the Americans were hardly disposed toward going to war with Japan to protect China or American interests there. Yuan Shih-k'ai, who had betrayed his emperor before the turn of the century, betrayed the Manchu Dynasty and then betrayed the republic, now betrayed China itself to advance his personal fortunes. In return for Japanese support for his new dynasty he submitted to almost all of the Japanese demands.

But, for the first time in his inglorious career, Yuan had moved too far too rapidly. Opposition to him proved unexpectedly strong. By now, of course, nobody trusted him. In scrambling for personal power, he had betrayed everyone.

The army rebelled and the rebellion spread in much the same manner as the revolt against the Manchu had in 1911. Indeed, by the spring of 1916 whole sections of the country had turned against Yuan. In the end, the northern provinces, his political base, abandoned him and left the grasping, rotund Yuan isolated in Peking.

The loss of the northern provinces brought his great adventure to an abrupt close. In one of his periodic uncontrollable rages, he vented his frustration by arming himself with a sword and, bursting into the room where his favorite concubine (he maintained a collection of twenty concubines) was lying with her newly delivered baby. "With a few savage blows, he butchered them both, leaving them lying in their gore, thus relieving the apoplectic stroke which threatened to overwhelm him." The report comes from a British observer, Bertram Lennox Simpson, the editor of the bilingual *Far Eastern Times*. A few weeks later, on June 6, 1916, Yuan Shih-k'ai, shattered, died of a stroke and expeditiously removed himself from the scene.

However, the idea of a restoration of the imperial system, having been seeded, acquired a growth of its own. "The news of Yuan Shih-k'ai's death was received with great rejoicing in the Forbidden City," P'u Yi later recalled. "The eunuchs rushed hither and thither spreading the news, the high consorts burned incense to the tutelary god, and there were no lessons in school that day." Within the Violet Enclosure, the consensus was that the time was indeed at hand for a restoration of the monarchy but that Yuan, unlike Napoleon III, who had rigged a plebiscite in restoring the French throne, had no ancestry on which to rely for support.

Thus, the tempo of life within the Forbidden City continued to quicken in anticipation of a recovery of the Great Inheritance. Household department officials were busier than ever conferring such honors as posthumous titles for the dead (a common practice in Imperial China), and for the living permission to wear a peacock's feather. They also busied themselves procuring young girls for the high consorts as ladies-in-waiting and recruiting more eunuchs despite the prohibition in the Articles of Favorable Treatment. In addition, there was an endless series of private dinners and public banquets for members of the republican government and parliament, as plots and counterplots were concocted with a view to the restoration. "Though I was told nothing about it officially," P'u Yi later wrote, "I was not completely in the dark."

In the connection, it is interesting that at the time Lenin, from afar, concluded that the advisers around P'u Yi "will probably unite the feudalists, bureaucracy and Chinese clergy [sic] and prepare for a restoration."

In 1917 the restoration movement reached its climax. Chang Hsun, a colorful Chinese warlord, now put himself at the disposal of P'u Yi. Chang had fought for the Manchu in Vietnam against a French invasion of Tonkin, the region around Hanoi, which had been a Chinese vassal state, and he had remained loyal to the Manchu cause during the revolution of 1911. A devout Confucianist, he was fond of saying, "All we republican officials are subjects of the Great Ch'ing emperor." Obviously not given to the subtleties of diplomacy, he demonstrated his continuing loyalty to the throne by refusing to cut off his queue. So did his 20,000-man army which was known in China as "the pigtailed army."

According to Manchu custom, nobody could be present when a high official was received in audience by the emperor. On the occasion of the pigtailed general's visit to the Forbidden City, P'u Yi was coached by the court on the proper behavior of an emperor toward a loyal subject who was also a republican field commander. Praise his loyalty to the throne, P'u Yi was instructed, and reply modestly to his questions so as to display divine virtue.

The boy sat on the Dragon Throne in court regalia and Chang Hsun knelt and kowtowed before him in the old manner. Since P'u Yi's abdication, the court had been so democratized that officials no longer had to report to the emperor on their knees. Graciously P'u Yi waved him to a chair. As he sat down, his gray mottled queue swung gently, revealing itself to the curiously pleased boy.

"Your imperial majesty is truly brilliant," Chang Hsun said as the dialogue opened.

P'u Yi, though only nine-and-a-half, already displayed an aptitude for diplomacy. "I am young," he replied, "and I know very little."

Chang Hsun was impressed by the emperor's humility and he recalled a previous emperor who had been enthroned at the age of five. "He, too, acceded to the throne when of tender years," Chang Hsun said.

"How can I be compared with my august ancestor?" inquired the boy.

And so the audience went.

The following day Chen Pao-shen, his principal tutor, and other court officials descended on P'u Yi "bearing smiles" and informed him that Chang Hsun had praised his modesty and intelligence.

The young boy was happy with his performance. He had a right to be. This was the first time he entered the political arena armed with words—guile, tact, and cunning. "I did not ask myself why Chang Hsun had come for an audience," P'u Yi said, "or why my tutors were so visibly excited, or why the imperial household department had given him such lavish gifts, or why the high consorts had held a banquet for him."

About a fortnight later, on July 1 Chang Hsun returned to the Forbidden City—at the head of his army. "Chang Hsun has returned," the boy was told. P'u Yi guessed that he had come to pay his respects.

Instead, he learned to his great amazement that the pigtailed general had come to return his Great Inheritance, to replace him on the Dragon Throne, to restore the Great Pure Dynasty.

"I was stunned by this completely unexpected good news," P'u Yi said later.

Chang Hsun requested an audience. "A republic does not suit our country," he told the emperor. "Only your imperial majesty's restoration will save the people. All that is necessary is for Your Majesty to grant this request."

"I am too young," the boy replied gracefully. "I have neither talent nor virtue. . . . But if things are so I must force myself to do as you say."

The audience was no sooner completed than a eunuch rushed into the Cloudless Heaven Palace with a pile of previously prepared imperial edicts, nine in number. The first of these proclaimed P'u Yi's return to the throne, and another created a board of seven regents, in Orwellian-Politburo style, with Chang Hsun as first among equals.

Once again, in the Chinese tradition, a great diplomatic measure was transacted between midnight and daylight. At 4:00 A.M. on July 1, as Chang Hsun's pigtailed army set up roadblocks in and around Peking, P'u Yi was enthroned within the Forbidden City, for the second time in his young lifetime, in the presence of a small assembly of Manchu nobles and their Chinese collaborators.

That morning the Chinese capital awoke to find pigtailed military patrols guarding the main buildings and the banner with a five-clawed dragon on a yellow field, hoisted over the Forbidden City. In their newspapers, at breakfast, Peking's citizenry pored over an imperial edict which read:

> While yet in our boyhood the Great Inheritance was unfortu-nately placed in our possession and since we were then alone, we were unable to weather the numerous difficulties . . . [which arose]. The power of the state was therefore voluntarily given to the whole country with the hope that disputes might disappear, disturb-ances might stop, and people might be enabled to live in peace. But ever since the form of the state was changed into a republic,

continuous strife has prevailed and several wars have taken place. Forcible seizures, excessive taxation, and bribery have been an everyday occurrence. . . .

Thus we have prayed to heaven day and night in the close confines of the palace, meditating and weeping in silent suffering [for the people]. We are now resolved that a new beginning will be made with our people."

In Peking, which was basically a Tartar or Manchu city, the outpouring in support of the *ancien régime* was unmistakable. Tailors sold dragon flags as fast as they could sew them; second-hand clothing shops were stormed for Manchu court attire; theatrical houses were crowded with people who begged for false horsehair queues. Newspapers brought out special editions. Over shops and homes, there was a lavish display of brilliant yellow bunting. The reaction astonished the foreign community, astonished China, and astonished the world, preoccupied as it was with the ebb and flow of great battles on the Western front. The usually unflappable London *Times* was so flapped that it led off its "Late War News" column with a Reuter dispatch from Shanghai which reported: "It is announced that the young ex-Emperor issued a decree announcing his succession to the Throne."

Several days later, in an editorial, the *Times* wrote: "It is premature to call these developments a restoration of monarchial government, because only the form and not the spirit reappears. . . . We have yet to see what the people of the South will say to the change . . . [where] the Republic has always been more popular . . . than in the North." The paper, which at that time consistently reflected the views of the Foreign Office, observed, however, that "the Manchu Edict which notified that the dynasty had ceased to rule, never constituted complete abdication. Loopholes were always left for a possible restoration."

But London was dubious about the possibility and concluded, "What China really needs is a stable, incorruptible, and progressive government, and this is not likely to be satisfied under the discredited Manchu." At best, the paper surmised, P'u Yi would be a "puppet emperor in the hands of military adventurers."

For forty-eight hours, China was in a state of uproar and confusion. Then on July 3, the successor president to Yuan, Li Yuan-hung, under house arrest in Peking, made good his escape in the night and took sanctuary in the Japanese Legation, after being rebuffed by the French. From this sanctuary he revealed that as soon as the pigtailed army had entered Peking, he had dispatched his presidential seal by courier to the main republican army garrison at Tientsin. The incident pointed up the importance of the seal of office as a political factor in Chinese thinking. "As heaven does not scorn calamity, so has the monarchy been restored," President Li wrote. "I was entrusted by the people with great responsibilities and it is my natural duty to maintain the republic to the very end. . . . I have sent the seal to Tientsin, and I appoint General Tuan Chih-jui as Premier and order him to temporarily protect the seal."

The general, responding to the president's action, took prompt command of the divided republican army and issued a manifesto in which the premier declared that "internal strife is bound to invite foreign intervention and the end of the country will then be near." "In the face of this extraordinary crisis" he added "our indignation must be one." It was. Faced by the reality of a Manchu restoration and the reconsolidation of the spoils system under the absolute control of one family, the republican factions suddenly discovered a common ground.

The threat of civil war loomed. The republicans rightly felt that a violent deposition of the boy-emperor would enrage the peoples north of the Great Wall in Manchuria. The likely consequence would be the partition of China along the Great Wall, and the even more likely intervention of the Japanese to "protect" their interests in Manchuria. Tactfully, the premier's manifesto sought to save the boy-emperor's face and forestall Manchuria's defection from the republic. It accused the monarchists of "utilizing a young and helpless emperor" to fulfill their "sinister design" of overthrowing the republic. Observing that the dynasty "sincerely and modestly abdicated its power," the manifesto praised the

Manchu for peacefully bringing to an end more than twenty dynasties in Chinese history, and said "none can compare with the Great Pure Dynasty for peace and safety."

"That the boy-emperor has been dragged on the throne entirely against his wishes is undeniable," the republican government asserted.

"History tells us that no dynasty can live forever," the manifesto concluded. "It is an unprecedented privilege for the Great Pure Dynasty to be able to end with the gift of special treatment. How absurd to again place the Ch'ing house on the top of a high wall so that it may fall once more and [this time] disappear forever."

Thus, while absolving the boy in the matter, the republic warned the court that if they submitted peacefully the Articles of Favorable Treatment would remain in force. Otherwise, the boy and the Manchu house were in physical danger.

The united republican armies began to march on Peking. Ten days later, after a series of perfunctory engagements, they quickly enveloped the capital. But the fighting, foreshadowed a new kind of warfare on the battle-scarred Chinese land. On July 7 the republicans brought into play an "infernal flying machine" and carried out the first air raid in Chinese history. With this single plane, they dominated the sky and bombed the Forbidden City.

"On the day of the air raid, I was sitting in the schoolroom talking with my tutors when I heard an aeroplane and the unfamiliar sound of an explosion," P'u Yi recalled. "I was so terrified that I shook all over, and the color drained from my tutors' faces."

Everything was in chaos as the plane dove on the Cloudless Heaven Palace. Either the pilot did not mean business or was untrained in the art of bombing—aerial warfare was only of recent vintage on the Western Front—and "gave us," P'u Yi said, "nothing worse than a fright." The plane dropped three bombs. One fell outside the Gate of Honored Ancestors and injured a sedan-chair carrier. Another fell in the imperial garden and damaged a lotus pond. The third fell onto the roof of the western gate, where a group of eunuchs had gathered to gamble, but it failed to explode.

"Soon after this," P'u Yi said, "the sound of approaching gunfire was heard within the Forbidden City."

The restoration collapsed.

"The bombs dropped by the aircraft of the army to punish the rebels changed things completely," P'u Yi wrote. "Nobody came to kowtow to me any longer, there were no more imperial edicts to read, and all my regents disappeared, except for my loyal tutor, Chen Pao-shen, and one other."

Chang Hsun sought refuge in the Dutch Legation. When the victorious republican forces entered Peking on the morning of July 12, "one could pick up real queues all over the place," P'u Yi acidly commented. These were the pigtails cut off by Chang Hsun's soldiers as they fled the field.

In this situation, the court hastily prepared an abdication edict, the second in the brief life span of the boy-emperor. The abdication edict frightened P'u Yi and he started to cry. Perhaps he sensed then that he would never regain the Dragon Throne. Humpty Dumpty had fallen from the great wall and all the emperor's horses and men could not restore him to power again.

This abdication decree, like P'u Yi's preceding one, was couched in Confucian terminology. "As our years are tender and as we live deep in the Forbidden City," it read, "we followed the memorials of Chang Hsun and others who said the nation was in a state of fundamental disorder. . . . It was only because we were asked to save the nation and the people that we forced ourselves to accede to the requests made of us and assumed power."

But the prospect of civil war changed everything.

"Our people have suffered hardships for years, and their state is as desperate as that of the burning or drowning man," the edict continued. "How could we then compound the people's miseries with war? Thinking this we were disturbed and unable to rest.

"We resolved therefore that we would not keep this political power for ourselves."

The edict was never issued. Instead, the republic issued a

manifesto of its own which declared that the restoration rescript was "fraudulent" and that P'u Yi, "a child living deep in the Forbidden City, had no choice in the matter." For two reasons, the republicans, in effect, papered over the role of the court in the restoration attempt. First, they feared that the abortive restoration would encourage the breakaway of the provinces north of the Great Wall and their seizure by the Japanese. The second reason defies belief, but it reflects the political instability of post-Manchu China. The conspiracy to restore the empire was glossed over because many of the same republican generals who marched on Peking to restore the republic had taken part in it. They had been playing on both sides of the fence in a bid for power. Although blame for the restoration was placed on Chang Hsun, the republic treated him leniently; he possessed evidence that the highest officials of the republic were part of the conspiracy.

P'u Yi was fascinated to learn that many of the warlords and leading personalities of the republic were enthusiastic monarchists, and that they absolved the Manchu court of involvement in the affair to protect the emperor. In the meantime, they fought out among themselves the question of who would exercise the power of regent if a restoration did occur. The only conclusion the boy could draw was that his adversaries were not really so much opposed to a restoration as agitated by the question of who was to lead it.

As a Shanghai newspaper observed shortly after the collapse of the 1917 restoration, "Had the restoration been managed by Hsu Shih-chang, it would certainly not have been so clumsily handled."

Against this richly brocaded history, in the following year, Hsu Shih-chang who had once held the title of Grand Tutor at the Manchu court was inaugurated as president of the republic. A new wave of excitement flooded the Forbidden City. Among the new president's first acts was to pardon the leader of the "pigtail army," Chang Hsun, for his role in the abortive restoration. The president also sacrificed to heaven in the Confucian manner and called on the country to study anew the classics. In private, and public, the president referred to the Manchu house as the "present dynasty"

97

and to P'u Yi as if he were the reigning emperor. Clearly, a third restoration was in the making.

Indeed, at a dinner in the Great Within one evening, the president confided that he accepted the highest office in the republic so that he could restore the emperor and "act as regent on behalf of the young monarch."

This, it developed, was the sticking point. The Manchu court recoiled at the thought of a Chinese regent for a Manchu emperor. More suspiciously, the president proposed that P'u Yi take a Chinese girl, his daughter, perhaps, as empress. A Chinese girl to share the Chamber of Divine Repose with the Son of Heaven! Outrageous. The ancestors of P'u Yi would writhe in their tombs. "From this time onward," P'u Yi said, "the Forbidden City never spoke about Hsu Shih-chang again with the old enthusiasm."

Enthusiasm or lack of it notwithstanding, the president's position grew increasingly desperate as the republic plunged deeper into anarchy and disorder. In this turbulent setting, two figures slowly emerged from the welter of confusion and moved into the forefront. They were destined to engage each other relentlessly in a struggle for power which would extend half a century and more: Chiang Kai-shek and Mao Tse-tung.

In 1911, at the age of twenty-three, Chiang, who had attended a Manchu military school, cut off his queue and joined the revolution against the dynasty. At the time the warlords increased their power. By 1919 the ritual of civil war in China was as structured as the planting of rice in the South or millet in the North. With the rise of the warlords, however, a new feature appeared on the Chinese landscape, the emergence of political parties. The concept of political parties was of Western origin of course. But the parties bore little resemblance to their Western counterparts except for the Communist and Fascist parties which later proliferated in the Western world. The central objective of the Chinese parties, as one Chinese analyst in the period observed, was "to *seize power* so as to be able to bring their ideas to the attention of the masses." This manifestly reflected the Chinese imperial tradition in which it is the duty of those who achieve power to set an example which the people can follow. As a result, in this period, China was divided into any number of "independent" and "semi-independent" areas as warlord pressed against warlord and political party pressed against political party for mastery of the republic. In some instances parties acquired warlord characteristics. Thus, for example, Sun's Nationalist or Kuomintang Party, and later the Chinese Communist Party, created their own private militia. At the time of the restoration, Chiang was a junior grade army officer of considerable promise. The muscular, stocky Mao Tse-tung also wore a pigtail. He was at school getting a typically classical education in the period before the 1911 revolution. Like Chiang, he cut off his queue and joined the spreading agitation against the Manchu. A bully, he and his friends attacked defenseless boys who refused to sever their plaits. When students and soldiers clashed at a guild house where he was living, Mao later recalled that "I escaped by fleeing to the toilet, where I hid until the fight was over."

Shortly after the failure of P'u Yi's 1917 restoration, a twenty-six-year-old Mao arrived in Peking and gazed on the Forbidden City for the first time, the Violet Enclosure from where he would one day rule China like an emperor. Settling in the capital, Mao became an assistant librarian at Peking University and drifted into a Marxist study group. Although P'u Yi would never meet either Chiang or Mao face-to-face, the destiny of the three, and the destiny of China, were to be inextricably interwoven.

With peace restored in Europe and the Versailles Conference in progress, the Manchu continued to plot actively the restoration of the dynasty. Given the growing anarchy in the countryside, they had reason to believe that the mandate of heaven would swing in their favor. From a political standpoint, however, they felt that one mistake in the abortive 1917 restoration was their failure to elicit the support of a foreign power for the "glorious return of the old order." There was another need for foreign support—protection. After the 1917 affair, a number of extremist factions in China, such as the Anti-Manchu League, demanded that the republic abrogate the

Articles of Favorable Treatment and be done with the court once and for all, driving P'u Yi from the Forbidden City. In their view, which was not without justification, as long as the boy-emperor occupied the Great Within he posed a threat to the republic.

The recent overthrow of the Austro-Hungarian, German, and Russian empires did not faze the Manchu, who were determined to restore the throne. Their problem was that P'u Yi, confined to the Forbidden City and under constant republican surveillance, could not easily establish regular contact with a foreign power. The court needed a cover. They found one in the boy's education. P'u Yi would learn a foreign language and a foreign tutor would be engaged to teach him. Given the outcome of World War I, with the Anglo-Saxon powers in ascendancy, it seemed wisest for P'u Yi to study English.

First the post of tutor was offered to an American diplomat who reluctantly turned it down because he was about to be appointed *chargé d'affaires* at Peking. The selection of an experienced diplomat rather than a professional English teacher showed the court's true interest; it was not education, but politics.

Next, the court turned to the British and offered the post of English tutor to Reginald Fleming Johnston, a senior official of the Colonial Office who spoke fluent Chinese. Johnston had served twenty years in China, and was a high-ranking official in the administration of the British leased territory at Weihaiwei, a port city on the Yellow Sea.

Johnston readily accepted the appointment, pending the approval of the Colonial and Foreign Offices in London. They quickly approved, sensing the opportunity to plant an agent within the Forbidden City. The fact that Johnston was anything but a teacher, plagued him thereafter. He certainly did not cross the threshold of the imperial labyrinth to teach reading, writing, and arithmetic. Vigorously defending his role in the Forbidden City, he later wrote, "It would be wrong to assume that this educational scheme was part of a conspiracy to restore the young emperor to the throne."

But then he openly acknowledged:

"It is true that most of those who interested themselves in the proposal, not excepting the president [of the Republic] himself, were more or less dubious about the prospects of republicanism in China, and some of them, at least, were still at heart loyal to the monarchy.

"But," Johnston continued, "all they hoped to achieve by having their former sovereign taught something of the history and institutions of the Western world was that in the event of the failure of the republicans to establish a stable government acceptable to the people of China, following a popular revulsion of feeling in favor of the old ways, the emperor might be ready and qualified to play his appropriate part in the building up of a new China under a limited constitutional monarchy."

Clearly, Johnston entered the Forbidden City in a dual role—as a British conduit and as a Manchu instrument in plotting the recovery of P'u Yi's "ancestral heritage." In His Majesty's Service, however, he clearly lacked some of the more dashing attributes of James Bond. Then forty-four years old and unmarried, Johnston was without a mistress at a time when concubinage flourished and both Chinese and foreigners acquired Chinese or White Russian girls as easily as they purchased a catty of rice.

As for the eleven-year-old boy, as P'u Yi later put it, "I was very surprised and disconcerted when I was told that I was to have a foreigner as a tutor." But, young as he was, he recognized the need for foreign support for the Manchu court.

CHAPTER 11

The Foreign Devil

P'u Yi viewed Johnston's arrival within the Forbidden City with misgiving. The first time he had seen a foreign devil was at the last reception the Empress Dowager Lung Yu held for the wives of Peking's diplomatic community. "I thought their strange clothes and their hair and eyes of so many colors were both ugly and frightening," he said.

At that time he had never seen a Western man, but he confessed that he had a rough idea of what they looked like from illustrated magazines. "They wore moustaches on their upper lips," he recalled. "There was always a straight line down the legs of their trousers, and they invariably carried sticks." The eunuchs told him that their moustaches were so stiff that one could hang lanterns from the ends. Their legs were similarly rigid; indeed, a senior Manchu official at the time of the Boxer Rebellion counseled Old Buddha that the foreign devils were so stiff that "when fighting them it is only necessary to knock them over with bamboo poles for them to be incapable of getting up again." As for the sticks foreign men carried, the eunuchs confided to the credulous, slender boy that they were "civilization sticks" and were employed for beating people. Given the free use of the bamboo rod within the Forbidden City at least this made sense. Perhaps these Western foreign devils were human after all.

On March 4, 1919, according to P'u Yi—and March 3, according to Johnston's first report to the British Foreign Office—the tutor and pupil met for the first time.

Prince Ch'un, the boy's father, took Johnston in hand at the Palace for the Cultivation of Happiness, the "little red schoolhouse" of the Forbidden City, and introduced him to his charge.

Johnston found the boy astride a makeshift throne. According to the protocol for receiving foreigners, the Scot bowed to the boy. P'u Yi then rose from the throne, descended and shook his hand. Johnston bowed again, and withdrew. A few minutes later he returned and this time P'u Yi bowed to him, an act which acknowledged the boy's acceptance of him as a teacher.

Johnston impressed the boy. "Despite his age," P'u Yi said, "his movements were deft and skillful." But, as in the illustrated periodicals, his back was so straight that the boy wondered if he had hidden an iron frame under his clothes. Although Johnston had no moustache or "civilization stick," and his legs bent, he always gave the boy an impression of stiffness. "It was his blue eyes and graying fair hair in particular that made me feel uneasy," P'u Yi later said.

If there was uncertainty about Johnston's role as an agent in His Majesty's Service, his British Majesty, that is, Johnston himself dispelled this doubt in his illuminating memoir, *Twilight in the Forbidden City*, published in London in 1934 before his death in retirement on a small island off the English coast. "Shortly after [my first] interview I wrote, for the information of the British authorities, a brief account of my experiences," he said.

The intelligence report contained a lengthy paragraph in which Johnston recorded his impressions of the boy-emperor. Warm and sympathetic, the report made plain that Johnston and the Manchu youth had established almost immediate rapport. Johnston observed:

The young emperor has no knowledge whatever of English or any other European language, but he seems anxious to learn and is mentally active. He is allowed to read the Chinese newspapers, and evidently takes an intelligent interest in the news of the day, especially in politics, both domestic and foreign. He has a good general knowledge of geography, and is interested in travel and exploration. He understands something of the present state of Europe and the results of the great war, and seems to be free from false or exaggerated notions about the political position and relative importance of China. He appears to be physically robust and well-developed for his age. He is a very "human" boy, with vivacity, intelligence, and a keen sense of humour. Moreover, he has excellent manners and is entirely free from arrogance. This is rather remarkable in view of the extremely artificial nature of his surroundings and the pompous make-believe of the palace-routine. He is treated by the court functionaries with all the outward reverence supposed to be due to the "Son of Heaven," he never goes outside the "Forbidden City" and he has no chance of associating with other boys except on the rare occasions when his younger brother and two or three other youthful members of the imperial clan are allowed to pay him short visits. Even his daily visits to the schoolroom are made the occasion for a kind of state procession. He is carried there in a large chair draped in imperial yellow, and he is accompanied by a large retinue of attendants.

Soon thereafter the emperor and the foreign devil entered into a genuine, intimate friendship.

P'u Yi gradually realized, he wrote later, how diligently Johnston taught him, and he described himself as "pleased." Some of the training belonged to the theatre of the absurd, a page out of *Turandot, The Mikado* or *Anna and the King of Siam.* Johnston not only taught him English but also trained him to behave like an English gentleman.

For example, Johnston explained to the Lord of Ten Thousand Years that if he ever visited London he was bound to be invited to tea, and invariably on a Wednesday. "At them one can meet peers, scholars, celebrities and all sorts of people Your Majesty will need to meet," Johnston observed. There is no need to dress formally, he continued, "but manners are most important."

And P'u Yi, raised from the cradle to eat from a bowl with chopsticks, humorously recalled how Johnston scolded him on one occasion and admonished him not "to drink tea as if it were water, nor to eat cakes as if they were a real meal, or make too much noise with a fork or spoon."

The etiquette of the British version of a Japanese tea ceremony aside, Johnston made a deep impression on the boy's mind and the subjects they discussed ranged far afield from tea and crumpets.

"What brought about the closeness between teacher and pupil was his patience," P'u Yi said. "Looking back on it now, I realize that it can have been no easy matter for the testy Scot to adopt the attitude he did to a pupil like myself."

Johnston brought the boy English weeklies and when P'u Yi expressed intrigue "at these funny things"—photographs of aircraft, tanks, and artillery—Johnston, "seeing that I was interested, explained the things in the pictures to me and told me what tanks were for and so forth."

P'u Yi, who had never ventured beyond the Great Within after his midnight arrival in the compound at the age of three, ten years earlier, was fascinated.

The young emperor was also impressed by the advertisements in the foreign journals and ordered the eunuchs "to buy dogs and diamonds for me from abroad like the ones shown in the ads." He had a wooden floor laid down in the Mind Nurture Palace and ordered European furnishings with the result that his room became a mélange of styles, both Chinese and Western.

The boy also aped his tutor. Imitating Johnston, he bought all sorts of trinkets in the manner of the foreign devils, watches and chains, rings, tiepins, cuff links, and so forth. Everything about Johnston captivated the last emperor of China and the boy went so far as to consider the odor of mothballs on his clothes as sort of Western perfume.

"I do not think that he ever realized how deep an influence he exercised on me," the Son of Heaven wrote. "The woolen cloth that he wore made me doubt the value of all the silks and satins of China, and the fountain pen in his pocket actually made me ashamed of the Chinese writing brush."

Gradually, the lessons in the English language and English etiquette dissolved, and discussions on extracurricular topics, ever-widening in scope, occupied more and more hours. Johnston told P'u Yi about the life of the English royal family, the politics of different countries, the strength of the powers after World War I, of places and customs all over the world, of the great British Empire "on which the sun never set," of China's civil wars, and so forth.

The depth of Johnston's influence was so great that a mere remark by him that queues were "pigtails" was enough to make the boy cut his off.

Ever since the abdication of the dynasty in 1912, the home ministry of the republic continually wrote the imperial household department of the emperor asking for cooperation in persuading the Manchu bannermen to cut off their queues. They also hoped that the court of the Forbidden City would follow suit. The tone of the letters was courteous and no reference was ever made directly to the Son of Heaven himself. In reply, the court employed a myriad of excuses to put off the republic. For example, the Violet Enclosure argued that queues "were a useful way of distinguishing who should be allowed in and out of the Forbidden City." In 1919, when Johnston entered the imperial city, it was still a city of pigtails. Yet Johnston's mild expression of disapprobation was enough to induce P'u Yi to "have mine off." When the eunuchs recoiled in horror and refused to apply the shears, P'u Yi cut off his queue with his own hands.

Within several days, more than a thousand pigtails disappeared within the Forbidden City as princes, court officials, eunuchs followed the emperor's example. The high consorts wailed, the boy's tutors wore long, painful expressions. Only Chen Pao-shen, the emperor's faithful adviser, and a handful of other senior officials retained their queues.

Since the Chinese language has no alphabet and it often is impossible to transliterate Western proper nouns faithfully, the

Chinese usually accord a foreigner a name of their own choosing; or sometimes the foreigner selects a Chinese name.

Johnston coined for himself a literary name, Chuang Shih-tung, drawn from the Confucian admonition that "a scholar sets his mind on truth." And as the relationship between P'u Yi and Johnston deepened, the boy asked Johnston to give him an English name. The Scot prepared a list of the names of British kings. From the list P'u Yi selected the name "Henry." Henceforth, in the foreign tabloids and Sunday supplements, the last emperor of China became best known as Henry P'u Yi.

In the course of their classroom sessions, Johnston noticed that the boy strained hard to read the large clock in the room. Johnston suspected that his pupil was badly short-sighted and he counseled the imperial household department to summon a foreign ophthalmologist to examine the emperor's eyes. To Johnston's surprise, the suggestion created as much of an uproar as if he had tipped over a pan of boiling water. P'u Yi described the reaction: "The Forbidden City all but exploded," he said.

The court trembled at the thought that the eyes of the Celestial Countenance should be examined by a foreign devil. The Lord of Ten Thousand years was still in the vigor of youth. Why should he wear spectacles like an old man? At the boy's insistence, an ophthalmologist examined him and strongly recommended glasses; from then on, for the remainder of his life, P'u Yi wore glasses, either black-rimmed clear glasses indoors or prescription sun glasses outdoors. No photograph of him ever appeared thereafter, until his death, without the inevitable spectacles.

As Johnston's influence with the boy broadened, and was translated into action, the eunuchs and officials of the court developed a deepening dislike, or even hatred, for him. To make matters worse, Johnston continually pressed P'u Yi to institute a budget as a means of excercising fiscal control in the Forbidden City, where graft and corruption were ingrained. In those days the expenditure of the palace was still enormous and the payments from the republic, under the Articles of Favorable Treatment, were often in arrears. To meet the running expenses of the Great Within, the imperial household department sold and pawned antiques— paintings, calligraphy, jade and other semiprecious carvings, porcelains, and similar *objets d'art* to Chinese and foreigners, museum curators, private collectors, and tourists. "Gradually," P'u Yi wrote with delicate understatement, "I learned through Johnston that there was *'something fishy'* [in his memoirs he used the English phrase] about these sales."

On one occasion, for example, the imperial household department approached the emperor for permission to sell a solid gold five-and-a-half-foot high pagoda. The department proposed to sell the object by weight. According to Johnston, only a fool would act in this manner. "I therefore sent for the officials of the department and asked them how they intended to sell it," P'u Yi said. "When they said they would sell the pagoda according to its weight, I burst into fury: 'Only fools would do that! Haven't you got an ounce of sense?'"

Johnston, the court correctly surmised, was ruining their racket. Accordingly, their hatred for him became implacable.

Matters came to a head in 1923, when Johnston learned that many new curio shops had opened along Heavenly Peace Square adjoining the great square in front of the Forbidden City. This is where the emperors had celebrated public occasions in the past, the republic observed Double Ten in the present, and where, in the future, the Communists would commemorate the October 1 founding of their reign. The eunuchs, Johnston learned, had systematically looted the unused Palace of Established Happiness of its art objects, sometimes replacing the originals with fakes. When P'u Yi ordered the eunuchs questioned, and beaten as necessary, to uncover the criminal network, the palace, where the treasures of the brilliant Ch'ien Lung period were stored, mysteriously burned to the ground, destroying evidence of what had been looted. "The fire is as impenetrable a mystery as the amount of damage it did," P'u Yi wrote. "My suspicion is that it was deliberately started by thieves to cover their traces."

A few days later another fire started, this time above one of the windows of the No Idleness Study in the eastern wing of the Mind Nurture Palace. Fortunately for the boy emperor, it was detected early. "My suspicions instantly grew stronger," P'u Yi said, and he confided to Johnston and Chen Pao-shen: "Somebody started this fire not only to cover his traces but also to murder me."

In July, 1923, P'u Yi reached a momentous decision. He decided to deal with the problem once and for all by expelling the remaining eunuchs from the palace. The imperial guards rounded up the eunuchs, 1,000 in all, and drove them out of the Forbidden City in less than an hour. One hundred eunuchs were retained.

By this act, the benign boy-emperor, isolated and sheltered, whose photographs give the impression of a passive, vapid youth peering expressionlessly through his spectacles, breathed the fire of his ancestral line, the fire of a dragon. He acted with energy and determination, behavior which belied his outward appearance. The Chinese press, which had been watching this slow transformation in the boy, from the removal of his pigtail to the expulsion of the eunuchs from the Forbidden City, applauded vigorously and hailed him in print as "one of the very few progressive Manchu princes of the present day." One Peking newspaper went so far as to comment, "Probably there would have been no Chinese republic had he been born thirty or forty years earlier."

In this fashion, over the years, Johnston became, as P'u Yi fondly recalled, "the major part of my soul." As for Johnston, he came to call the boy "my young dragon." Unmarried, childless, Johnston became a father to the child, a rapidly maturing young man who was in desperate need of paternal love and guidance.

But if Johnston was educating P'u Yi, the education was a two-way street. As Confucius had forecast, China could never be conquered because the conqueror would become Chinese. Fascinated by Chinese culture and the Chinese language, which is exceptionally beautiful when written and lends itself admirably to poetry, P'u Yi noticed that after two or three months Johnston grew "more and more like my Chinese tutors." Johnston employed the same reverential forms in addressing the boy and "his ways of doing things became very Chinese."

During his twenty-eight years in China, Johnston revisited the West only twice. He was well versed in Chinese history; familiar with the Chinese landscape, having visited every province in the country at one time or another; expert in Confucianism, Buddhism, and Taoism; a connoisseur of Chinese poetry; a student of Chinese teas and peonies. "I do not know how many classical Chinese books he had read," P'u Yi said with a mixture of respect and amazement, "but I remember he used to wag his head as he'd chant T'ang dynasty poems just like a Chinese teacher, his voice rising, falling, and pausing."

When P'u Yi awarded Johnston a mandarin hat button of the highest grade, as a token of his appreciation, his tutor had a full set of Manchu court clothes made for the occasion. When the imperial household department rented an old-style Peking house for him, he furnished it as a veteran of the *Ta Ch'ing*, or Great Pure Dynasty: adorning the entrance with red tablets on which were written in black Chinese *tzu* or characters, "Companion of the Palace of the Cultivation of Happiness," "Entitled to Be Carried in a Chair with Two Porters," "Awarded the First Grade Hat Button," "Entitled to Wear a Sable Jacket," and so forth. Each time P'u Yi honored him with a present, Johnston wrote a memorial to the boy-emperor, thanking the youngster for his benevolence.

However deeply enamored Johnston was of China and things Chinese, he was still a product of Western civilization. Royalist that he was—King George V later knighted him for his work in China—Sir Reginald Fleming Johnston was inherently democratic. In China, like many Westerners before and after him, he found a common ground of understanding in the writings of China's "democratic philosopher," Mencius. And he brought Mencius's teachings fully to bear on his "young dragon." The boy's English copybooks were peppered with the dialogues and parables of the Chinese sage. In attractive, legible handwriting, for example, P'u Yi wrote in English: "Mencius said, 'The most important element in a state is the people; next come the altars of the national gods; least in importance is the king.' " Subtly, and not so subtly, Johnston prepared P'u Yi for a return to the Dragon Throne not as an absolute monarch, a political impossibility given the currents unleashed by the 1911 revolution, but as a limited constitutional monarch.

And like many a Western romantic enamored of the Asian way of life, the more attached and the more deeply he became involved in the Asian life style, the more he wanted to reform it. This conflict within Johnston is reflected in his reports to the British Foreign Office. By illustration, Johnston openly expressed alarm to London about the "moral dangers" which confronted his young ward as the youth matured—the pernicious influence of the eunuchs, the prospect that the boy would be exposed to harem life, and the terrifying isolation of the Forbidden City from the real world.

"Although the emperor does not appear to have been spoiled, as yet, by the follies and futilities of his surroundings," Johnston said in a dispatch, "I am afraid there is no hope that he will come unscathed through the moral dangers of the next years of his life—necessarily very critical years for a boy in his early teens—unless he can be withdrawn from the influence of the hordes of eunuchs and other useless functionaries who are now almost his only associates."

But underlying their personal relations, like a silent, swift, underground stream, coursed the politics of restoration, as P'u Yi matured and realized the dimensions of his Great Inheritance. Johnston encouraged his thoughts about a restoration, with deliberation.

"One can see clearly from all the papers," Johnston lectured him, "that the Chinese people are thinking again of the dynasty and that everybody is tired of the republic. I do not think there is any need for Your Majesty to worry about republicans and warlords. Tutor Chen Pao-shao is quite right in saying that the most important thing is for Your Majesty daily to renew your sage virtue."

While China was racked by turmoil, disruption, banditry, famine, and civil war, Johnston found within the Forbidden City the "one fragment of Chinese soil which preserved at least the outward appearance of stability and dignity, one virgin fortress in which the manners and rituals of a vanishing past still formed part of the daily routine."

Clearly, in the checkered and irrigated fields of China, these were troubled times. As a North China daily expressed it in 1921, "Of the peasantry, eight or nine out of every ten are illiterate and as obtuse as deer or pigs. It is a pitiful state of things. They have no conception whatever of the meaning of liberty, political rights and government. All they know is that they pay their land tax [to a war lord] and must provide themselves with the means of livelihood from day to day." In a coded dispatch to the State Department, the American Legation at Peking reported coincidentally that "there is far more corruption under the republic than under the Manchu régime." And in the marketplace, people were commonly overheard to ask: "How is the Emperor Hsüan Tung [P'u Yi]?" "Who is now ruling the imperial house?" "Would the country be at peace if the true dragon sat on the throne?" Even the most deeply anti-Manchu, antimonarchical people were disappointed in the republic. "The reason some people talked about a restoration," the politically astute P'u Yi said, "is that they were sick of the disasters inflicted by warlordism."

In this light, in 1921 the powerful Tientsin newspaper *North China Daily News*, taking note of the general dissatisfaction across the land, observed, "The only conclusion to be drawn from this is that republicanism in China has been tried and found wanting." Significantly, the paper added, "The mercantile classes and the gentry, the backbone of the land, are weary of all this internecine strife and we firmly believe that they would give their wholehearted support to any form of government which would ensure peace." In the light of the public response when peace and order finally came to China after the Second World War, the editorial proved an accurate prophecy.

P'u Yi, lean and bespectacled, was fifteen at the time. Already he was sensitive to the explosive situation. He did not believe that people wanted a restoration of the throne as much as that "they were sick of the disasters inflicted by warlordism." He also realized what should be, what was and what could be. And, having known no world other than the Forbidden City, he felt stifled and suffocated. "I grew to hate the sight of the high palace wall," he wrote. His father, Prince Ch'un, his tutors, Chen Pao-shen and Johnston, the high consorts, the eunuchs and other aides came and went freely through the massive gates of the Great Within. He alone was imprisoned. "Prison, prison, prison," he lamented increasingly as he climbed atop an artificial hill in the palace grounds and looked yearningly at the walls around him. Actually, Johnston's tales about the outer world whetted the boy's interest in the Great Without. Accordingly, with his brother P'u Chieh, his only childhood companion, he plotted an escape with an adventurous air of innocence to which only a Mark Twain could do justice in the retelling.

While P'u Chieh was permitted to move about freely, he had been trained from his infancy to remain completely faithful to the emperor, his brother, and never to forget that P'u Yi had been chosen by heaven as the head of the Aisin-Gioro clan.

The first step in their planned escape was to secure money. Like the corrupt eunuchs around him, he gathered a collection of valuable calligraphy and paintings from the imperial collection, including rare books dating from the Sung Dynasty. His brother secreted the scrolls under his flowing gown and deposited them outside the Forbidden City. With their finances secured, the two boys bribed the guards at the Gate of Divine Valor to let them pass as the opportunity arose. "My idea was a little too simple," P'u Yi recalled with tenderness. "I thought that all I had to do to win the guards over was to give them some money."

The youngsters had no sooner left the Mind Nurture Palace on the night of their escape when they learned that the whole Violet Enclosure was placed on a siege footing. All the gates, inner and outer, were sealed, and imperial guards patrolled the palaces and thoroughfares of the imperial compound.

The guards at the Gate of Divine Valor had betrayed him. More than ever, P'u Yi realized that though the outer world might view his life as the ruler of his own city-state with envy, actually he was nothing more than a prisoner of historical forces over which he exercised no control.

Failing in his plot to escape, the boy became more despondent. He grew bored with his environment. As this mood of restlessness and resignation deepened, his father and the high consorts attributed his behavioral change largely to puberty and applied the time-tested imperial remedy. They put a girl in his bed—not one girl, but two.

CHAPTER 12

The Phoenix and the Dragon

Traditionally, in China's age of imperial splendor, when an emperor was seeking a bride who would be honored with the title of empress, couriers were dispatched throughout the Celestial Empire and the most attractive, best educated, and well-mannered girls were borne by sedan chair into the Forbidden City. From this collection, the emperor selected the maiden of his choice. He either handed her a jade mushroom, whose significance is now lost in the dust of the past, or he hung a brocaded pouch on her jade buckle. Often, the selection was decided on political grounds—to strengthen relations with a clan or distant province. Often, too, the emperor's mother made the choice for him, and several girls would be selected, one as empress, another as second consort, another as third consort, and so forth.

The Grand Nuptials normally lasted several days, days filled with feasts, theatricals, the granting of new titles, and general merriment within and outside the walls of the Forbidden City. Viceroys, governors, generals, and mandarins flocked to the Cloud- less Heaven Palace to witness the event.

In a huge sedan chair with elaborate brocaded lining, borne by twenty-two eunuchs, the bride was carried through the gates of the Violet Enclosure. On the serpentine corners of the canopy were perched four magnificent silver birds, *feng,* the mythical queen of birds who symbolized happiness and fertility.

As in the case of other important imperial acts, the actual marriage ceremony was conducted in the middle of the night. After the rites of the Golden Scroll and the Golden Seal, the bride was borne to the Palace of Earthly Peace and there the Son of Heaven greeted her. The couple withdrew to the privacy of a brocaded dragon-and-*feng* couch where the emperor removed the bride's ornate headdress and gazed into her eyes for the first time.

P'u Yi reacted with disinterest in the matrimonial project as it was outlined by his father and the high consorts. But he had little choice in the matter. His Grand Nuptials were set for December 3, 1921, shortly before his seventeenth birthday. As a concession to modernity, the personal inspection ceremony was discarded. Instead, the boy made his choice from a group of photographs. "I was to pencil a mark on the picture of the girl I liked best," he said.

The photographs of four candidates were placed in his youthful hands, Manchu girls approved by the high consorts and the imperial household department. P'u Yi was disappointed. The photographs were of poor quality (he could not see their faces clearly) and in their elaborate ceremonial dresses, "their bodies looked as shapeless as tubes," he said. The reference to their shape is the only expression of desire—latent or repressed—which he made about the affair. For a young man of seventeen (according to Chinese reckoning), he seemed unnaturally disinterested. "I hardly thought about my impending marriage," he conceded later. "I gave no thought to the relations between husband and wife."

After studying the photographs, he casually drew a circle "on a pretty picture." Beauty is in the eye of the beholder, the sages of all lands tell us, and P'u Yi's choice was Wen Hsiu, a moon-faced princess of the Ordet clan, a girl three years his junior.

The court demurred, described her as "ugly," and proposed the selection of Wan Jung, the daughter of a rich and powerful family, graceful, statuesque, a true Manchu beauty by any norm, and the same age as P'u Yi. Thus, even when it came to the selection of a wife, he discovered he was not a free agent. The suffocating atmosphere overcame him once more but, as usual, he bowed to the "advice of the princes," and wondered aloud why they had not explained the situation at the beginning instead of letting him think that "there was nothing to this business of making a pencil mark." Respecting his elders, in the Confucian tradition, he dutifully penciled a circle on the photograph of Wan Jung.

P'u Yi still did not appreciate the true motivation behind the marriage arrangements: relieving him of restlessness and boredom as a prisoner of history.

"Since the Celestial Countenance has marked Wen Hsiu's photograph," he was then informed, "it would not do for her to marry one of his imperial majesty's subjects, so his imperial majesty had better take her as a consort."

Disinterested in the project from the outset, the boy now strongly objected. "I did not feel that I had much need for one wife, let alone two," he said. "I was not at all keen on this proposal." In all probability, the court had hoped that he would select one of the four as empress and the other three as consorts, in the tradition of most Sons of Heaven.

If P'u Yi was upset, so was his overly protective bachelor tutor, Reginald Johnston. "He acquiesced without enthusiasm in his betrothal," Johnston wrote, "but he surprised and shocked the court by vehemently protesting against being provided with more than a single fiancée."

Within the Forbidden City, Johnston was counted mainly responsible for having inspired the boy with monogamous ideas. This, Johnston protested, was unfair and untrue.

"The only opinion I expressed at court, or in conversation with the emperor, on any aspect of the matrimonial project," he said, "was that as he was only a boy of sixteen [Western-style age] the question of his marriage was one which might advantageously be discussed at a later date." Apparently, the tutor-father did not want a rival for the affection of his "young dragon."

Unmoved though he was by the physical aspects of the enterprise, P'u Yi displayed a marked appreciation of its political importance. The Grand Nuptials marked his coming of age. Now he would become his own master. "It meant," he said with relief, "that others could no longer control me as if I were still a child." Thus, when the Manchu princes pointed out to him that according to ancestral custom, the emperor must have an empress and a consort, he found the argument politically irresistible. Since he wanted all the prerogatives of an emperor, he agreed to take a consort too.

Briefly, for the fleetest of moments, the occasion of the Grand Nuptials provided the court with the opportunity to relive the radiance and splendor of the past. The yellow standards of the Great Pure Dynasty flew again from the crenellated walls of the Forbidden City and the sedan chairs bearing empress and consort were paraded through the streets of Peking, with large numbers of republican troops and police serving as a bodyguard, despite the political contradiction of the situation. Two princes, dressed in Manchu robes and bearing staffs of office in their hands, rode on Mongolian ponies behind two republican army bands. They in turn were followed by additional musical bands, a troop of republican cavalry, and mounted police. Then came seventy-two dragon-and-*feng* parasols and banners, four yellow pavilion sedan chairs containing the two girls and the Golden Scroll and Golden Seal, and thirty pairs of brightly lit yellow lanterns. The need for lanterns was manifest. The wedding ceremony was carried out in the light of a waning moon at 4:00 A.M., the hour selected as most propitious by court astrologers.

Peking turned out to witness the spectacle. Among the foreigners, particularly, tongues wagged incessantly when it was learned that the consort had entered the Forbidden City the day *before* the wedding. This gave rise during the cocktail hour in the legation compounds to ribald suggestions that the consort provided the young dragon with an opportunity for an introductory course into the rites of love. Johnston was upset by this "ignorant and nonsensical chatter" and hastened to explain to all who would listen that "the true reason why the *fei* (concubine) entered the palace first is that she might be able, on the empress's arrival, to place herself at the head of all the palace women and be the first to welcome her."

The Grand Nuptials not only provided the court with an opportunity to air the yellow bunting gathering mildew in the imperial storerooms, but it provided an occasion for the monarchists in the republican administration to fly their own colors. President Li Yuan-hung, China's Chief Executive during the abortive 1917 restoration, who had been reelected to office, sent P'u Yi a red card addressed to the "Emperor Hsüan Tung" and presented him with a wedding gift of four vessels in cloisonné, two bolts of silk and satin, a brocaded curtain, and a pair of scrolls wishing the Lord of Ten Thousand Years longevity, prosperity, and good fortune. The former president, Hsu Shih-chang, sent a gift of $20,000 and twenty-eight porcelain vases and a sumptuous hand-woven carpet with a dragon-and-*feng* design. From the different provinces, the warlords also sent rich gifts. All told, P'u Yi received more than $1 million in cash and literally a palace full of porcelains, scrolls, gold and silver objects, jade and other semiprecious stone carvings and, of course, bronzes. The only notable exception on the list of those who gave gifts—a "Little Red Book" listing the donors and their presents was published—was the name of Sun Yat-sen, who was then in the south trying desperately to retrieve his republic from the anarchy which was rapidly enveloping it; heart-broken, he died a year later, his dreams of creating a single-minded, unified China free from foreign control, unfulfilled. With prescience, in his last will and testament, he held that "our revolution is not yet finished." As Sun Yat-sen was aware, the nation was still torn between loyalty to the past and loyalty to the present. Thus, when the delegate of the president arrived at the Forbidden City to congratulate P'u Yi formally on the occasion of his wedding, he first addressed the boy as he would the head of a foreign state, bowing when he completed his address. "That was on behalf of the republic," he said. "Now your slave greets your imperial majesty in his private capacity." With that, the republican dignitary bent his knee three times and kowtowed nine times before the young man.

Such acts of fealty elated P'u Yi and the court. The tangible gifts from the republican revolutionaries were unimportant compared with these surprising demonstrations that the emperor still retained his hold on the Chinese. They seemed to imply that P'u Yi's prospects were bright.

The presence of foreign diplomats at the wedding ceremony excited the court still further. This marked the first time that foreign officials had appeared within the Violet Enclosure since the revolution of 1911. At a reception for the diplomatic community, P'u Yi addressed the assembled guests. "I, the emperor, feel honored by your presence," he said forcefully in English. The foreigners were impressed and some of them no longer completely ruled out the possibility of a restoration of the monarchy.

The only politically discordant note that December was that both the empress and consort were Manchu girls. Many monarchists hoped that, for the first time since 1644, a Manchu emperor would take to his couch a Chinese girl, even if only as a consort. But the Manchu racial tradition was too strong, and the desire to maintain the "purity" of the royal bloodline too overpowering to be sacrificed even for strategic political advantage. In such an event, the Manchu house would no longer be Manchu; its last vestige of distinctiveness would disappear; it would be assimilated by the Chinese as Confucius forecast. As it turned out, the court had little cause for concern. Like his predecessor, Kuang Hsu, P'u Yi fathered no children. There is even doubt that he ever consummated his marriage to the seductive-looking empress, Wan Jung, or with his young consort Wen Hsiu.

According to custom, the emperor and empress spent their wedding night in the Palace of Earthly Peace. The bridal chamber, some thirty feet square, was unfurnished except for an oversized bed more than seven feet square. Everything in the bridal suite, except the brilliant yellow tiles—the inevitable touch of imperial yellow— was dark red: red bed-curtains, red pillows, red flowers. When P'u Yi and his Manchu bride retired to the "peculiar room," as P'u Yi described it, he felt "stifled."

"The bride sat on the bed, her head bent down," he remembered, painfully recalling their first night. "I looked around me and saw that everything was red . . . it all looked like a melted red wax candle. I did not know whether to stand or sit."

He suddenly recoiled at the scene, and rushed out of the room, leaving his bride alone, unattended on her wedding night. As P'u Yi fled, perhaps for the first time he realized that the eunuchs, who had been fondling him from the crib through adolescence, had triumphed over him, and had gained a sense of revenge for their own sorrowful state. Generally, modern psychiatry considers homosexuality a symptom of inner conflict or the by-product of genetic, biological, cultural, and environmental factors. Reared by eunuchs, isolated from the heterosexual world, P'u Yi's sexual variation was more likely than not environmental in origin.

Homosexuality was not by any means unknown in China, nor were P'u Yi and his predecessor on the Dragon Throne, Kuang Hsu, the only emperors with homosexual proclivities. The most notorious episodes of homosexuality among the emperors of China were recorded during the spring and autumn period and the Han Dynasty, contemporary with the classical era of Western history when homosexuality was commonplace in both Greece and Rome. In Peking, within the Forbidden City, homosexuality was delicately referred to as the "shared peach" or "sheared sleeve." According to chroniclers of the empire, a duke strolling through the garden of his estate one day, in the company of a young male courtier, plucked a ripened peach, ate half the fruit and presented the other half to the young man. Hence the phrase, "shared peach." The phrase "the sheared sleeve" originated with an emperor, whose reign ended one year before Jesus went to the Cross. He awoke from a nap and found his favorite male companion sleeping at his side with his head on the emperor's sleeve. Fearful of disturbing the slumber of his lover, the emperor cut off the sleeve of his jacket.

In his autobiography, P'u Yi recalled thinking at the time of his panic, "how did Wan Jung feel, abandoned in the bridal chamber?" A mail-order bride, Wan Jung viewed the wedding from a different perspective. Like any Manchu girl of the royal blood, she had been prepared from childhood for a possible summons to the Forbidden City; that was the highest honor a dragon emperor could bestow on a Manchu woman. She was therefore both surprised and thrilled when the couriers of the Great Within brought the news that she was the chosen one.

"My wedding in 1922," she recounted to a friend some years later, "was perhaps the last Manchu pageant. Everything was done with care to fulfill the rites which have been elaborated through centuries to make the Son of Heaven's wedding the most marvelous of spectacles. Flowers perfumed the court. All the Banners came, bringing their wives and children. Everyone was dressed in robes jeweled and encrusted with gold, according to rank."

And Wan Jung continued with obvious relish, "I was the bride in it, and I enjoyed it all. It was fairy tale, such as my nurse used to tell me, come true."

As for her relationship with P'u Yi, she recalled life within the Violet Enclosure in those early years: "We had one part of the Forbidden City. There is a lovely lake there—pink with lotus in early summer. We skated on it when it was frozen, and drifted on it in a purple boat on warm spring evenings. We wrote and gave plays in the blue-domed theatre. . . . We lived a secluded life. We did not find it confining, but natural. The Son of Heaven and his bride, according to Manchu custom, usually lived a secluded life."

Her most interesting remark is that she did not find their relationship confining, but natural. Wan Jung was probably aware of the shared-peach and sheared-sleeve tradition behind the walled city.

Their personal relationship aside, politics gnawed at P'u Yi's innards. "If there had been no revolution I would be starting to rule with full power," he repeatedly told himself. "I must recover my ancestral heritage."

This chord became the dominant motif in his life. Eventually, he would undertake any risk, any gamble, ally himself with any camp, pursue any path, do anything required of him by whomever required it, if, in his own mind, it brought him closer to recovering his ancestral heritage. Of course, this was in open conflict with his strong desire to escape from the Forbidden City, to cut his moorings to the past, and to win his personal freedom. The conflict, which tormented him throughout his life, was never truly resolved, nor could it be.

While P'u Yi seriously considered his future, the warring political factions within the republican camp, however divided among themselves, were equally concerned about him. The dragon had attained maturity. Now he posed a more dangerous threat to the republic. If he could be deprived of his lair—expelled from the Forbidden City—the humiliation would weaken him immeasurably and reduce the possibility of another attempted restoration.

CHAPTER 13

The Flight from Peking

At the time of the wedding, old residents of Peking in 1921 commonly remarked that the city and the Violet Enclosure had not known such gaiety since the year before the outbreak of the disastrous Sino-Japanese War in 1895, the war which, in the last analysis, unhinged the Manchu Dynasty. But as Johnston himself astutely observed, "For three winter days, the twilight of the Manchu court seemed to have broadened into something that looked like daylight—but was not." He was prescient. Less than a year after his wedding day, P'u Yi was to be driven from the Forbidden City.

As it developed, after the Grand Nuptials and his coming of age, P'u Yi made the first use of his new authority in reorganizing the Forbidden City to carry out the "great enterprise." There was little doubt about the nature of the enterprise. A court document of the period, dated "First Month of the Sixteenth Year of Hsüan Tung"—1924—pointedly observed: "The most important task today is to plan secretly the restoration." P'u Yi gave first priority to consolidating his base by protecting the court. The next priority went to putting the Forbidden City's treasury in order to finance overt monarchist groups and secret societies that supported the restoration.

Ruthlessly, P'u Yi reorganized the imperial household department. He cut back the staff from 700 to 300. He broke precedent and appointed a Chinese chief-of-staff, Cheng Hsiao-hsu, particularly recommended by Johnston who described him as the man he most admired in China, with "his character, learning and ability . . . unmatched in the country." A former Manchu foreign-office functionary who had served largely in Japan, Cheng Hsiao-hsu declined to remain in the service of the republic after 1911 and eked out a meager living by selling calligraphy. After his appointment, Cheng Hsiao-hsu reorganized the imperial staff and instituted enormous economies. The imperial viands room was virtually closed down. The number of cooks was reduced from 200 to 37.

In an era when public relations was in its infancy, P'u Yi launched a public relations campaign that would be the envy of Madison Avenue. P'u Yi had always engaged in acts of charity in the royal manner, and the great majority of his gifts were bestowed anonymously. On the advice of his counselors he dropped the anonymity. Thereafter, he occasionally sent money directly to a newspaper office for distribution to an impoverished family or village the paper had reported about. On other occasions he sent emissaries with money direct to the destitute families. In either case, the newspapers carried a story within the next day or two about his bounty. At little cost he kept his name before the public.

But his gifts went beyond the realm of simple public relations. On September 3, 1923, Tokyo, rapidly developing into one of the world's major cities, was devastated by an earthquake which claimed 140,000 lives. For weeks, the disaster made the front pages everywhere. P'u Yi ordered antiquities, calligraphy, and other art treasures from the imperial collection to be sent to Japan to be put on the market to raise money for the families of the victims. Cheng Hsiao-hsu, with his Japanese diplomatic background, may have originated the idea. The gifts raised $250,000. In response, the

Japanese Diet sent a delegation to Peking to thank the young emperor for his liberality and sympathy. Chen Pao-shen, P'u Yi's senior tutor, praised his pupil for the "magnificence of the imperial bounty and the humanity of the celestial mind." Then, dryly, he added, "This action will make its influence felt in the future."

Simplistically, or perhaps because he was so dazzled by his lofty existence within the Forbidden City, Johnston refused to view the gesture toward Tokyo as political. "I can confidently assert that there is no political motive underlying the emperor's action in this matter," he wrote.

Despite these activities and the Grand Nuptials, P'u Yi grew more restless than ever. He had achieved his majority but he still lived in grand isolation with no immediate hope of a restoration. In fits of extreme despondency, he even contemplated renouncing the title and leaving China altogether. Johnston sympathized with his ward's plight and tried to console him with the reflection that all emperors lead lives of rigid isolation. But Johnston privately admitted to himself that the obvious answer to that was that P'u Yi's imperial ancestors were compensated. "They were real monarchs and exercised real power," Johnston acknowledged, "whereas their unhappy descendant of today is well aware that he has nothing but an empty title [and] that his only subjects are eunuchs and court officials." Even so, Johnston counseled delay, confident that the pendulum would swing in P'u Yi's favor as anarchy engulfed the republic. But the young emperor's desire to restore the ancestral heritage, on the one hand, and to renounce the throne and go abroad, on the other hand, acquired, in that period, another dimension: fear for his life.

A new round of civil war enveloped China in 1924, this time focusing on the north, including Manchuria. Intuitively, P'u Yi felt that his life was in jeopardy. As power within the republic, like a shuttlecock, flew back and forth among the contending factions, he feared that one faction or another would come to power and seek to do away with him as a relic of the past, as a symbol of hated foreign,

Manchu domination and as a living threat to reestablish the monarchy.

In parliament, where chaos reigned, various groups pressed for the abolition of the Articles of Favorable Treatment. Outside parliament, the newly established Chinese Communist Party, founded three years earlier, echoed this sentiment. In the mind of P'u Yi and his coterie of Manchu and Chinese advisers, he would be done for, if an implacably hostile faction, the Communists, for example, came to power. Accordingly, P'u Yi began to think of a way out.

As it developed, he did not have long to wait. On November 5, 1924, one of the more colorful warlords of North China, General (later Marshal) Feng Yu-hsiang, marched on Peking, deposed the president in a lightening coup, and surrounded the Forbidden City. Feng Yu-hsiang's troops marched to the tune of "Onward Christian Soldiers" and his army included a division baptized by immersion in the Yellow River. Popularly known as the "Christian General," confused politically and philosophically, Feng's concepts were an amalgam of the teachings of Jesus, Sun Yat-sen and Karl Marx. A man of action, he staunchly supported the republic; he converted to Christianity, yet also studied at Moscow during the Lenin era. When he was accused of being a Communist, a prominent missionary of the day responded, in a classic retort which still rings in Chinese history, "Yes, he is red, indeed, red with the blood of Jesus!" Such was a measure of the confused state of affairs after the collapse of the dynastic system as China groped toward a new form of government.

However varied his political philosophy, the Christian General was a confirmed anti-Manchu. With his troops in control of Peking, the Manchu population inside and outside the Forbidden City was terrified. They feared a massacre.

The Son of Heaven was forced to abandon Peking, the center of the universe. For China and the Chinese it was one of those great watersheds of their history. At the moment history is made on a grand scale, the participants are apt to remember at most some small detail—Americans remember what they were doing when they learned Pearl Harbor was bombed, for example, or that Jack Kennedy was murdered.

P'u Yi remembered the incident well. He was sitting in the Palace of Accumulated Elegance at nine that morning eating fruit with his young empress when a senior court official burst in with a document in hand. "I jumped up," he said, "dropped my half-eaten apple to the floor, and grabbed the paper." Wan Jung, the empress, provides a variation on a theme. "When we were at breakfast, my old nurse ran in, screaming that Chinese soldiers were pushing in through the gates to take us," she recalled. "I thought that she had gone silly, and told her to be quiet. I was eating an especially delicious baked apple, and I went on eating it. But she was right."

And the Chinese writer, Chiang Monlin, in his memoirs, published in 1947, almost a generation later, recalled that a few days after the expulsion of the Lord of Ten Thousand Years, he ventured into the Forbidden City to witness a government committee sealing, palace by palace, the doors of the halls, and that he found the apple that the young emperor had left behind.

"The living quarters of P'u Yi looked vulgar," Chiang Monlin wrote. "A cheap-looking long foreign table stood in the middle of the hall with a few ugly chairs at either side. A pair of pink glass vases decorated the table. It was more like a second-rate country inn in America than the residence of an emperor of China. All the fine furniture and art treasures had been pushed aside and bundled up in the background. The vulgar Western civilization of the treaty ports had invaded the palace; nothing could be more out of place. Cheap magazines were scattered about. Half an apple, freshly cut, and a newly opened box of biscuits lay on the table. Apparently the Emperor had been taken by surprise and left the palace as it was at the moment."

The paper P'u Yi had grabbed was an ultimatum proposing a revision of the Articles of Favorable Treatment. The revision "abolished in perpetuity" the imperial title; reduced P'u Yi's annual subsidy from $4 million to $500,000; ordered him to leave the Forbidden City; pledged to "continue forever" sacrifices at the ancestral temples and tombs; and promised to accord him "the *special* protection of the government of the republic." But as a citizen of the republic, why would he need *"special"* protection?

Indignity was heaped upon indignity. Through an aide P'u Yi was informed to vacate the Violet Enclosure by noon. The emperor's first thought was to contact Johnston but he discovered that the telephone lines into the palace had been cut. Then he thought of sending a courier, but he was informed that soldiers had been posted at the gates.

After a parley at the main gate, the eviction edict was extended to three in the afternoon. The soldiers guarding the enclave permitted Prince Ch'un, Chen Pao-shen and others to enter the Violet Enclosure but they specifically barred Johnston.

Before the deadline hour, an aide reported that the Christian General said, "We can only have another twenty minutes and that if we are not out by then, they will open fire with artillery."

Feng provided five limousines for P'u Yi and his wives and staff. Before leaving the Great Within, the young emperor filled an attaché case with precious stones, and his most valuable possession—the imperial seal. The convoy then left from the front steps of the Palace of Supreme Harmony and drove, significantly, not through the central gate of the Forbidden City which was reserved only for the emperor, but through a minor gate, and into the outside world. It was P'u Yi's first trip outside the Forbidden City since he had been brought there as a child. The limousines deposited P'u Yi and his family at the Northern Mansion, the home of his father, Prince Ch'un. As P'u Yi alighted from the car, the envoy of the Christian General approached, shook hands and addressed him, for the first time in his life, as "Mr. P'u Yi." Outside the protective moats, towers and walls of the Great Within, P'u Yi's fairyland touched by the wand of reality, dissolved. P'u Yi turned into a pumpkin.

"Mr. P'u Yi," the representative of the republic repeated, "do you intend to be an emperor in the future or will you be an ordinary citizen?"

"From today onwards," the Son of Heaven replied, "I want to be an ordinary citizen."

"Good. Then we shall protect you. As a citizen, you will have the right to vote and stand for election. You could even be elected president one day."

This moment of humiliation, his sudden devaluation from Son of Heaven to mister, produced within him a strange sensation. He felt as though an enormous weight had been lifted from his shoulders. Like a hydrogen or helium-filled balloon, he felt lighter-than-air. He was free. He had soared over his prison wall. He had escaped the Forbidden City. More than that, he had escaped history. In those fleeting seconds he was deliriously happy. "I had no freedom as emperor," he blurted out as if shouting to the world. "Now I have found my freedom!" At the gates of the Northern Mansion, the Christian General's guards, who had listened attentively to the dialogue as if they were in a theater, burst into spontaneous applause. Startled, the Lord of Ten Thousand Years, turned in their direction and bowed courteously. They bowed back.

But inside the Northern Mansion, the atmosphere altered radically. The moment he crossed the threshold, as his aides and advisers welcomed him to safety, he felt the old weight return, the grave responsibility he had inherited from the emperors of the past. His immediate thought was to assess how dangerous the situation was. The most encouraging news was brought that evening by Johnston. The Dutch minister, doyen of the diplomatic corps, and the British and Japanese ministers, had lodged a "protest" with the republic over the expulsion of P'u Yi from the Forbidden City in violation of the Articles of Favorable Treatment which were internationally recognized as an agreement binding on two foreign entities, the emperor and the republican government. The Japanese legation, which had established a message-transmission belt to P'u Yi after his relief donation to the victims of the Tokyo earthquake, sent word that the Japanese cavalry posted in their legation compound patrolled near Prince Ch'un's Northern Mansion and that if the Christian General "started anything, we will take decisive action."

After several days of tension, the Peking situation appeared to ease, and control at the gates of the Northern Mansion relaxed. In truth, like so many other half-organized coups in that period, indeed like the abortive 1917 restoration attempt by the Pigtail General, the Peking coup by the Christian General collapsed of its own weight. The foreign diplomatic community refused to attend a banquet in honor of the new government. Confronted by pressure from inside and outside the country, Feng Yu-hsiang retreated from Peking on November 28, only twenty-three days after he had set his power play in motion. That day the Northern Mansion sent the new republican home minister a telegram which repudiated the revisionist document, implying that it was extorted through "violence and terror" and declared that therefore the Manchu house was "unable to recognize its legal validity."

P'u Yi had reached a crossroad. "Three roads stretched out before me," he said. One road was to follow the path of the revised Articles of Favorable Treatment, that is, abandon the title and the desire to recover his ancestral heritage. He would thus win personal freedom. Moreover, he possessed wealth and private lands. Life could be very attractive. But as he and his advisers viewed him, he was the true and only Celestial Emperor, ruler of a quarter of mankind, if not the world. To abandon the Dragon Throne without a fight, and disgrace his ancestors, was a path not worthy of serious consideration. The court rejected the first road out-of-hand.

At the ends of the other two roads were potential rainbows. He could return to the Forbidden City and reestablish his base in the center of Peking. There he would resume his "old life," as he put it to Johnston and Chen Pao-shen, and bide his time. The third course was the most tortuous and uncertain—to go abroad and stage a comeback in alliance with a foreign power. This strategy was known by the phrase "using foreign power." Through it he might return to the Forbidden City in a manner worthy of his forefathers, as a conqueror, as a Manchu, a Master.

Interestingly, there was a fourth road of which neither P'u Yi nor any of his principal advisers, including Johnston and Cheng Hsiao-hsu, both of whom wrote elaborate journals covering the period, ever made any mention: fleeing to Manchuria and reestablishing the dynasty in the ancestral homeland of the Manchu. The situation appeared to strongly favor such a course.

At the beginning of the 1911 revolution, Manchuria openly opposed the creation of a republic. But when the emperor abdicated, the Manchurians accepted the republic as a *fait accompli,* although they retained their personal loyalty to the emperor as lineal descendant of the Exalted Founder. Indeed, if the dynasty had refused to abdicate in 1912 and had transferred the court to Manchuria, the history of China and, perhaps, of the world since then, may have been quite different.

By 1924, Manchuria was ruled independently of the rest of China by a powerful warlord, Marshal Chang Tso-lin, who was sympathetic to the young emperor. Although the marshal had declared Manchuria "independent" and even negotiated separate treaties with foreign powers, his concept of independence did not, as the League of Nations later reported at the outbreak of the Sino-Japanese War of 1931, mean that "he or the people of Manchuria wished to be separated from China." Manchuria's so-called independence was part of the on-going Chinese civil war. Like the warlords of other provinces, the Manchurian leader alternately supported the republic, attacked it or declared his territory independent of it, but he never acted in such a way as to threaten the partition of China into separate states. On the contrary, most Chinese civil wars were connected with some ambitious scheme to unify the country under a strong, central government. Through all its wars and periods of "independence," therefore, Manchuria remained an integral part of China.

In this murky situation, P'u Yi conceivably could have

attempted—however improbable success—to reconquer China as the founder of the Manchu Dynasty did in the seventeenth century from an "independent" Manchurian base. Yet, surprisingly, there is no evidence among the principals that such a plan was even discussed. This is particularly odd since P'u Yi was within a few years destined to ascend a Manchurian throne, not in alliance with Manchurians or Chinese, but in collaboration with the Japanese.

Throughout that November night in 1924 the emperor's aides debated his future course of action. "Although I had no definite ideas about my future," P'u Yi recalled, "one thing was clear in my mind from the moment I entered the portals of the Northern Mansion: come what may, I was going to leave."

"I had not left a big Forbidden City for one in miniature," he explained, "particularly when I was in such danger there."

Soon, however, a fresh development menaced P'u Yi. China was on the brink of a new upheaval and Sun Yat-sen hurried north in an effort to forestall the country's further descent into chaos.

After an intense round of negotiations in 1924 aimed at unifying the country, Sun Yat-sen appeared to be nearing an agreement with the northern warlords, including Marshal Chang Tso-lin. Whether such an accord was possible is doubtful. History will never know. Sun died in the spring of the following year, after forty years of immersion in the revolutionary movement. Clearly, a united front of Sun Yat-sen and the northern warlords would have made short shrift of P'u Yi's hope to restore the Dragon Throne.

Of even more sinister import to the court was a dramatic shift by Sun Yat-sen and his Kuomintang toward the Soviet Union. Sun had appealed in vain to the West, notably to the United States, for recognition and support in unifying the country. At this juncture, the Kremlin proffered assistance and Sun, in desperation, accepted the offer, although he was wary of Communists and Communist dogma. With the aid of Soviet advisers, he modeled the Kuomintang along Communist lines. Members of the newly established Chinese Communist Party were permitted to enter the Kuomintang, while retaining their own Communist Party identity and discipline, thereby forming a "bloc within" the Kuomintang. Soviet military advisers were accorded the opportunity to provide assistance in establishing a military academy for the training of Kuomintang cadres under the direction of that rising young Cantonese officer, Chiang Kai-shek.

Despite Sun Yat-sen's policy shift, the Kremlin, beneath the surface, played the same imperial game *vis-à-vis* China as the Czars had before it. As part of their new-found alliance, Moscow and Sun's Kuomintang signed a smokescreen agreement which canceled all previous Sino-Russian treaties. The Russians surrendered their leases, concessions and extraterritorial rights in China. However magnanimous a gesture, it was a matter of facing reality for the Russians—a Russian strength of character under Czars or Commissars.

After the Bolshevik Revolution and the overthrow of the Czars in 1917, the Chinese had systematically withdrawn their recognition from Czarist officials within China and gradually recovered Russian leases and concessions. Thus, the Kremlin was giving up something it no longer possessed. Even so, despite the existence of an "anti-imperialist" Communist government in Moscow, the Kremlin maintained a weathered eye on Russia's strategic interests. Despite the 1924 agreement, the Soviet Union retained a firm hold on Mongolia and the Chinese Eastern Railway in Manchuria, the shortest route between Moscow and Vladivostok, Russia's only warm water port in Asia, strategically situated astride the Sea of Japan. Thus, the agreement provided for continued joint Soviet-Chinese management of the railroad. Furthermore, in addition to signing a formal agreement with the republic, the Kremlin entered into a separate agreement with Chang Tso-lin's "independent" Manchuria. The terms were almost identical except that the Russian lease on the railway was shortened from eighty to sixty years. By making a separate agreement with Manchuria, the Soviet Union encouraged the independence of the region, as one step toward detaching it from China and making their own influence paramount there.

In 1921 Soviet troops had entered Mongolia in pursuit of remnant Czarist forces. For all practical purposes, the Russians, since then, have never left. Moscow set up a puppet Provisional Mongolian People's Republic, and Lenin concluded a treaty of friendship with the new regime, in which there was no reference to China. By the terms of the 1924 agreement, Moscow paid lip service to China by recognizing Outer Mongolia as "an integral part of the republic of China," and stated that it "respects China's sovereignty therein." But the Kremlin treated the region as "autonomous" or semi-independent and therefore entitled to freedom from Chinese interferences in its foreign affairs. Moscow opened direct relations with the new government and the Mongolians dropped the word "provisional" from the country's name. By transforming Mongolia into a satellite, the commissars completed the grand design of the Czars and turned Mongolia's 1.5 million square miles into a gigantic buffer zone between Russia and China.

Thus, the endless Russian and Chinese struggle for the twilight zone between them—Mongolia and Manchuria, borderlands where P'u Yi exercised hereditary influence—continued unabated despite the collapse of "imperialist" governments in St. Petersburg and Peking, and the emergence of "revolutionary" regimes in both Russia and China.

Despite the continuing friction over Mongolia and Manchuria, Sun Yat-sen and his Kuomintang moved into an increasingly closer embrace with the Soviet Union and the Chinese Communists.

If the prospect of a pact between Sun Yat-sen and the warlords alarmed P'u Yi and demolished his hopes for a restoration of his ancestral heritage, the republic's tilt toward the Communists, both within and without China, panicked him and the Manchu court.

P'u Yi was visibly nervous. He had learned to smoke cigarettes, which were then the rage in China, and in moments of tension he chain-smoked. After a draw or two on it, he discarded the cigarette. Often he simply paced around the room and crumpled one unlighted cigarette after another in his right fist. Clearly, he was frightened and could not make up his own mind about the best course of action. The desire to restore the throne was always with him, but so was the urge to renounce the whole business and flee abroad. Then there was the constant fear for his life in the roiled politics of the day. Gradually, the desire for physical survival dominated his every action.

China was in the throes of a post-revolutionary reign of terror. A fairly typical example of the atmosphere is mirrored in the book of a Chinese political analyst of the period who openly wrote that the Christian General and others plotted the execution of a number of political personalities, including "the ex-emperor Hsüan Tung now known as Mr. Henry P'u Yi." As a result of in-fighting among the different factions, however, the conspiracy against the former emperor collapsed and, the analyst freely wrote, "as a consequence . . . Henry P'u Yi [was] saved from the fate of the firing squad." In the press of Peking, Shanghai, and Canton, in this period P'u Yi repeatedly read about plans to eradicate the last vestige of Manchu rule. In particular, an anti-monarchist group, the Anti-Manchu League, campaigned publicly for the detention and execution of monarchists as "traitors to the republic." As for P'u Yi, they formally pressed for his expulsion from China. But he feared he would be murdered once he was in their hands, ostensibly waiting for deportation.

Little wonder that P'u Yi, who was hardly a forceful character, was frightened. When the elephants fight, the grass is trampled, and, in this situation, he felt like a blade of grass.

Against this tumultuous background, a monumental decision was made by P'u Yi's Manchu, Chinese, and British advisers, Chen Pao-shen, Cheng Hsiao-hsu, and Johnston: The nineteen-year-old emperor would take sanctuary in a foreign legation.

Unsurprisingly, given Johnston's influence on the boy, P'u Yi's first thought was to seek British asylum.

But the British minister in Peking in 1924, Sir Ronald MacLeavy, turned down his request for refuge because "the legation was too small to accommodate" the emperor and his entourage. Sir Ronald suggested that he "had better go to the Japanese."

At this juncture, Johnston stepped in and made the arrangements. As the evidence demonstrates, the British played an instrumental role in putting the last emperor of China—the last Manchu emperor—in Japanese hands. Johnston, in his memoirs, candidly admitted his role. "I first went to the Japanese legation to arrange for the emperor's flight," he wrote. "I did so," he weakly explained, "because I felt that of all the foreign ministers, the Japanese minister was the one who was most likely to be able and (I hoped) willing not only to receive the emperor but also to give him effectual protection." Johnston acknowledged that he then reported his activity to Sir Ronald and that the British minister told him that if everything went as arranged, he expected Johnston to become his guest at the British Legation, which was situated a few yards from the Japanese compound in Peking's exclusive diplomatic quarter, "in order that I might be as near as possible to the emperor."

Why were the British so interested in putting P'u Yi in Japanese hands? The answer is still open to debate but the consensus at the time was that Britain was playing its old balance-of-power game in the Far East. The Foreign Office entertained high hope that the Japanese, whose interest in Manchuria was manifest, would place P'u Yi on a Manchurian throne under their aegis, a situation which in turn would produce sparks between Japan and Russia along the Manchurian frontier. This would open up a second front to preoccupy Lenin and his Bolsheviks and curtail the Kremlin's revolutionary activities in the West.

Johnston proposed a ruse to get P'u Yi out of his father's Northern Mansion. P'u Yi would order a limousine and claim that he was going house-hunting in Peking. En route, feigning illness, he would stop at the German Hospital, less than a half-mile from the Japanese and British compounds. The emperor would slip out of the back door of the hospital and drive in another vehicle to the Japanese legation.

On November 29, 1924, the plan was put into operation. A strong wind blew that morning and the air was hazy with yellow dust, conveniently camouflaging the occupants of the limousine. P'u

Yi, Johnston, and Chen Pao-shen, the ever-faithful tutor, passed through the gates of the Northern Mansion and arrived at the German Hospital where Johnston sent for the director, a Dr. Dipper. Johnston picks up the thread of the story in short, staccato sentences which read like something out of a 1920s E. Philipps Oppenheim thriller. ". . . I sent my card to Dr. Dipper. He came out of his room and recognized the emperor. I asked him to take us at once to a private room as I had something important to say. He took us upstairs to an empty ward. I told him briefly what had happened and what we proposed to do. 'Meanwhile,' I said, '. . . I leave the emperor in your charge. Please see that he is well protected.' "

Johnston then took out the bundle of pearls and jewels which the emperor had entrusted to him and handed it to Dipper. The bundle included the most valuable treasure of all—the seal of the emperor.

Thereupon Johnston left for the Japanese legation and begged the Japanese minister to extend to the emperor the hospitality of his legation. The Japanese diplomat did not answer immediately.

"He walked up and down the room considering the matter and then gave me his decision," Johnston recalled. "He would receive the emperor."

Johnston "joyfully" returned to the German Hospital and was stunned to discover that P'u Yi had vanished. "But I have just made arrangements for him to get to the Japanese legation," Johnston exclaimed in shock.

"That is precisely where he has gone," said a hospital attendant.

Johnston was puzzled and returned to the Japanese minister's house within the Japanese compound. He did not find P'u Yi.

The mystery was soon solved, however.

Independently, perhaps in collusion with P'u Yi, who was already well versed in the art of palace intrigue, Cheng Hsiao-hsu, his Chinese adviser and the man whom he had appointed Keeper of the Seals, the most trusted position within the Forbidden City, arranged with Colonel Takemoto, the Japanese military attaché and commander of the legation's security force, for P'u Yi to take sanctuary at the Japanese legation.

Later, in his journal, Cheng Hsiao-hsu described his role: "I recommended to His Majesty that he go to the Japanese legation and he ordered me to go and tell the Japanese. I immediately called on Colonel Takemoto. Takemoto asked me to invite the emperor to come to the legation forthwith. A strong wind was blowing at the time and the sky was filled with yellow sand so that one could see for a distance of a few paces." Arriving at the Japanese compound, he recalled, "Takemoto met the emperor and took him to the barracks."

The year, it should be restated, was 1924. Within Japan the struggle for supremacy between the civilians and the militarists touched off by the modernization of the country, was still undecided. One manifestation of the confrontation was the wave of political assassinations which swept Japan, starting with the murder of the first commoner to hold the premiership, Hara Takashi. Between 1921 and 1932 Japan had ten premiers as the power struggle unfolded. Two of these were commoners and both were murdered in office. The civilian-military schism was mirrored at the Japanese legation. The relationship between the military and civil officials in the compound was so strained that Colonel Takemoto did not report his private arrangement with Cheng Hsiao-hsu to the Japanese minister, a civilian and the senior representative of the Japanese government in China. But the militarists had yet to dominate Japan. As soon as the minister heard that P'u Yi had arrived at the barracks, he promptly invited him to occupy his own residence in the compound. P'u Yi, who felt more at ease among Japanese civilians than army officers, accepted the invitation with alacrity.

P'u Yi then sent for his two wives. When the republican guards—now aware of P'u Yi's ruse—refused to permit them to leave the Northern Mansion, the Japanese brought diplomatic pressure to bear on the republican government. Weakened by internal strife, and fearful of provoking the Japanese militarists, Peking bowed to the pressure.

The Japanese enclave was soon flooded with P'u Yi's staff and the Japanese had to set aside a whole compound building for them: Companions of the Southern Study, senior officials of the imperial household department, attendants, personal guards, eunuchs, ladies-in-waiting, maids, and scullions. Thus, the essential administrative offices of the Great Ch'ing Emperor functioned once more as in the Forbidden City. This time it functioned for the first time on foreign territory, the diplomatic compound of Japan.

Both the Japanese civilian and military officials treated P'u Yi with hospitality and deference, and the care with which the Japanese legation looked after their guest stirred many Manchu into viewing the Japanese as a vehicle for "using foreign power to plan a restoration." As one of P'u Yi's advisers wrote in a memorial: "The Japanese Minister does not only take Your Majesty's past glory into account, he sees you as the future ruler of China: how can your subjects and officials fail to be gratified?"

P'u Yi's nineteenth birthday fell thirteen days after the Chinese New Year in 1925. "As I was in a stranger's house, I had not intended to celebrate it," but his hosts insisted and offered him the main hall of the legation in which to receive the felicitations of visitors. The hall was furnished with magnificent carpets and behind an overstuffed armchair with a yellow cushion, which served as a jury-rigged throne, stood a yellow screen. All the pages wore Manchu hats with red tassels. Former Manchu officials and local Manchu veterans, members of Peking's diplomatic community, and others, totaling more than 500 people, crowded into the miniature throne room.

For the occasion, P'u Yi wore a blue silk gown with a yellow dragon motif and black satin jacket. All the princes, court officials, and Manchu veterans wore the same except for the yellow dragon. "Imperial yellow, queues and ninefold kowtows combined to give me feelings of anguish and heartbreaking melancholy," P'u Yi reminisced. Now a new ingredient was added to the rapidly maturing character of the emperor. Clearly, he was no longer a boy. The desire to restore his Great Inheritance, the desire for personal liberty, the fear for his life, amid conflicting moods of elation and despondency, combined to confuse and torture him. And yet, at nineteen (twenty, by Chinese reckoning) his life was just beginning.

As reported in the Shanghai press, P'u Yi addressed the birthday throng in an impromptu speech.

"I am fully aware that in the modern world emperors can exist no longer and I am resolved not to run the risks involved in being one," he said and added, "My life deep in the Great Within was that of a prisoner, and I took no delight in my lack of freedom."

Then he described the humiliation he suffered at the hands of the Christian General and said, "I do not wish to complain, but I cannot miss this opportunity to reveal the sorrows that lie in my heart." He appealed to the republic to equitably settle the matter of the Articles of Favorable Treatment so that the clothes, vessels, calligraphy, and books "left by my ancestors" may be returned to their owner. And he startled the assembly by adding: "I have an important announcement to make.

"I will," he pledged, "never agree to any proposal that I should seek foreign intervention on my behalf: I could never use foreign power to intervene in domestic Chinese politics."

The Chinese press viewed his pledge with mistrust. The *Peking Daily*, for example, looked on his presence in Japanese hands as "part of the plot to keep him until there is an incident in a particular province [Manchuria], when a certain country [Japan] will send him there with armed protection and revive the rank and title of his distant ancestors." The paper concluded this accurate reading of the future with the observation that "P'u Yi's terror and flight were the result of deliberate intimidation by certain people—he has fallen into their trap, which was a part of a prearranged long-term plan."

As evidence later indicated, the so-called plots on P'u Yi's life may have been organized by Japanese *agents provocateurs* for the purpose of driving him, by intimidation, into their hands. As for the British role, although London vehemently denied it, then and later, the suspicion has persisted that Britain gave up on the possibility of P'u Yi's restoration, sensing that control of China would see-saw between Nationalists and Communists, and adopted an artful strategy of its own. The Foreign Office was preoccupied with the containment of the Bolshevik revolution and the expansion of the Soviet sphere of influence in Asia. In this situation, the belief persists, Britain employed P'u Yi as bait in the expectation that the Japanese would grab him as a moral and legal cover for their creation of an "independent" Manchuria under their own aegis. In such an event, Britain would encourage a Soviet-Japanese confrontation in Manchuria and Mongolia relieving Soviet pressure on the West and on China proper, which would then remain largely a British sphere of influence.

Among many Japanese civilians, the last emperor of China was looked on as a useful political tool in the event that anarchy in China led to a restoration of the dynasty. But the Japanese militarists viewed the situation within a narrower context. They saw in P'u Yi an instrument for Manchuria's detachment from China and the creation of a satellite Manchurian régime under a legitimate emperor of Manchurian blood. If the Soviet Union could detach Mongolia with insouciant concern, as China writhed in chaos, Japan could do the same in Manchuria. The militarists viewed Manchuria as a vast, largely underpopulated territory, rich in agriculture and in untapped industrial raw materials and granaries. Manchuria, in their view, provided the ideal solution to the mounting pressures on an increasingly urbanized and industrialized Japan, the desperate need for raw materials and food to feed Japan's burgeoning population of seventy million people.

Within the Japanese militarist faction was the largely autonomous, semi-independent Kwantung army, stationed in Manchuria since the end of the Russo-Japanese War to protect Japanese investments and interests in the region, especially in the Kwantung Leased Territory. This territory embraced the southern end of

Liaotung peninsula and encompassed 1,300 square miles. In addition to the peninsula, the Japanese had won the right to administer a narrow strip of land containing the tracks of the South Manchuria Railway. The total area was 108 miles, although the tracks stretched out into the immensity of the Manchurian plain for 690 miles. The Japanese militarists and industrialists favored employing P'u Yi as a vehicle for the creation of an "independent" Manchuria.

Whatever the strategies of the day, as the great powers jockeyed along the path leading to World War II, indisputably the British pushed P'u Yi into Japan's outstretched arms. At first, at any rate, P'u Yi went willingly. If P'u Yi truly wanted to renounce the throne and escape the burden of history, he need only have sought refuge in the American Legation in Peking which already had the reputation of a sanctuary for Chinese of different political persuasions who were caught up, willingly or unwillingly, in the tumultuous politics of the period. But there is no hard evidence that at any time P'u Yi or his advisers considered American protection, although one writer of the period quoted Elizabeth as claiming she raised the idea with P'u Yi.

The final verdict on P'u Yi is found in the historical events themselves, whatever his motivations. The inconvenient nature of the Japanese compound for himself and his large retinue was a factor. After twelve weeks in the cramped legation quarter, Peking acceded to Tokyo's "request" that the Celestial Lord and his entourage be permitted to leave the republican capital and travel freely by rail to Tientsin, on the China coast, where the Japanese maintained a large concession under the legal canopy of extraterritoriality. There, P'u Yi rented Chang Garden, a sumptuous Chinese mansion which covered more than three acres, surrounded by a high wall and containing several smaller buildings.

On February 23, 1925, the last Manchu emperor took his leave of the Japanese minister and his wife and left by the back gate for the short drive to the Peking railway depot. He was accompanied by the police chief of the Japanese consulate-general in Tientsin and a number of plainclothesmen drawn from the notorious *kempeitai*, the

Japanese army's secret police. At every station along the seventy miles of track additional Japanese policemen, and special agents in black civilian clothes, boarded the train. "By the time we reached Tientsin," P'u Yi said, "the carriage was almost full of them."

Twenty years later, at the end of World War II, looking back on his flight from Peking, P'u Yi observed, "I had entered the tiger's mouth." But at the time, he considered his flight a flight to freedom.

PART III

THE MANCHURIAN CANDIDATE

1 *(above left)* P'u Yi, 1908, on the eve of his first enthronement as emperor. On the lap of his father, Prince Ch'un, is P'u Chieh, P'u Yi's brother and lifelong companion. 2 *(above right)* Celestial Emperor, age three. In the background, a screen depicting cranes in flight, birds symbolic of happiness and longevity.

3 *(left)* The great seal of the last emperor, possession of which is proof of the owner's legitimacy as absolute ruler of China. Today the seal is in the possession of the Communist government and is kept in the Forbidden City.

4 *(above)* On November 14, 1908, Empress Dowager Tzu Hsi, who ruled China for more than half a century, handpicked P'u Yi as emperor-designate. Two days later she died.

Mencius said "The most important element in a state is the people; next come the alters of the national Gods; least in importance is the king."

5 *(above)* Under the tutelage of Johnston, who dubbed P'u Yi "Henry," the boy-emperor studied English. In a composition book, P'u Yi copied the thoughts of Mencius, China's democratic philosopher and one of the targets of Chairman Mao's anti-Confucian campaign in China.

6 *(above left)* Sir Reginald Johnston, P'u Yi's tutor and confidant, and British agent. 7 *(above right)* While the world was preoccupied by World War I, a royalist coup restored P'u Yi to the throne on July 1, 1917. The coup collapsed shortly thereafter. The incident is best remembered for being the occasion of the first bombing in Chinese history. Republican aircraft attacked the Forbidden City. 8 *(below)* Articles of Favorable Treatment which toppled the throne, February 12, 1912. Under the articles, P'u Yi abdicated but was permitted to retain the title of emperor, to continue to live in the Forbidden City, and to retain his personal bodyguard, an arrangement unique in the annals of republican revolution.

關於大清皇帝辭位後優待之條件

　　本年十二月二十日公布

　　今因大清皇帝宣布贊成共和國體中華民國於大清

　　皇帝辭退之後優待條件如左

第一款　大清皇帝辭位之後尊號仍存不廢中華

　　民國以待各外國君主之禮相待

第二款　大清皇帝辭位之後歲用四百萬兩俟改鑄

　　新幣後改為四百萬元此款由中華民國撥用

第三款　大清皇帝辭位之後暫居宮禁日後移居頤

　　和園侍衛人等照常留用

第四款　大清皇帝辭位之後其宗廟陵寢永遠奉祀

　　由中華民國酌設衛兵妥慎保護

第五款　德宗崇陵未完工程如制妥修其奉安典禮

　　仍如舊制所有實用經費均由中華民國支出

第六款　以前宮內所用各項執事人員可照常留用

　　惟以後不得再招閹人

第七款　大清皇帝辭位之後其原有之私產由中華

　　民國特別保護

第八款　原有之禁衛軍歸中華民國陸軍部編制

　　額數俸餉仍如其舊

9 *(left)* In the attire of an English squire, P'u Yi sits astride his favorite pony. Horseback riding, golf, and tennis were his favorite sports; his only hobby was collecting mechanical toys, especially Lionel and American Flyer train sets.

10 *(below)* Raised by eunuchs, exhibiting homosexual tendencies at an early age, the sixteen-year-old P'u Yi, on December 1, 1922, acquired the first of his five wives, the Manchu beauty Wan Jung, later known as "Elizabeth." This is a wedding picture. The day before their nuptials, P'u Yi was given his first concubine.

11 *(above)* Surrounded by plainclothes detectives, P'u Yi and his empress prepare to board a train in 1932 for a quick tour of the new nation of Manchukuo.

12 *(above)* After P'u Yi had signed secret protocols giving Japan control of Manchukuo, the Japanese army presided at a luncheon in his honor. On his left is General Akira Muto, whom the Allies hanged as a war criminal at the end of World War II. On his right is General Kuniaki Koiso, later wartime prime minister of Japan, whom the Allies sentenced to life in prison.   13 *(opposite, top)* For the first time in history, two Sons of Heaven—the emperors of China and Japan—meet during P'u Yi's state visit to Japan in 1935. With Hirohito on his right, P'u Yi rides through Tokyo with the pomp of a true Lord of Ten Thousand Years.   14 *(opposite, bottom)* Over Japanese objections, P'u Yi donned Manchu dragon robes and announced to heaven in 1934 his accession as the emperor of Manchukuo. This was the third time he mounted a throne.

16 (above) On August 16, 1946, P'u Yi, left, meets for the first time since 1931 with a representative of Generalissimo Chiang Kai-shek, who had branded him a traitor to China. The setting was the American-occupied zone in Japan. The Nationalist representative is H. Chiu, an Allied prosecutor at the Tojo Trial. In the center is the Russian head of P'u Yi's prisoner detail, Major Yezev.

15 *(right)* After P'u Yi was captured by the Russians on August 16, 1945, a Red army major general, A. D. Pritual, made arrangements with two unidentified Japanese generals to fly P'u Yi to the Soviet Union. P'u Yi, seen sitting at right, listens disconsolately.

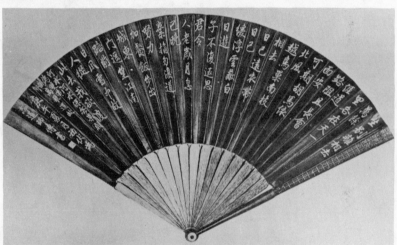

17 *(above)* The controversial fan which P'u Yi presented to Johnston at their farewell in 1932 and which was introduced by the Japanese defense at the Tojo Trial in 1946 to authenticate P'u Yi's personal seal on documents in order to indicate that he willingly conspired with the Japanese in founding Manchukuo.

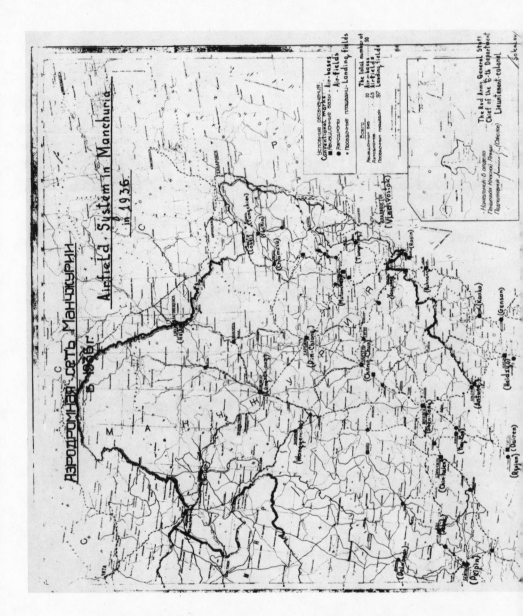

18 *(above)* In the midst of his mass murder trials in the thirties, Stalin kept an eye on the Japanese buildup in P'u Yi's Manchukuo. This is a 1936 Red army intelligence report. Two years later Soviet and Japanese armies fought on the Manchurian border. In 1969 Soviet and Chinese Communist forces clashed in the same area.

19 *(above)* P'u Yi spent nine years, from 1950 to 1959, in a Chinese Communist jail. During the Korean War, when Peking feared an American invasion of Manchuria, he was transferred briefly to the Harbin "thought control" center. In prison he did menial labor. 20 *(below)* With Sino-Soviet tension mounting in the Manchurian border areas, Chairman Mao pardoned P'u Yi, with a view to winning the allegiance of 2.4 million Manchu. The official pardon declares that he had "repented and acknowledged his crimes against the Chinese people."

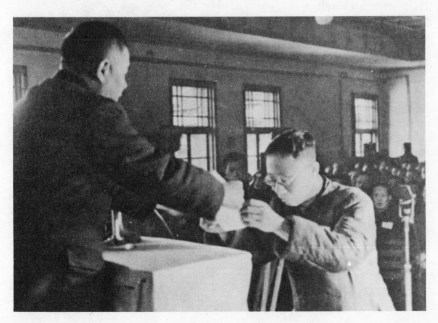

21 (above) For the first time, a Manchu emperor is married to a Chinese subject, destroying for all time the imperial Manchu claim to an undiluted blood line. P'u Yi and his bride, Li Chu-hsien, left, a Communist Party member, celebrate at a wedding party. 22 (right) As the Sino-Soviet schism deepened, P'u Yi was restored to full citizenship and was given official duties, including membership in the National People's Congress. His voter registration card is a curious mixture of Arabic numerals and Chinese characters. The date on it is November 26, 1960.

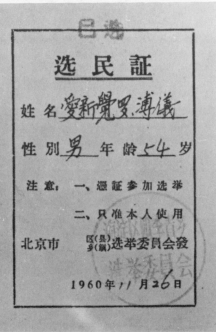

选 民 証

姓 名 愛新覺羅·溥儀

性 别 男 年 龄 54 岁

注意: 一、憑証参加选举

二、只准本人使用

北京市　区(县)　选举委员会發
　　　　乡(鎮)

1960年 11 月 26 日

CHAPTER 14

Tientsin Interlude

Accompanied by his aides and Japanese escorts, the bespectacled nineteen-year-old P'u Yi, whose spare figure made him seem taller than he was, negotiated without incident the seventy-mile journey by rail from Peking to Tientsin, the longest trip of his life. Peering through the windows of his private car, he was fascinated. For the first time, the only surviving occupant of the Dragon Throne, the true Son of Heaven, gazed out on the mosaic of rice fields, truck gardens, impoverished villages, and ornate pagodas which make up the Chinese landscape. Occasionally, he caught a glimpse of the Yun Ho, or Grand Canal, flowing parallel to the track, a waterway over which people had glided between north and south, between Peking and Hangchow, a distance of 1,100 miles, since the seventh century.

In 1925, as now, Tientsin ranked with Shanghai and Canton among China's principal ports of entry. Situated in a coal-rich area astride the confluence of the Pai and Hai rivers, it was a dusty city of broad streets and substantial buildings. The bustling port area, with its wharves stretching two miles along the riverbanks, served as a transit center for the shipment of goods to Mongolia, Manchuria,

147

and, in those years, Siberia, although for several weeks of the year, even Tientsin was closed by ice. The city's traffic was congested. Trucks, cars, bicycles, horse carts, trams, and rickshaws flowed like water and formed such a solid mass that they looked like a dragon.

Then, as now, Tientsin was also a major marshaling yard and its roundhouses provided rail links between Peking and Mukden, the capital of Manchuria under the Manchu, and between Peking and Shan Hai Kwan, the easternmost limit of the Great Wall through whose portals P'u Yi's ancestors had streamed during their seventeenth century conquest of China.

When P'u Yi's coal-burning locomotive pulled into the station, the port city was a hub of foreign activity. Here the raw power of extraterritoriality was on display. Strung out for a length of five miles were the settlements of the British, the Japanese, French, Italians, Belgians, and others. Again the Americans were conspicuous by their absence. Each concession flew the national colors of its occupying power. Within each enclave the foreigners lived under their own laws and maintained order with their own troops and mercenaries.

For an effete, wide-eyed young man, raised within the restricted confines of the Forbidden City, with its choking accumulation of the dust of the ages, the beat of Tientsin was as strange, exciting and alien as the view from the train had been. The port was ablaze at dusk with garish electric signboards; the architecture of the city was a mix of Victorian and Chinese styles; the Bund, or main thoroughfare, along the waterfront was crowded with streethawkers and streetwalkers, theaters, brothels, gambling dens and curio shops; the business district was a jumble of banks, accounting houses and the offices of trading cartels. Like Shanghai and Canton, though on a lesser scale, Tientsin was lusty, brawling and full-bodied.

As P'u Yi left the crowded railroad depot, with a phalanx of Japanese plainclothesmen clearing a path before him, he met with the first disappointment in his journey into the outer world. Chang Gardens, in the process of refurbishment, was not yet ready for occupancy and he was forced to spend his first night away from

Peking in a commercial hotel, a Japanese hostelry no less, the fashionable Yamato, which boasted several austerely furnished rooms in the Japanese-style, with bamboo screens, *tatami* floors, and sliding panels. His escorts' selection of the Yamato was hardly surprising. Throughout his sojourn in Tientsin, P'u Yi was under the constant surveillance of the *kempeitai*. The night he registered at the hotel, for example, the Japanese secret police moved into a house across the road from Chang Gardens (which, incidentally, had briefly sheltered Sun Yat-sen earlier in the year). The Japanese kept a log of P'u Yi's visitors. And whenever P'u Yi left Chang Gardens, a Japanese plainclothesman sat up front with his chauffeur. Whenever he visited the theater or shopping district, a Japanese agent followed at a discreet distance behind him.

In the light of the sanctuary he found among the Japanese first in Peking and then in Tientsin, logic demanded that he plunge directly into close collaboration with his hosts to advance his restoration to the throne. But he did not do so. In the first place, the conflict between the army and the cabinet in Tokyo was not yet resolved, and there was no consensus among the Japanese as to their ultimate course of action. Also P'u Yi was still uncertain about collaboration with a foreign power to achieve a restoration. He felt, perhaps wrongly, that he still commanded the allegiance of sufficient numbers of Manchu, Mongols, and Chinese, and sufficient wealth (in addition to the imperial seal, he carried to Tientsin a veritable Nibelungen hoard of gold, jade and precious stones) to remount the Dragon Throne on his own. He needed only to prepare for the inevitable collapse of the republic.

Moreover, his advisers themselves, like the Japanese, were divided. Several Manchu and Mongolian princes strongly urged P'u Yi to collaborate with the Japanese to restore the ancestral heritage. Others, just as strongly, believed that his expulsion from the Violet Enclosure and his subsequent flight from Peking ended all hope of restoration. This faction implored him to work with the republic for the restoration not of the throne but of the Articles of Favorable Treatment. Their objective was a return to the Forbidden City where P'u Yi, at a minimum, could continue to propitiate the memory of his ancestors and preserve a shell of the dignity and respect his forebears had enjoyed. In their view, P'u Yi could continue to rule in spirit like the Pope or the Dalai Lama. This line of reasoning, however, was faulty. The Pope and Dalai Lama symbolized spiritual power. P'u Yi embodied both spiritual and temporal authority.

Whatever the merits of the conflicting arguments, it was clear that P'u Yi could never remount the throne as the Great Ch'ing Emperor under the aegis of the Japanese. The obvious reason was that Japan also boasted an emperor who, like P'u Yi, was considered the Son of Heaven. There is only one sun in heaven, argued Chen Pao-shen in Tientsin as he had in Peking, and P'u Yi had to address himself to the Japanese cautiously. Yet if he rejected outright collaboration with Japan and was not prepared to return to the Forbidden City as mock emperor, what other course was open to him in promoting the "great enterprise"? In the confusion of the period, there was still another nettle to grasp: "Contact and buy over the warlords," P'u Yi ordered his advisers.

At this stage China verged on anarchy. The Nationalists and Communists competed against each other with their own paramilitary organizations, and assorted warlords, some political in nature and others apolitical, controlled pockets of territory. The situation was bitingly summarized by a dismayed Sun Yat-sen in 1924—a year before P'u Yi fled to Tientsin—at the first national congress of the Kuomintang party: "The initial goal of the revolution was the overthrow of the Manchu Dynasty and its emperor," Sun observed. "But after the Manchu Dynasty was overthrown, numerous small emperors emerged."

Among the "numerous small emperors" were Chinese, Manchu, Mongol, and even White Russian warlords. One with whom P'u Yi established contact was the notorious Russian, Gregorii Mikhalovich Semenov.

At the time of the Bolshevik Revolution, Semenov commanded a force of several thousand in a group known as the Special

Manchurian Detachment. In this turbulent era, when Red and White Russians hunted down and butchered each other, Semenov established himself as a petty warlord in Siberia. Defeated by the Bolsheviks in 1922, he fled to the United States.

Several American consular officers in Siberia were shocked to learn that Semenov sought sanctuary in the United States. They denounced him as a mass murderer and the incident caused a sensation, as if, in a present-day context, Martin Bormann was discovered living in Los Angeles. Demands for Semenov's ouster led to a U.S. Senate inquiry, and to his deportation.

Semenov drifted back to Manchuria. By 1927 he had regrouped some of his old comrades and reestablished himself along the Manchurian-Mongolian frontier. As a free agent, he sold his services to the highest bidders and received independent financial assistance from both the Kwantung army and P'u Yi. There is also evidence that Semenov worked with Japan's rabid nationalist Black Dragon Society. In 1934, for example, in the Stalinist period, Moscow published a book, *Militarism and Fascism in Japan,* which linked him and the society with a plot to put P'u Yi on a Manchurian throne.

"I cannot remember how much money I spent or how much jade, pearls and jewelry I gave away in trying to win the friendship of warlords and buy them over," P'u Yi wrote thirty years later in his autobiography. "But I do know that the one who got the most was the White Russian, Semenov."

Indeed, P'u Yi was so impressed with Semenov's enthusiasm for a restoration of the great Ch'ing Dynasty that on their first meeting at Chang Gardens, P'u Yi handed $50,000 over to him to finance his activities.

Through Semenov, who reported directly to P'u Yi, the court expected to rally the petty warlords of the Manchurian border areas and weld them into a private army strong enough to wrest control of the region in the name of the emperor. However fanciful the scheme, the plan reflected P'u Yi's desperate search for allies in this period.

The most important of the "numerous small emperors" was Marshal Chang Tso-lin, the Manchurian Tiger, as some called him, a man whose physical appearance belied his reputation. Small in stature, with narrow, sloping shoulders, he lacked military bearing and was deceptively mild-mannered and cultured; he collected Confucian classics, for example. During the Russo-Japanese War, which was principally waged on the Manchurian plain, Chang Tso-lin served the Japanese as a guerrilla leader and harassed Russian communication lines. After the overthrow of the Manchu Dynasty, he was appointed a *tuchun*, or military governor, by the republic. But his personal influence extended much further, and he hated both the Japanese and the Russians.

The Manchurian Tiger maintained an army of 250,000 men at a cost of about $200 million annually, a large part of the funds raised in mafioso-style, through an intricate network of "protection associations." Under his rule, organized murder and extortion were commonplace. And yet, in his own way, he was a patriot. In 1923, the marshal explained to the editor of the *China Weekly Review,* an influential English-language journal, "my only interest is in unifying China."

Although the marshal allied himself at times with the Nationalists, he did not approve of Sun Yat-sen's philosophies which, he contended, failed to "harmonize with the spirit of the Chinese people." Parliaments, political parties, secret ballots, Robert's Rules of Order were all foreign devil concoctions. At heart a Confucianist, he believed in the *Wang Tao,* Heavenly or True Way, and he leaned toward a restoration of the monarchy.

P'u Yi's flight to Tientsin moved Chang Tso-lin to lend the troubled dragon assistance in plotting a dynastic restoration. There were other warlords of a similar disposition, of course, and P'u Yi courted them, but Chang Tso-lin was by far the most important, if only because his satrapy was the size of France and Germany combined. Manchuria contained 30 million inhabitants—3 to 5 million Manchu, 20-plus million Chinese, 800,000 Koreans (who were Japanese subjects since Korea was a Japanese colony), 230,000

Japanese, concentrated along the South Manchurian Railway, which they owned and operated, and about 150,000 White Russians, camped largely astride the Chinese Eastern Railway, a joint Sino-Russian venture. This was an empire in itself.

Four months after P'u Yi's arrival in Tientsin, the marshal sent a courier to him with a package of $100,000 in bills and a request for an audience. Either Chang Tso-lin felt he was not strong enough to maintain his hold on Manchuria and that an alliance with the hereditary Manchu ruler would consolidate his position, or he wanted to ingratiate himself with the ex-emperor to counterbalance the Nationalists and Communists who had just agreed to bury their grievances, at least temporarily, and join forces to eradicate the warlords.

P'u Yi readily agreed to grant Chang Tso-lin an audience, and a meeting between dragon and tiger was arranged in the Chinese quarter of the port city.

"This was the first time I had gone out to visit an important republican figure," P'u Yi said. To his astonishment, when P'u Yi drove through the gate of his host's compound and alighted from his limousine, the marshal without hesitation bent his knee three times and kowtowed nine times, the traditional ritual of fealty to the Lord of Ten Thousand Years.

"I hastened to help him to his feet and we walked into the reception room together," P'u Yi recalled. "I was in very good spirits and grateful for what he had just done to end my uneasy feeling that I had lowered my dignity by coming to see him." What made the emperor even more pleased, of course, was to discover that the marshal had not forgotten the past.

In a reproachful tone of voice, however, Chang Tso-lin told the last Manchu emperor that he should not have courted Japanese protection at a time when he, the Manchurian Tiger, had plenty of troops of his own with which to ensure his majesty's safety. As their first conference broke up, Chang said, "If the celestial heart requires anything in the future, contact me."

As the marshal escorted P'u Yi to his black limousine, Chang

Tso-lin observed for the first time that a Japanese plainclothesman was seated next to the chauffeur. In a deliberately loud voice, as he closed the door to the car, Chang said, "If those Japanese put a finger on you, let me know and I'll sort them out."

Within a few hours of P'u Yi's return home, the Japanese police agent reported the tenor of the incident to his superiors. The following day, a Japanese consular official arrived at Chang Gardens and delivered P'u Yi a discreet warning. "If your imperial majesty makes another secret trip into Chinese territory," he politely threatened, "the Japanese government will no longer be able to guarantee your personal safety."

Tokyo's Manchurian policy was based on collaboration with the marshal to protect Japan's special interests in the territory. The ruling clique of the Japanese Kwantung army, with headquarters at Mukden, was dissatisfied with this bland arrangement. Moreover, they feared that the marshal plotted a restoration of P'u Yi, which would complicate their own grandiose scheme of incorporating Manchuria into the Japanese empire. The Japanese cabinet had little stomach for the situation. They were not particularly interested in military expansion, but the Kwantung army felt that with China in disarray, the moment was approaching to defy Tokyo, seize Manchuria and, in a stroke, resolve Japan's internal problems caused by the lack of living space, the scarcity of arable land, and the shortage of industrial raw materials.

As a first step in their elaborately structured shadow play, a clique of senior officers plotted the murder of Chang Tso-lin. The Japanese principals in the affair were Colonels Kenichi Doihara and Seishiro Itagaki, two men who were later to play a central role in P'u Yi's life.

Doihara, a rotund, flabby man, was director of the Kwantung army's intelligence service, the army's bureau of "dirty tricks." Itagaki, a strategist, was the architect of the army's expansionist Manchurian policy. Unlike Doihara, Itagaki possessed a face that could never be forgotten. His skin was the color of aged parchment, his eyebrows black and bushy, his head bald. Itagaki affected urbanity, civility, and sophistication; Doihara, disingenuity; but both were zealous and ruthless. They exemplified the hard-core militarist faction of Japan's radical nationalist movement. It was they, and men like them, rather than the emperor or cabinet, who formulated Japan's Manchurian policy.

The radical nationalists arranged for Chang Tso-lin's assassination on June 4, 1928. A train carrying the marshal to Mukden exploded en route, killing him and his bodyguards in a single stroke.

"This incident, plotted and instituted by a clique in the Kwantung army," Japanese Admiral Kisuke Okada, a former premier of Japan, told Allied interrogators in 1946, "represented the first overt army move . . . to project itself into the formulation of the policies of the government."

The Tokyo cabinet was shaken by the army's defiance of the government's Manchurian policy and Emperor Hirohito, who had ascended the throne only two years before, urged the cabinet to take strong disciplinary action with respect to the military. But the army's spirit of *gekokujo* (according to Japanese tradition, an act of insubordination motivated by a sense of patriotism and idealism) was so deeply embedded that the government was unable to impose disciplinary action. As a consequence, the cabinet resigned shortly thereafter.

With the assassination of Chang Tso-lin, the army's influence in the formulation of Manchurian policy grew progressively stronger. "During this period," Okada testified, "it became apparent to all in Japan who concerned themselves with matters of state that it was only a question of time until the army should undertake the occupation of Manchuria."

Chang Tso-lin's murder startled not only the cabinet in Japan but also P'u Yi's courtiers, notably Chen Pao-shen. "They tried to make me see a warning in it," P'u Yi said, but he ignored their advice to disengage himself from the clutches of the Japanese. Now twenty-three years old, P'u Yi imagined that he had developed into an astute strategist. Presidents and premiers, commissars and warlords come and go, he reasoned, but he was unique. "I alone am the emperor, and neither the Japanese nor anyone else can find another in the whole of China," he said. This was P'u Yi's trump card and he played it repeatedly thereafter as he scrambled for advantage in the political arena.

P'u Yi calculated that though the Japanese were strong enough to take Manchuria, they were incapable of running it alone; ultimately they would have to come to terms with him to legitimize and consolidate their conquest. While they used him, he would use them to promote the "great enterprise."

Yet his deep involvement with such sordid characters as Semenov and Chang Tso-lin showed that P'u Yi still preferred to launch a restoration without exclusive reliance on a foreign power (though he was aware that both warlords maintained a relationship with the Kwantung army). Thus, the record indicates, during the first three years of his stay in Tientsin, P'u Yi's relations with the Japanese were correct, not much beyond that.

Tientsin's bright lights and the sense of personal freedom after imprisonment in the Violet Enclosure, intoxicated not only the emperor but also his graceful empress, Wan Jung, who was now called "Elizabeth" by the popular press, and his secondary consort, the pudgy, dimpled Wen Hsiu, who never acquired a Western name. Both of them had followed him to Tientsin, together with his eldest brother and most intimate confidant, P'u Chieh, who had acquired the name "William." Later, they were joined by two other brothers and five sisters. P'u Yi's father, Prince Ch'un, and three other children, preferred to remain in Peking and try to come to terms with the republic.

The triangular relationship between P'u Yi and his two consorts was out of date and a source of embarrassment for the two women, especially for Wen Hsiu, who, it will be recalled, had been P'u Yi's first choice as empress. She resented deferring to Wan Jung at public receptions, dinner parties, and on other social occasions. Jealous of the empress, she found their strained family relationship and their artificial matrimonial life intolerable in cosmopolitan, gossip-ridden Tientsin. Adopting a modern life-style, she summoned the nerve to demand a divorce. Never before in the dynastic history of China had an empress, much less a consort, of the dragon emperor petitioned for a divorce. P'u Yi was infuriated. It was unthinkable.

Yet, divorce was simple enough; under Chinese law, a divorce was arranged if both partners agreed to the dissolution of their marital status and, in the presence of two witnesses, signed a statement to that effect. Determined to escape history, Wen Hsiu threatened to file publicly for divorce in the Tientsin District Court, unless P'u Yi and his advisers acceded. He consented. The papers were no sooner drawn up than Wen Hsiu packed her few personal belongings and left Chang Gardens. P'u Yi never saw her again. She returned to Peking and never remarried. In 1950 she died only a few months after witnessing the arrival of a new occupant in the Forbidden City, Mao Tse-tung.

The relationship between P'u Yi and his empress also displayed early signs of stress. Frustrated by an impotent and disinterested husband, she engaged in periodic domestic quarrels and taunted him with the chilling word "Eunuch!" Rumors flooded Tientsin's diplomatic corps that she was an opium addict. But there is no convincing evidence that Elizabeth smoked opium in this period, though she did turn to it later in life. Like P'u Yi, she had an eye on the throne and as long as there was a prospect of restoration—however slim—she played the role of empress with enthusiasm. As P'u Yi later said of her "Wan Jung attached great significance to her position as empress and was prepared to be a wife, in name only, for the sake of it."

The oft-repeated tale that Wan Jung turned to opium in Tientsin (Japanese intelligence reported "P'u Yi's number one wife is a dope addict and a bundle of nerves") is not supported by the American Nora Waln, the adopted daughter of a Chinese family in Tientsin, a discerning observer of China and the Chinese, and a friend of the empress. Nora Waln in 1933 wrote one of those warm, intimate books about Chinese life, *The House in Exile,* which fitted snugly into the Sino-American love affair and was part of the genre which produced Pearl Buck, the Soong Sisters, Charlie Chan, and the Flying Tigers.

"I have never seen any woman, of any race, equal to the loveliness of the Manchu ex-empress in 1927," Miss Waln wrote. The engaging Wan Jung was tall and slim, with ebony hair, rose-petal skin and slender arched feet. Each finger of her exquisite hands possessed perfect half-moons at the base of each nail, and her eyes were soft, liquid brown.

Nora and Elizabeth became fast friends. They exchanged gifts; Nora, for example, introduced Elizabeth to lace-trimmed silk underwear. At no time, however, does Nora suggest that Wan Jung was addicted to the pipe. Certainly not in Tientsin where the dark clouds of P'u Yi's political future still bore a silver lining. Yet for all her beauty, Wan Jung had resented her rival, Wen Hsiu. From the outset she ignored her and rarely spoke to her. Wan Jung had not been P'u Yi's first choice, and she resented it.

Conceivably, P'u Yi may have feared that he could not gratify her sexually and therefore bypassed her for a less vivacious and apparently less active bedmate. Whatever the case, Elizabeth celebrated Wen Hsiu's departure from the household by going on a shopping spree.

In the midst of these domestic rumbles, as he maneuvered for support among the warlords, P'u Yi was shaken by a macbre incident which overnight dissolved his misgivings and apprehensions about the Japanese and made him more than ever determined to regain the throne, even at the cost of destroying himself in the process. Thoughts of returning to Peking under the Articles of Favorable Treatment evaporated; the impulse to abandon power politics dissolved. Perhaps no other single event so stunningly seared his psyche as the grotesque "affair of the tombs."

In the summer of 1928, a number of exotic pieces of jade and other *objets d'art* turned up in Peking curio shops. Several pieces were instantly recognized, including a cache of sixty-five pounds of pearls of such rare luster that one pearl alone fetched a price of $50,000. The jewelry had formed part of the treasure buried in the

Eastern Tombs with the Old Buddha, the Empress Dowager Tzu Hsi.

At one time or another in Chinese history, most of the tombs of earlier dynasties were plundered by bandits. But until 1928 there was no instance on record of organized vandalism motivated by politics, racism, or ideology rather than profit. The collapse of the dynasty in 1912 meant the collapse, however, not only of the imperial system but also of Confucianism, the moral and social order which over the centuries had given China a set of ethical values. Into the vacuum tumbled Western concepts about democracy, which were inexplicable to the overwhelming majority of Chinese, and Marxism-Leninism which, among other things, sought to stifle the individualism, initiative and originality which, in the course of millennia, had shaped the contours of the Chinese character. The Chinese were caught up in an unmanageable, self-generating, destructive cultural revolution.

Nineteen twenty-eight epitomized the new climate. The forces occupying the area in the vicinity of the Eastern Tombs launched a cultural revolution of their own. They dynamited open the tombs of Ch'ien Lung and Tzu Hsi, among others, and not only rifled them of priceless treasures but also smashed unmovable tomb statues, hacked the lacquer off the pillars of the tombs, ruined scroll paintings with graffiti, flung open the coffins of the dead, and threw their bones into the air.

Mortified, P'u Yi dispatched a group of Manchu nobles to the scene to verify the authenticity of the sensational reports about the incidents that were sweeping Peking. At the Eastern Tombs, the nobles broke down and wept. The naked body of Tzu Hsi was found lying on the lid of her coffin, half-covered with a faded, torn, yellow dragon robe of longevity. Her unrotted hair still retained a lustrous black sheen. But her body had turned purple, and her lined and gnarled face—which P'u Yi as a child had found so hideous— was bruised and battered. Sections of the republican press applauded the desecration of the dead as "heavenly justice" and hailed the destruction of the tombs as an act of "divine retribution for the past misdeeds of the Manchu rulers." All the treasures, of course, vanished, including two apple-green jade melons, each the size of the average cantaloupe, inlaid with diamonds and emeralds. Between $17 and $50 million worth of art and jewelry disappeared, the greatest single art theft of the century. But transcending the theft for private gain was the mutilation of the corpses.

Only one tomb remained intact, that of the Emperor K'ang Hsi who, with Ch'ien Lung, raised China's cultural accomplishments—in literature, in ceramics, and in other art forms—to new levels of excellence. When the looting soldiery battered open the door to the mausoleum, a spring of muddy water, "the color of imperial yellow," one witness declared, gushed forth. In terror, the officers and men fled.

For a devout Confucianist and Buddhist such as P'u Yi, raised in a belief in ancestor worship and filial piety, a man who burned joss sticks each evening to propitiate the spirits of his forebears, the incident was traumatic. Understandably, the royal clans in the borderlands of Manchuria and former Manchu officials living in China were aroused. Delegates of every banner, even those that had been lying low since the court's abdication in 1912, flocked to Tientsin to offer condolences. Money poured in from all over China to restore the mausoleums and P'u Yi provided personal funds for the reburial of the bones of his illustrious ancestors, seventeen in number, emperors, empresses, and concubines. Spirit tablets for the dead were erected at Chang Gardens with tables for burning incense and mats for the pious to kneel on as they prayed, in their sorrow, to the disturbed spirits of the dead. Veteran Manchu visited P'u Yi in a seemingly unending stream to bow, kowtow, and weep "as if it were a funeral," P'u Yi remembered with bitterness. Mongolian princes and Han scholars joined in the mourning.

For his part, P'u Yi dispatched a telegram to Chiang Kai-shek and demanded the punishment of the culprits, including the generals in command of the troops who had perpetuated the outrage. Chiang ordered an inquiry but nothing came of it. The republic did not even send a note of sympathy to the bereaved Manchu court.

From then on, P'u Yi held Chiang in contempt. Perhaps, subconsciously, his distaste for the Generalissimo was conditioned in part by frequent references in the Chinese and foreign press to the gradual emergence in China of a "Soong Dynasty" with Chiang Kai-shek at its head. Chiang had married Soong Mei-ling, the sister of Soong Ching-ling, Sun Yat-sen's wife. Another of these attractive, articulate sisters, Soong Ai-ling, married H. H. Kung, the republic's minister of industry, labor and commerce. Their brother, T. V. Soong, as finance minister, held the purse strings of the republic and, for good measure, served as acting minister of foreign affairs. Clearly, a Soong Dynasty was in the making, or so it seemed.

P'u Yi's hatred for the Chinese, for Chiang Kai-shek and the republic—all of whom he blamed for the sacrilege—was indescribable. "My heart smouldered with a hatred I had never known before," he wrote in his memoirs. "Standing before the dark and gloomy funerary hall I made an oath before my weeping clansmen: 'If I do not avenge this wrong I am not an Aisin-Gioro,' " i.e., a faithful member of the imperial Manchu clan.

At this juncture, in this troubled state of mind, P'u Yi made the crucial political decision of his life.

"My experience of the past few years and the story of Chiang Kai-shek's rise to power combined to make me believe that if one wanted to achieve anything it was necessary to have military power," P'u Yi wrote. Significantly the sentence was published in 1964, on the eve of the Great Proletarian Cultural Revolution at a time when Mao Tse-tung, was preaching, "Power grows out of the barrel of a gun."

Overcome by remorse, seething with a desire for revenge, P'u Yi seized the initiative in his relations with the Japanese. He established direct and intimate relations with the Kwangtung army, then protecting Japan's "special rights" in Manchuria, and in March, 1929, seven months after the desecration of the tombs, dispatched his younger brother, P'u Chieh—the boy with whom he had played hide-and-seek in his childhood in the Forbidden City—to Japan as his unofficial representative.

Reginald Johnston, who had left P'u Yi's service after the flight from Peking, rushed to Tientsin to offer his sympathy. Johnston was stunned by the dramatic change in his former pupil, who appeared to have aged appreciably overnight. "The change was very marked," Johnston wrote, and he was a man unaccustomed to exaggeration. "So marked was it that it seemed to me as though he had been in communion with the spirits of his outraged ancestors and that they had urged him to turn away from the China that had disgraced herself and them and to fix his gaze on the land in which they had laid the strong foundations of their empire three hundred years ago."

"The magnitude of the catastrophe," Johnston continued, "can hardly be estimated except by those who know something of the Chinese cult of ancestors and the deep reverence with which the Chinese and Manchu regard the graves of their forefathers.

"Everything else could be forgiven—insults, ridicule, threats of death, confiscation of property, the tearing up of agreements—but not this appalling act of savagery and sacrilege," he said.

When a situation reaches the limit there is bound to be a reaction—P'u Yi began conspiring in earnest to return to his ancestral homeland with the assistance of "foreign power," the semiautonomous, insubordinate Kwantung army.

CHAPTER 15

Incident at Mukden

Following the desecration of the imperial tombs, P'u Yi moved into a deepening relationship with the Kwantung army and with such radical nationalist Japanese groups as the Black Dragon Society, named, significantly, for the Black Dragon River, which demarcates the Russian-Manchurian border and is known in Russian as the Amur.

In effect, P'u Yi operated as a government-in-exile. The Kwantung army established a special bureau to deal with him. Mino Residence, a fashionable apartment building in Tientsin, which never appeared to have a vacancy, served as the special bureau's secret headquarters.

In his discussions with the Japanese, P'u Yi was immeasurably heartened. His contacts stressed the military superiority of Japan and the feebleness and degeneracy of China and ascribed China's condition to her lack of an emperor. "These talks gave me a strong belief in the might of the Japanese armed forces," P'u Yi wrote, "and gave me great confidence."

The Kwantung army's intimacy with P'u Yi was only one of

several developments between 1929 and 1931 which influenced the army to strike in Manchuria. Among the others were Chiang Kai-shek's apparent progress in neutralizing petty warlords; the rising spirit of Chinese nationalism, especially among the youth; the decision by Marshal Chang Tso-lin's heir to incorporate Manchuria into the Chinese republic; Soviet rivalry in Manchuria; the growing influence of the Chinese Communist Party; and the internal situation in Japan.

Swept up by the Great Depression, Japan was racked by economic, political, and social unrest. Unemployment was widespread and the youth and the army restless. Radical nationalist groups expressed contempt for the system of parliamentary democracy adopted from the West and denounced big-business interests which appeared concerned only with profit. Radical groups in the army and among the youth forged a common front and favored the creation of a military-socialist state in which the great industries were nationalized and such imported political philosophies as representative government and civil liberties were obliterated. Insularity and chauvinism, coupled with easy victories over such relatively inferior adversaries as Korea and China, had heightened Japan's warrior tradition. The Japanese man-in-the-street came to believe in the invincibility of the imperial army. Enlightened civilians, members of the nobility and the heads of the big-business combines sensed otherwise but they were powerless to resist the popular ground swell.

If the Japanese at home were restive, the Kwantung army was even more impatient. With one eye cast south to the Chinese and the other north toward the Russians, the army felt that it had to move quickly to get Manchuria for Japan.

In 1929, a year after the incident of the tombs, the Chinese republican government, riding the crest of a wave of militant nationalism, put pressure on the Soviet Union to live up to Lenin's pledge to abandon Russia's special rights in Manchuria. The Chinese closed down Soviet enterprises in Manchuria, seized the Soviet-owned telegraph and telephone systems along the Chinese Eastern Railway, and deported Russian citizens. The pressure placed on the Russians was an integral part of Chiang Kai-shek's domestic policy of suppressing the Communists at home.

Stalin reacted vigorously. Soviet troops launched a series of border raids along the Soviet-Manchurian frontier; by the end of 1929, the raids had developed into a military invasion of Manchuria. Chiang Kai-shek characterized the invasion as "proof that Soviet Russia is continuing Czarist Russia's aggressive policy toward China." In firefight after firefight, the Soviet army routed the Chinese. Forced to the conference table, Chiang Kai-shek accepted a protocol which restored the Russian *status quo ante* in Manchuria. At this juncture, with China again humiliated by the foreign devils, the Communists south of the Great Wall established their first soviet on Chinese soil.

As viewed by the Kwantung army, especially by the radical nationalist clique headed by Doihara and Itagaki, the Soviet invasion of Manchuria and the developing strength of the Chinese Communists were portents of things to come. The Kwantung army envisioned Stalin's detachment of Manchuria from China and its use as a base for the Communist struggle in China against Chiang Kai-shek. It was a repeat of the old game in Manchuria, the question of who would get there first: the Russians, the Japanese or the Chinese. The Manchu themselves were merely pawns. Thus, Doihara and Itagaki planned a preemptive strike in Manchuria, with their leading pawn the Manchu emperor, P'u Yi.

In the summer of 1931, P'u Yi's younger brother, P'u Chieh, resplendent in the uniform of a Japanese military academy, returned to Tientsin and brought with him a message from his contacts in the Japanese army and the Black Dragon Society. "Please inform your brother," he was instructed, "that his situation is by no means hopeless."

The gist of the message was confirmed by Nora Waln, who had received an invitation on July 6 from "Mr. and Mrs. P'u Yi" to join them at Sunday brunch. "They had received a gift of raspberries from the country and were going to have raspberry *fu yung,* in which I delight," she wrote.

Raspberry *fu yung* aside, she observed: "The ex-empress told me that her husband had been unofficially approached by Japanese callers, as well as by his relatives, who work continuously for a monarchial restoration, and by [monarchist] Chinese, regarding acceptance of a throne in Manchuria."

But, Miss Waln continued, "Elizabeth confided that she and her husband were both anxious to keep free from all politics." Nothing, of course, could be further from the truth. While they may not have shared the same bed, P'u Yi and his empress shared the same political objective, the throne. In retrospect, it appears that P'u Yi shrewdly used Elizabeth's relationship with the talkative, socially active Nora Waln to lay down a smokescreen in Tientsin's diplomatic community about his future plans.

As summer waned, Doihara tipped the Kwantung army's hand in an interview with one of Japan's leading newspapers. The forty-eight-year-old colonel, who, along with Itagaki, had just been appointed to a post in the Kwantung army's headquarters at Mukden, said, "There is no telling what might happen in Manchuria." Only a few days later on September 11, in a coded dispatch, the American minister to China, Nelson T. Johnson, notified Washington that Chiang Kai-shek's intelligence apparatus expressed the belief that "Japan would occupy Manchuria within the next three months." Johnson reacted to the information with disbelief.

"I thought such action on the part of the Japanese highly improbable," he wrote. "It seemed fantastic that at this time the Japanese would act in this way, particularly as they were able to exploit Manchuria while all of the expenses of administration and government remain on Chinese shoulders." Johnson, of course, was reacting rationally in the manner of an intelligent, urbane observer, almost in scholarly fashion. He did not appreciate the gut and gutter politics of Japan's radicals and paid little attention to their pursuit of glory, their desire for power and public adulation, their obsession with remaking the world, and their fanaticism. That same year, though, the Black Dragon Society issued a pamphlet which declared, "The organization of an independent Manchurian-Mongolian state is a matter that brooks no delay."

Dutifully, Johnson kept relaying to Washingson the latest information that he received. On September 12, he passed along a Nanking *aide-mémoire* which "drew attention to the possibility of grave developments in Manchuria" and reported that the Japanese army in Korea had been quietly strengthened by two divisions and had assumed positions along the Yalu River, which separates Manchuria from Korea.

Then on September 18, 1931, there occurred the opportunity for which P'u Yi had been impatiently waiting for nineteen years—the Mukden Incident, one of those great watersheds in human affairs. The episode was manufactured by Doihara and Itagaki as a pretext for Japan's seizure of Manchuria.

According to the official Kwantung army version, a lieutenant and six men went out on patrol that night north of Mukden along a section of track of the Japanese-controlled South Manchurian Railway. The night was "dark but clear." Suddenly they heard a large explosion. Rushing to the scene, they discovered a thirty-one-inch gap blown in the track. As they studied the damage, the patrol was pinned down by rifle fire. At this moment, the lights of a southbound express appeared on the horizon. At full speed the train raced toward the spot. When it reached the site, the train swayed, righted itself and raced on, arriving punctually at Mukden at 10:30 P.M. As the train passed, the firing resumed and the lieutenant radioed Mukden for assistance. Manchuria's capital was quickly overrun. The commander-in-chief of the Japanese garrison in Korea was asked to rush reinforcements, although the Kwantung army encountered almost no opposition at home or from the great powers who were in a position to stop them. In a matter of weeks, the Japanese army had occupied Manchuria at hardly any cost in men or material. The *Manchurian Daily News,* a Japanese-subsidized, English-language newspaper, aptly summed up the incident. "All is fair in war and love," the paper said. "This is the truth in a nutshell."

Japan's Kwantung army provided a dazzling exercise in what Hitler's generals would later term "Blitzkrieg," nine years before the Germans minted the word and a decade before the Japanese displayed the most stunning example of it, the occupation of the whole of Southeast Asia in a matter of weeks.

The diplomatic community in China was shocked. Johnson cabled Washington that "we believe the real reason for the Japanese attack was the desire of the Japanese army to strike a fatal blow to the Chinese." And now, for the first time, P'u Yi's name crept into the coded diplomatic dispatches. The American consul general at Mukden reported that "the Japanese were scheming to place the ex-Emperor, Hsüan Tung, at the head of a new Manchurian government."

If the Chinese, Americans and others were shaken by the Kwantung army's lightning thrust, so was the Japanese government. In the words of Kisuke Okada, the former premier of Japan, "the so-called Mukden Incident did not take any enlightened public official of Japan by surprise." But the role of the Japanese army detachments stationed in Korea, which crossed into Manchuria without the sanction of the emperor and in defiance of the cabinet, generated a crisis in Tokyo. "The army during these years," Okada said, "was completely out of government control and no restraint could be placed upon it."

Several foreign correspondents in Manchuria at the time felt that Tokyo's surprise pointed to a split between the civilian moderates and the army radicals and that a vigorous protest by the great powers, or even by the United States alone, would force the Kwantung army to retreat. But appeasement was in the wind. Many Americans felt that so remote an incident, in so obscure a place, was of little consequence. Nelson Johnson, from Peking, succinctly summed up this viewpoint: "Whether China rules Manchuria, or whether Japan rules Manchuria, or whether Russia rules Manchuria is not a matter of United States concern." Most of his countrymen agreed.

Yet, for one brief moment, the Kwantung army's forward momentum was checked. In Washington, at a news conference, President Herbert Hoover expressed the offhand belief that the Japanese army had "run amok." But in the words of a *Manchester Guardian*'s correspondent at Mukden, "when the Kwantung army discovered that America was only bluffing again, they proceeded with their program."

The Mukden Incident had profound consequences. Mukden was the starting point for the ultimate creation of a Japanese empire which embraced the western rim of the Pacific from Korea to New Guinea. Mukden led directly to Pearl Harbor. Mukden also led to the demise of the League of Nations. After weeks of debate, during which the Kwantung army consolidated its hold on Manchuria, the League on December 10, 1931, appointed a commission of inquiry headed by the Earl of Lytton. The commission's measured, final report was delivered October 1, 1932, after the Kwantung army had completed the occupation of Manchuria. On the basis of the Lytton Report, the League branded Japan an aggressor and Tokyo simply walked out of the League. The League never recovered.

The seizure of Manchuria also provided the Japanese army with a major foothold on the Asian mainland, a jumping-off place for the conquest of China south of the Great Wall. And perhaps the most profound consequence of all, given the atmosphere of the times, is that Mukden became a model for Mussolini and Hitler. The Japanese were accused later of aping Mussolini and Hitler. Actually, as the record shows, it was the other way around. And, lastly, within the context of the life and times of the last Manchu emperor of China, the Mukden Incident put P'u Yi back on a throne and provided him with a base from which he hoped to avenge the spirits of his ancestors, recover his heritage and reoccupy the Forbidden City in Peking.

In a broader perspective, the first gunshots of World War II were fired during the incident at Mukden. With a rhythm that defies rational explanation, the war opened and closed on the same note. The last shot of the global conflict also rang out on the Manchurian plain. Incredibly, P'u Yi, overshadowed by events though he might be, was on stage both times as the curtain rose on the war and as the curtain fell.

CHAPTER 16

The Dragon Returns Home

As war clouds gathered, P'u Yi and his consort, Elizabeth, like the decadent characters in a Vicki Baum novel, lived a life of extravagance and, on the surface, of insouciant concern. They were the toast of the Tientsin's smart set.

Attired in the latest Gene Sarazen fashion, with knickers, peaked cap and black-and-white saddle shoes, P'u Yi was a familiar sight on the golf links at Tientsin. Fond of horses, he frequented the Tientsin race track and wore striped trousers, morning coat, and top hat as the occasion demanded. In riding habit and white helmet, he played polo in the foreign quarter with British diplomats, French bankers, and Danish shipowners. He became so enthusiastic about the game that he imported a large thorough-bred from England and, for some unknown reason, christened him Ponto. His foreign friends addressed the horse as "Mr. Ponto," and it was a standing joke in Tientsin that visitors would casually ask, "And how is your good friend Mr. Ponto?" Newcomers to Tientsin, of course, were puzzled by the reference.

On occasion, to Elizabeth's amusement, P'u Yi was reported in the gossip columns as having been seen the night before in the city's red-light district. But, she knew, he visited the area not so much for the pleasures of the boudoir as for those of the gaming tables.

As for Elizabeth, as the last empress of China, she was the pride of the international cocktail circuit and the prize conversation piece at parties and dinners. Quickly, she developed into a social butterfly and appeared alternately in public in exquisitely brocaded Manchu robes and the latest Parisian style, calf-length dresses, silk stockings, and perky derby hats. With her slender figure and graceful walk, she could have been mistaken in the West for a model. Her English was good—far better than Henry's despite the lack of tutoring—and she was especially fond of arranging for picnics aboard her motor launch.

Tientsin's exhilarating climate was conducive to the kind of active, meaningless social life in which the participants were preoccupied only with their guest list, gossip, and the weather. Like New York, the temperature climbed into the nineties in summer and the rivers were clogged with ice in the winter. This provided the city with a singular appeal: it demanded a four-season wardrobe.

Both Henry and Elizabeth were oblivious to the crash of 1929. Although P'u Yi constantly complained of his empress's extravagance, his secret cache of pearls and cut and uncut jewels was sufficient to maintain their luxurious, fast-paced life, and, in the bargain, to support a legion of relatives and camp followers.

The Mukden Incident, which electrified P'u Yi and his courtiers, put an end to all of that. Swiftly, the political climate in Tientsin changed. "Sooner or later," said the eighty-four-year-old Cheng Hsiao-hsu, who had emerged as P'u Yi's principal adviser, "the Japanese are bound to invite your imperial majesty to go to Manchuria."

As the Japanese army swept across Manchuria, the local administrations dissolved into confusion. The vacuum was temporarily filled by a makeshift Japanese military administration. Doihara, for example, turned up as the mayor of Mukden, a rather odd posting for the director of the Kwangtung army's secret service, whom the press of the period nick-named, incongruously, both the "master murderer" and "Lawrence of Manchuria." Such incongruities reflected the confusion on the scene—and in Tokyo—arising out of the army's rash act.

In Japan, the power of the army rested principally on the right of the chief of the general staff and the army divisional commanders, including the commander of the Kwantung army, to enter the presence of the emperor and obtain his sanction for military policies without the interference of the civilian cabinet. As the American ambassador to Japan, W. Cameron Forbes, suggested to Washington on December 17, 1931, in a coded dispatch, "This right of direct access has had, I am convinced, a very vital connection with the incident at Mukden."

Already troubled by the murder of Chang Tso-lin, Hirohito had urged moderation and restraint on his army commanders, however. Rebuffed, the army expressed concern over Japanese lives and property in Manchuria as the situation in China deteriorated. As a consequence, the army obtained an imperial sanction, as Forbes concluded, "to take whatever measures might be necessary for protection of Japanese lives and property in case of Chinese aggression." Thus, when the "incident" at Mukden developed, the army possessed imperial permission to take "whatever action might be deemed necessary."

P'u Yi was aware of the special army-emperor relationship in Japan. In the original Chinese language version of his memoirs P'u Yi makes plain that the Japanese War Office's direct link to Hirohito was uppermost in the minds of himself and his advisers. P'u Yi believed that the army had won the secret approval of Hirohito for the Manchurian venture, and for his restoration.

Six days after the Mukden Incident, the Kwantung army installed at Mukden a civilian Committee for the Maintenance of Peace and Order. The Japanese press, taking a cue from the War Office, promptly acclaimed the committee as "the first step in a separatist movement."

P'u Yi did not have long to wait for the next move. On

September 30, twelve days after the Mukden Incident and six days after the "first step" toward independence, with the Japanese army still fanning out across the Manchurian plain, Itagaki made the move which P'u Yi and his advisers awaited. Doihara was dispatched as an envoy to P'u Yi to inform him that "the people of Manchuria clamor for your imperial majesty's return."

"Everything is settled," P'u Yi jubilantly told his advisers. I need only take a Japanese warship to Talien [Manchuria]."

But to his surprise, both his advisers Chen Pao-shen and Cheng Hsiao-hsu were visibly embarrassed. "It has always been the hope of your humble slave that the old order would be restored as it is only natural that heaven will comply with the wishes of the people," Cheng Hsiao-hsu said. "But to act rashly in the present confusion might lead to inextricable difficulties." Chen Pao-shen was astonishingly direct, perhaps out of exasperation. "Your imperial majesty should not put trust too heavily in the representative of a mere colonel," he said.

Itagaki, of course, was more than "a mere colonel." Nevertheless, Chen Pao-shen again lectured P'u Yi on the widening split in Japan between army and civilians. In truth, the extent of this rift was wider than even he imagined. From Tokyo, the American ambassador informed Washington that the Japanese foreign minister, Baron Shidehara, had known nothing about the Mukden Incident; this situation was echoed a decade later in 1941 when special envoys from the Japanese emperor and the foreign office arrived in Washington to negotiate peace and found themselves as much in the dark as their hosts were about the attack on Pearl Harbor. But P'u Yi was unimpressed with his advisers' analysis. He was convinced that power grew out of the barrel of a gun. "My fate is in the hands of soldiers," he said, bitingly, "not politicians."

As P'u Yi analyzed his situation, the decisive element was the Kwantung army. Chiang Kai-shek, he concluded, was so preoccupied with the struggle against the Communists that the Chinese republic was in no condition to fight Japan; therefore it would passively accept the loss of Manchuria. As for the great powers—the

Europeans and Americans—P'u Yi was convinced that they would not block the Japanese expansion along the Soviet border. He believed that the paramount Western power in the Orient, Britain, secretly supported the restoration of his dynasty. Undoubtedly, he was influenced in this judgment by Johnston, intentionally or otherwise.

Any doubt about the British was probably removed when Johnston—"on a rather unexpected," as he phrased it—mission for the Foreign Office, arrived in Tientsin October 7, a week to the day after Doihara's visit. "I spent the next two days in his company," Johnston wrote a year later, "and was given information which enabled me to foresee what was to happen in the near future." Johnston does not explicitly state what that information was but by implication he leaves no doubt in the reader's mind. "As may be readily understood," he said, "there was only one topic of conversation." Although Johnston discreetly refused to spell out the topic, at least in public, the last chapter of his memoirs is appropriately entitled, "The Dragon Goes Home."

Their parting on that occasion was touched with poignancy. They felt they would never meet again, although they were destined to do so once more, in Manchuria. As a farewell gift, P'u Yi presented his most intimate Western friend a fan in which, in beautifully measured strokes, he copied a T'ang Dynasty poem which reflected the undercurrent of melancholy never too far below the surface of his own existence. P'u Yi was history's pawn, and he could never dispel that knowledge. In the style of a love sonnet, the poem read:

> I wanted to follow him across the river,
> But the river was deep and had no bridge.
> Oh, that we were a pair of herons,
> That we could fly home together.

Did P'u Yi invite Johnston to go "home" with him to Manchuria? Or did he imply that he wished they could both fly from politics altogether? We can only speculate, although there is evidence, in P'u Yi's writings and other sources, that Johnston made him a standing offer: The gates of London always stood ajar in the event that P'u Yi was forced to flee abroad or desired to escape his destiny.

Johnston was not the only foreign caller P'u Yi received in this period of stress. Nora Waln reappeared in his life. "I found him and his wife much perturbed by callers who were using every possible means of persuasion and pressure to get him to agree to be crowned Emperor of Manchuria," she said of their last meeting. And the American embassy in Tokyo, in a confidential dispatch to Washington the following month, reported that "the ex-emperor of China would be set up at Kirin [Manchuria] within thirty days under the aegis of the Japanese." The new state, the message concluded, "would decidedly not go the way of Korea," which Japan had annexed as a colony after its conquest and occupation around the century's turn.

Chiang Kai-shek was alarmed by the flurry of reports and rumors at home and abroad that Japan had invited or intended to invite P'u Yi to reascend a Dragon Throne in Manchuria. Secretly, he dispatched a personal emissary to P'u Yi and offered to revive the Articles of Favorable Treatment; in a rather crude and cumbersome manner, he also offered the ex-emperor an additional lump sum in cash—the amount to be determined—on condition he live anywhere "except in Manchuria or Japan." In his autobiography, P'u Yi confirmed the existence of this offer but said, "I remembered the desecration of the mausoleums by Kuomintang groups and distrusted Chiang Kai-shek." Thus, he said, "I gave the emissary a noncommittal answer." Another source, the *Shanghai Evening Post & Mercury,* perhaps the most famous English-language daily on the China coast, reported that the Nationalists offered temporarily to restore the conditions of favorable treatment, including a payment of 4 million taels but that P'u Yi haughtily asserted that Chiang Kai-shek could best fulfill his responsibilities by concerning himself with the welfare of the people, by giving them good government, and by restoring internal peace.

The Nationalists have never formally acknowledged that such an offer was made; but there is no doubt that Chiang tried to get Johnston to keep P'u Yi out of Manchuria. On November 10, 1931, Johnston "received an urgent request to visit Mr. T. V. Soong." At the interview, the acting republican foreign minister showed Johnston a telegram reporting that P'u Yi was "in danger and in need of Johnston's help." Soong expected Johnston to rush to P'u Yi's side at Tientsin and, perhaps, dissuade him from accepting the Japanese invitation to go to Manchuria. "I told Mr. Soong," Johnston wrote disdainfully, "that the emperor knew of my movements and could communicate with me direct at any time. . . . If he was in danger and needed help, he only had to say the word and I would go to him. But the word must come from himself."

P'u Yi's noncommittal reply and Johnston's rebuff alarmed Chiang Kai-shek, who sent an *aide-mémoire* to the United States government and declared: "In the event that the establishment of P'u Yi's bogus government is confirmed, the National government will regard such a government as a seditionist institution and at the same time as an auxiliary organ of the Japanese government in disguise, while all the acts of such a government which are necessarily illegal will be repudiated by the Nationalist government and the entire responsibility therefore will be on the shoulders of the Japanese government."

Chiang Kai-shek had cause for alarm. During the first week of November, Doihara paid another personal visit on P'u Yi and appeared to place the Kwantung army's cards on the table. The deck included a king.

The meeting took place within P'u Yi's compound. Doihara, surprisingly, turned up in a Western business suit with a briefcase under his arm, like a traveling salesman. P'u Yi greeted him in his sitting room and Doihara bowed politely as he entered the august presence. The Japanese envoy played his role of courtier with gentlemanly precision. First, he inquired about P'u Yi's health, then, he engaged the emperor in other equally innocuous exchanges. P'u Yi fidgeted and then stood up and began to pace the room, breaking unlighted cigarettes between his fingers. Doihara recognized the symptoms of tension and turned to the business at hand.

Japan had no territorial ambitions in Manchuria and "sincerely wanted to help the Manchurian people set up their own independent state," Doihara began. Then he expressed the hope that P'u Yi would not pass up the opportunity to become involved. Since antiquity, he pointed out, Manchuria had provided an ideal springboard for the subjugation of China. This was P'u Yi's "chance of ten thousand years." As for the fledgling state's security against attack by Stalin or Chiang Kai-shek, Japan pledged to enter into a mutual defense treaty with the new nation and guarantee its sovereignty and territorial integrity.

P'u Yi was impressed. Only one question required clarification. What form would the new state take? Monarchy or republic? For the first time, Doihara hesitated. "This problem will be solved after your majesty comes to Shengyang [Mukden]."

"No," P'u Yi snapped with an upsurge of daring. "I will go only if there is a restoration."

Doihara smiled. "Of course," he said, "the new state will be a monarchy."

Reassured, P'u Yi agreed to embark clandestinely for Manchuria on November 10.

In arriving at this decision, P'u Yi was probably influenced by the rash of threatening letters and telephone calls he had been receiving in this period; on one occasion, a basket of fruit containing two bombs was sent to his residence; fortunately the bombs were detected before they exploded. On another occasion a shot was fired at him. Fifteen years later, at the Tojo Trial, P'u Yi concluded with hindsight, that Doihara had contrived the campaign of terror to pressure him into leaving an "unsafe" Tientsin and an unhospitable China. If Doihara and Itagaki could stage-manage such a spectacular production as the Mukden Incident and its aftermath, sending bombs in a basket of fruit was a sideshow.

According to captured World War II documents, the Japanese Foreign Office was kept largely in the dark about the negotiations between P'u Yi and the Kwantung army; P'u Yi was a partner in their deception. For example, in early November, besieged by newsmen, P'u Yi held a rare news conference and vigorously denied any intention of returning to Manchuria. Members of his entourage also spread the tale, subsequently published abroad, that the ex-emperor and empress entered into a compact to commit suicide rather than consent to his restoration in Manchuria.

While these distracting balls were tossed into the air, Doihara skillfully organized disturbances in the Chinese quarter of Tientsin. As the disorders spread, Chiang Kai-shek proclaimed martial law and several of the foreign concessions, including that of the Japanese, followed suit. Deftly, Doihara had placed P'u Yi incommunicado.

As prearranged, on November 10, the Lord of Ten Thousand Years, attired in a Japanese army greatcoat and peaked cap, hid in the trunk of a black convertible roadster, with large headlights and flat running boards, and was driven at night to the British concession. The driver of the vehicle was so nervous that he struck a telephone pole en route and P'u Yi banged his head badly against the trunk top. Along with other members of his entourage, the Empress Elizabeth remained behind under guard in the Japanese concession. The Japanese did not trust Elizabeth, perhaps because she had too many American friends. In a postwar memoir published in Tokyo, a director of Japanese intelligence, Tanaka Takayoshi (Ryukichi), quoted Doihara as telling him, "She is trying to persuade P'u Yi not to accept our plan."

While occasional exchanges of rifle fire were still heard in the Chinese quarter the roadster carrying P'u Yi pulled up alongside a nondescript wharf and an unlighted motor launch chugged into view. The deck of the launch was piled high with sandbags concealing a platoon of Japanese soldiers. Several of P'u Yi's advisers, including Cheng Hsiao-hsu, waved from the ship's bridge; but Chen Pao-shen, whom P'u Yi once described as "the tutor who had the deepest influence on me next to Johnston," was conspicuously absent. Unknown to P'u Yi, there was a large drum of gasoline lashed to the limber holes in the bilges. In the event of a challenge by Chinese shore batteries, the boat would blow up.

Slipping her lines, the launch gathered headway and moved as quietly as possible down stream to the mouth of the Pai. The blinking lights of the foreign settlements dropped astern and ahead loomed the dark, Chinese-held banks. After two hours of silent running, a shout from the bank, in Chinese, commanded: "*Chih! Halt!*"

"My heart jumped into my mouth," P'u Yi said later. "I lay on the deck paralyzed as if all my nerves had been cut."

Obeying the shoreside summons, the Japanese skipper backed down his engines and spun the wheel to port. As the vessel glided toward the bank, he suddenly spun the wheel hard to starboard in a deft maneuver, and opened up the throttle. The launch lifted her nose and roared away through the mouth of the river, and gained the open sea. P'u Yi was safe, from the Chinese at any rate.

Once out on the open sea, the launch rendezvoused with a Japanese merchantman, *Awachi Maru,* a 1,948-ton freighter with a black hull, red boot, and dirty white superstructure. Built in 1906, the *Awachi Maru* was a familiar sight along the China coast.

That night the emperor's escape was celebrated at sea in modest Japanese style: *miso* soup, pickled cabbage, and warm bottles of sake. Under the influence of the bland rice wine, the aged Cheng Hsiao-hsu grew voluble and spoke enthusiastically of the racial and cultural links between China and Japan. On the spot, in Chinese classical style he composed a poem to commemorate the exploit, describing it as an "heroic enterprise."

Two and a half days later the coastal tramp steamer tied up at the railway dock at Yingkow, a south Manchurian port, after an uneventful voyage of 250 miles. It had been P'u Yi's first experience on the sea. No crowds, bands or flags greeted the return of the Manchu's illustrious heir to reclaim what was rightfully his. But a special train swiftly bore him to the hot springs resort town of Tangkangtzu, two hours from the coast. There the entire top floor of the principal hotel was reserved for him. That night he dined on Japanese food, superbly prepared but a far cry from the subtle imperial viands of the Forbidden City.

From the hotel window he gazed out on Manchuria for the first time and found himself boxed in by wild, dark mountains, the T'ien Shan or "Thousand Ridge" chain, a series of lofty, forbidding peaks interrupted here and there with patches of green and roaring cataracts.

CHAPTER 17

Checkmated

The following morning, exhilarated by events, the descendant of the Exalted Founder of the Manchu Dynasty dressed hurriedly to go out for his first stroll across the rich soil of his ancestral Manchuria. Like many Chinese and Manchu, P'u Yi was thoroughly familiar with the historic hot springs of Tangkangtzu whose waters were said to contain great medicinal value. In antiquity members of the Manchu nobility often took "the cure" here.

Nestling within the Thousand Ridges, he knew, were clusters of Buddhist and Taoist temples where the traveler could find hospitality while visiting the hot springs. A day or night spent at any of these temples, it was said, was like a page out of the past. In this setting, the Japanese had built a modern, four-story inn with serpentine roofs and—the hotel's brochure boasted—"American improvements," which meant plumbing. Before the Great Depression, cruises to the Orient usually had included a stopover at Tangkangtzu, whose renown approached that of Baden-Baden or Saratoga Springs.

For the day's outing, P'u Yi slipped into a polo shirt with open

182

throat, a thick British woolen sweater, cream-colored slacks, and brown-and-white saddle shoes, the costume of the typical tourist. In this guise, the emperor would blend into any group of tourists in the main lounge and lose himself among the peddlers and hawkers in the narrow streets below, for whom tourists were standard fare. But he promptly found himself up against the harsh reality of the great game he was involved in. Ostensibly for reasons of security, Japanese officials barred him from leaving his hotel suite. How long would he be quarantined at the inn? "That depends on Colonel Itagaki," he was informed. When was he to leave for the capital? "That depends on Itagaki." For every question he asked, the reply was the same. P'u Yi might as well have been under house arrest.

Out of touch with developments since his flight from Tientsin, P'u Yi was unaware of the new depths of confusion into which Japan had been thrown by the Mukden Incident. Externally, Japan was isolated. The climate of world opinion tilted strongly against Tokyo. The great powers frowned on the Manchurian venture; so did the League of Nations. Within China, students and workers staged demonstrations and strikes, demanding that Chiang Kai-shek redeem face and declare war on Japan. Clearly, the tide of Chinese nationalism ran high. Internally, Japan was in crisis. The cabinet and the army were at odds and the emperor humiliated by the fact that his army had crossed the Korean border into Manchuria without his permission.

Indeed, the stiuation in Japan was so delicate that the government forbade the press to publish "any comment on Japanese aid in connection with the ex-emperor of China leaving Tientsin." By now, of course, the foreign press was filled with reports that the Japanese had taken P'u Yi to Manchuria under duress. In an effort to undercut sagging morale in China, the republic had spread the story that P'u Yi had been kidnapped. For the Chinese, the humiliation suffered by Japan's conquest of Manchuria was bad enough. For the world to learn that the last emperor of China had defected to the Japanese was even more humiliating. The Japanese, meanwhile, constructed a different version of events. On November 18, 1931, the Japanese foreign minister informed the American ambassador that "the departure of the young emperor was wholly on his own initiative and due to fear for the safety of his life which has been repeatedly threatened in Tientsin until he could not sleep." And Baron Shidehara added: "He was not assisted by Japanese troops or civil authorities in this move but is now being 'protected' by them at [a] resort in Manchuria."

Describing P'u Yi as "weak and inexperienced," the foreign minister disclosed that neither the Japanese civil nor military authorities favored his restoration as emperor. However, he said—and it was the tip of the iceberg—"a plain 'Mr. P'u Yi' might be selected by members of the various independence committees in Manchuria as a sort of general chairman." This was the first official intimation that Japan was not interested in a restoration of the Great Ch'ing Dynasty.

Back in London, Johnston also derided the reports that his former pupil had been abducted. "Had he wished to escape from the danger of being kidnaped and carried off to Manchuria," Johnston said, "all he had to do was to walk on board a British steamer bound for Shanghai."

"He left Tientsin and went to Manchuria of his own free will," he added with finality.

Johnston's strong statement notwithstanding, the diplomatic corps in Tientsin continued to lean heavily on the kidnapping theory. The vernacular Chinese press carried headlines which—not inaccurately—reported that P'u Yi had been transported to Manchuria by a Japanese freighter "under escort of Japanese guards." When a high-ranking officer in the British garrison advised an American consular official that P'u Yi "had been taken to Mukden," the American immediately contacted a Japanese colleague and reported back to Washington that the Japanese official was "noncommittal."

Whether he had been abducted or not, Manchuria prepared for the imminent restoration of the "boy-emperor" and local tailors were deluged with orders for yellow imperial dragon flags. Wigmakers and theatrical supply houses, however, detected no sudden upsurge in business; even if the emperor were restored, apparently the queue would not be.

With the Kwantung army racing across Manchuria, the League of Nations paralyzed, the students in China on the rampage, the Japanese cabinet in disarray and P'u Yi incommunicado, the Chinese Communists seized an initiative. They announced the formation of China's first soviet republic in Kiangsi province—three days before P'u Yi's dash for Manchuria. Mao, who had struggled incessantly for the leadership, emerged as chairman, a position, that for all practical purposes, he has held ever since.

Historically important in the light of future developments, the constitution of the first soviet betrayed concern about the non-Chinese minorities who inhabit China's borderlands—"Manchurians, Mongolians, Moslems [sic], Tibetans."

These groups, the new regime averred, would be "equal before Soviet law and shall be citizens of the Soviet Republic [of China]." The use of the term "Manchurians" is a fair indication of the preoccupation of Mao Tse-tung and his companions even then with the territory which comprised China's vulnerable northern frontier. The charter also recognized "the right of self-determination of the national minorities in China, their right to complete separation from China, and to the formation of an independent state for each national minority." Ritualistically, the constitution listed again the various ethnic minority groups by name, but this time the Manchurians were omitted from the list. Apparently Mongolians and Tibetans exercised the right to "either join the Union of Chinese Soviets or secede from it and form their own state as they may prefer"—but the Manchurians did not.

In part, of course, the Communists were concerned lest the Japanese point to this provision as additional evidence of Manchuria's separate identity. In any event, in the light of the Russian incursion into Manchuria in 1929, the Japanese invasion in 1931, the Russian occupation of the territory in 1945, and the Sino-Russian clashes along the Manchurian frontier in 1969, the omission is of more than passing significance. This preoccupation with the "Outer Palisades Country," as the Chinese sometimes referred to the territory, by Russians, Japanese, and both the Chinese Nationalists and Communists, also explained their political interest in the last Manchu emperor. He commanded the loyalty and support of the Manchu and Mongol clans in Manchuria's border regions and he was a pawn of incalculable advantage to whichever party possessed him.

Despite his isolation in this turbulent period, P'u Yi again displayed an aptitude for political analysis. Something had gone wrong, he reasoned. The Japanese at the inn no longer acted as respectfully toward him as the Japanese had in Peking and Tientsin. Imperceptibly, he felt, the atmosphere had changed. His advisers sought to console him. "The Kwantung army is our host for the time being and until his imperial majesty reascends the throne, he should regard himself as their guest," Cheng Hsiao-hsu comforted P'u Yi—and probably himself.

"Although I still felt impatient," P'u Yi reluctantly, but realistically, concluded, "I had no choice but to force myself to wait."

In effect, P'u Yi was in suspended animation. He was neither a free agent nor a prisoner of the Kwantung army. The line between compulsion and free will was blurred. The world at large suspected that he was a captive, and in a sense he was: a captive of history.

As the days of idleness turned into weeks and the weeks into months, P'u Yi became increasingly morose and frustrated. Confined to the top floor of the hotel, he paced interminably up and down, like a madman, endlessly smoking—making each pack do double service by breaking cigarettes in half. "I seethed with hatred of Doihara and Itagaki," he said of this period. Suddenly, as in the past when he expelled the eunuchs from the Forbidden City, he grew bold. He played his trump in the struggle for survival—uniqueness.

"I decided to let the Kwantung army know that if they did not agree to my demands to restore the throne," he said, "I was going back to Tientsin."

But the train of events enveloped him before he could deliver his ultimatum. During his period of idleness, a series of "independence committees" had sprung up in Manchuria like bamboo shoots after the rain. Before P'u Yi could deliver his ultimatum, the committees—little more than Japanese front organizations—issued a proclamation of independence on February 18, 1932, and adopted the name of "Manchukuo," land of the Manchu. The following day, the Supreme Council of the new regime unanimously agreed to invite P'u Yi to become the "Chief Executive" of Manchukuo. Surprisingly, it also selected Changch'un, a minor town of narrow streets and unimportant buildings, as the capital of the new country and not Mukden, which had been the first capital of Nurhachu, the founder of the Manchu empire.

P'u Yi was presented with a *fait accompli*. Resentful toward heaven, he blamed others. In anger, he berated his advisers, especially Cheng Hsiao-hsu who had been instrumental in encouraging him to keep the faith with the Kwantung army. But it was too late for regrets. To run afoul of the Kwantung army, as Marshal Chang Tso-lin had, was dangerous; moreover, if P'u Yi failed to follow through with the Japanese, all hope of a restoration was lost.

Five days after the formation of Manchukuo, the issue between P'u Yi and the Kwantung army came to a head. On February 23, a cold and clear day, with patches of snow covering the Manchurian plain, Itagaki made his first call on the former emperor. "He was the most neatly dressed Japanese officer I had ever seen," P'u Yi observed; "his shirt cuffs were of dazzling whiteness and the creases in his trousers were razor sharp." Although P'u Yi did not say so, Itagaki's ochre-colored uniform and white shirt must have made his normally black brows even blacker.

After an exchange of salutations, Itagaki opened the dialogue by explaining the "sincerity of the Kwantung army in helping the Manchurian people win their freedom from Chinese rule." There was an element of disingenuity in the exchange which both accepted—Manchuria consisted largely of Chinese; why would Chinese free themselves from Chinese? Itagaki's oration was polished, and P'u Yi shifted uneasily in his high-backed, teak chair. As Itagaki spoke, P'u Yi nodded formally; he was waiting for Itagaki to get to the point that really interested him.

Then, like a salesman displaying his samples, Itagaki opened his traveling case and produced a "Declaration of Indepencence of the Manchu and Mongolian Peoples," and the five-barred flag of the new state, each color representing one of the five races of Manchukuo—Manchu, Chinese, Mongols, Japanese, and Koreans, a play on the traditional Chinese concept of the five "races" which make up China: the Chinese, Manchu, Mongols, Tibetans, and "Moslems." * In view of their special position in Manchuria and their role as midwife at the birth of the new nation, Itagaki continued, the Japanese would exercise the same rights as other nationalities in Manchukuo, including the right to hold office.

Thrusting aside the flag and documents, bursting with indignation, P'u Yi cried out, "What kind of a state is this?"

"Of course," Itagaki replied evenly, "this will not be a restoration of the Great Ch'ing Empire. This will be a new state and Your Excellency will be the Chief Executive."

For the first time in his life P'u Yi was addressed as "Your Excellency." As Itagaki's lips framed the words, the blood rushed to P'u Yi's head.

The next three hours sizzled. The people of Manchuria did not simply long for him as an individual but as the Great Ch'ing Emperor, P'u Yi argued shrilly. Itagaki responded cooly with the observation that the Manchurian people had expressed their desire to have him head the new state and the Kwantung army was "in full

* Thus, when the republic was founded in 1912, the five-barred red-yellow-blue-white-black flag was adopted, each color denoting a "race," and when the Communists came to power in 1949, the five-pointed star was adopted, each point representing a "race."

accord with their decision." P'u Yi found it inexplicable that Japan, a monarchy, would sponsor the creation of a detestable republic. Itagaki agreed and suggested that the term "republic" be dropped from the title of the new nation. As point and counterpoint were exhausted, P'u Yi touched on the intangible core of their confrontation. "The imperial title,", he said, his voice quivering, "has been handed down to me by my ancestors and were I to abandon it I would be lacking in loyalty and filial piety."

Itagaki came prepared. As he replied, the tide went out and the rock was revealed. The office of Chief Executive of the State of Manchukuo, he quietly assured P'u Yi, would be temporary in character; after the creation of the national assembly, a new constitution would opt for the imperial system.

Thus, the situation, as foretold by the venerable Chen Pao-shen, came down to this: The Samurai warriors of the emperor of Japan, the true Son of Heaven, were not prepared to sponsor a rival claimant to the title. They recalled that the Chinese had looked down upon their ancestors as "half-civilized barbarians," and still looked on them that way. The Great Ch'ing Dynasty was dead, beyond resurrection. At some later date, as the emperor of Manchukuo, P'u Yi might remount the throne but it would be by popular or Japanese consent and not by divine right.

Itagaki painstakingly restuffed his briefcase. The smile evaporated from his face and he frostily proposed that they resume their talk the following morning.

P'u Yi's distraught advisers, mindful of the fate of Chang Tso-lin, cautioned him not to get on bad terms with the Kwantung army. That night P'u Yi entertained Itagaki at a lavish banquet, which included two dozen courses, from spring rolls to melon soup. In front of each setting was a bottle of Martell three-star cognac, a must at Chinese banquets. The dinner was a stag affair. During the fete, the subject of the day's negotiations was carefully avoided.

When the conversations resumed the following morning, Itagaki came directly to the point. The army's position was final. There was nothing further to discuss. "We will regard its rejection as evidence of a hostile attitude," he said softly, "and we will act accordingly." Itagaki had made P'u Yi an offer he could not refuse.

P'u Yi was stunned by the remark. "My legs turned to jelly," he said, "and I collapsed speechless into an armchair."

After Itagaki's departure, the twenty-six-year-old Lord of Ten Thousand Years, and his courtiers, sat in silence. Finally, Cheng Hsiao-hsu spoke. "Your slave may regret the present situation," he said, "but there is nothing we can do about it."

However tenuous the hint that the national assembly would opt for an imperial system, Itagaki's offer held out P'u Yi's only hope for the future. P'u Yi's credentials were unimpeachable after all and everyone recognized his person as that of the Great Ch'ing Emperor. He was unique, and he must not forget it. For the present, he had to mark time. Even so, he would rule a land of 30 million people. Perhaps these comforting thoughts were true. But inwardly P'u Yi sensed that the gain might not be worth the loss. Timorously, he played his worn trump card. He agreed to accept the office of Chief Executive on the condition that he would resign if he were not given the title of emperor within a year. This threat of resignation, hopefully, would provide him with a modicum of leverage against the Japanese.

Cheng Hsiao-hsu carried the message to Itagaki while P'u Yi, filled with remorse and melancholy, hatred and despair, resumed his incessant pacing back and forth in his hotel room. His adviser returned shortly, his face beaming. Itagaki agreed to the condition and planned to give the future Chief Executive a "little banquet" that evening in honor of the occasion.

Itagaki's private banquet was lavish, like P'u Yi's the night before. Unlike P'u Yi's, however, it included girls. Raised among eunuchs and disinterested in his wives, P'u Yi found the affair distasteful. Itagaki, in high spirits, drank freely and became boisterous. The geishas of the evening were *korobi*, trained not only to offer songs, poems, and lively table talk, but also their bodies. "Itagaki fondled and embraced the girls," P'u Yi observed uncomfortably, "without bothering about the conventions of polite behavior."

Thus, among prostitutes and drunken army officers, the last emperor of China prepared to remount a throne.

CHAPTER 18

A Jade Throne

On February 28, the All-Manchurian Assembly, a "spontaneous" Japanese creation, unanimously nominated P'u Yi as regent of the new state with the title of Chief Executive. A nine-man delegation was sent to the former emperor requesting him to accede to "the popular demand of the Manchurian people." In a scene which has been replayed often in history, P'u Yi rejected the office. Probably, he felt he had to exhibit modesty and humility. In literature, Shakespeare has repeatedly extracted dramatic moment from this sort of scene. Mark Antony observed that Caesar refused the crown when it was first offered, and when Richard III, then Duke of Gloucester, was proferred the throne, he too declined to accept it at first. Like Shakespeare's characters, P'u Yi was not insensitive to dramatic values.

In his memoirs, he candidly recalls the delegation's arrival. "I met them myself," he said, "and both sides made set speeches. . . . They 'earnestly beseeched' me, and I 'modestly refused.' "

Four days later, on March 5, the delegation dutifully repeated the charade. This time P'u Yi acceded, and the following day

Manchuria's newspapers carried the text of his acceptance speech. "As you entrust me with this great responsibility," he said, "how could I venture to refuse for the sake of idleness and leisure?" Shakespeare could not have written a better scene.

In his speech, however, P'u Yi deftly tried to paint the Japanese into a corner. He accepted the post of Chief Executive "temporarily," he declared, and if, at the end of one year, the constitution of Manchukuo was not amended in accordance with "my original intention, I shall then carefully reconsider my virtue and my strength."

En route to Changch'un, the seat of the new government, which had been renamed Hsinking (New Capital), P'u Yi's train halted briefly at Mukden, a city of massive walls, drum towers, temples, pagodas, and palaces. A short distance from the city's walls, in a thick forest, stood the magnificent mausoleum of the founder of the Great Ch'ing Empire. P'u Yi made a pilgrimage there and knelt before the tomb of Nurhachu, burning an offering and praying to the spirit of his illustrious ancestor, in an act of filial piety.

As he reboarded the train, P'u Yi's thoughts were on his expulsion from the Forbidden City, the flight from Peking, the despoiling of the tombs, "and the oath I swore as a result." As he stared out the window at the Manchurian plain, with its dark and jagged mountains on the horizon, he saw not the landscape, only his own life history. But the tumultuous welcome he received as his train pulled into Hsinking awakened him from his reverie.

The depot was bedecked with five-barred Manchukuo banners, military bands played, and a large crowd cheered. The whole city, or so it seemed, turned out to greet him, the throng arriving in old Russian droskies, spike-wheeled Peking carts, fragile rickshas, and the latest model Western motor cars. In addition to the Manchukuo flags, there was a spattering of old yellow dragon banners and clusters of Japanese *hinomaru*, a red ball on a white field, waved energetically by groups of Japanese school children, the boys attired in black pants and black jackets with brass buttons and the girls in black skirts and white middy blouses. Representatives of the eight

Manchu banners, attired in ceremonial dress, and riding Mongolian ponies, their banners flapping in the cold air, drew to attention and dipped their standards as P'u Yi alighted, hardy warriors who had waited almost twenty years to the day for the reemergence of their hereditary leader. P'u Yi was as moved as he had been when he celebrated his first birthday outside the Forbidden City seven years earlier. "Their presence brought tears to my eyes," he said. Now he was convinced more than ever that his collaboration with foreigners to restore the throne had been justified.

The inaugural ceremony was brief. In the presence of his bannermen and the representatives of the Mongol clans who also considered him their hereditary chieftain, he was sworn into office as Chief Executive and presented with the gold seal of office, wrapped in a bolt of yellow silk. The generals of the Kwantung army witnessed the ceremony; from the back row, Doihara and Itagaki looked on with triumph. That night the event was celebrated with a black tie dinner. In an editorial, the London *Times* pointed to an anomaly in the situation. "Mr. P'u Yi," the newspaper said, "thus undergoes the extraordinary vicissitude of becoming the first ruler of the infant state after having formerly been the infant ruler of a most ancient state." Describing him as a cultured and intelligent student of politics, the *Times* nevertheless concluded that his new government was installed "at the instigation, no doubt, of Japan."

China's reaction to the inaugural ceremonies was undisguised. The Chiang Kai-shek government branded P'u Yi a traitor and termed the "so-called 'State' of 'Manchukuo' a fake." Under no circumstances would China recognize the new nation, Chiang-Kai-shek declared. And at Geneva, before the assembled League of Nations, the Chinese delegate denounced Manchukuo as a "puppet state" and accused Japan of "conceiving, organizing and carrying through the independence movement." "The issue is no longer a Sino-Japanese issue—it is an issue in which the whole civilized world stands confronted by Japan," the Chinese spokesman declared. In the face of this outburst and of the League's condemnation of Japan, Japan withdrew from the world body, setting a pattern of defiance of international opinion which Mussolini and Hitler imitated shortly thereafter.

Was P'u Yi a traitor? Once again, the answer is blurred. Most Chinese felt he was. But others thought differently, such as George Bronson Rea, an American who had founded the *Far Eastern Review* in 1904, served as an adviser to Sun Yat-sen and Yuan Shih-k'ai, and finally emerged as a counselor to Manchukuo's Ministry of Foreign Affairs. He became a passionate defender of P'u Yi. The world ridiculed P'u Yi as a puppet, reviled him as a traitor and arraigned him as a weakling who dared not call his soul his own. "No thought seems to be given to the fact that P'u Yi is not a Chinese," Rea said, "that he owes no allegiance to China, that he and his forebears were Manchu and that the Chinese republic entered into a solemn treaty with his family to recognize and respect his status as a foreign sovereign," a treaty which the Chinese tore up.

Rea's transformation into a Manchukuo adviser was dictated by his conclusion, after a generation of service to China, that the American policy of building a "strong China" was wrong because a "strong China" would dominate the Far East, and be Communist to boot. Above all, Rea feared that America's sentimental attitude toward China would reap a whirlwind with Japan. "It is not the business of the United States to go to war with Japan over matters which do not affect its vital security and interests," he declared.

Rea's defense of P'u Yi notwithstanding, Manchukuo was a Japanese army creation from beginning to end and the success of the Japanese militarists in Manchuria whetted their appetite for more glorious adventures—the conquest of China. "Manchukuo's vaunted independence exists only in the imagination of Japanese propagandists," H. J. Timperley, the *Manchester Guardian*'s Peking correspondent wrote; "the Manchukuo 'government' amounts to little more than a polite fiction invented to obscure the fact that Japan has gone in for imperialism in a big way." Of course, the truth was that Japan had gone in for imperialism at a time when the dominant Western powers, imperialist themselves, were barring the club to new members.

The question of whether or not P'u Yi was a traitor also intrigued G. H. W. Woodhead, the influential English editor of the *Peking & Tientsin Times,* an acquaintance of P'u Yi in his Tientsin period, and a man upon whose head the Japanese placed a reward when they overran Britain's Far Eastern territories in 1941–1942. At Hsinking, on October 2, 1932, Woodhead submitted P'u Yi to extensive cross-examination. Brusquely, he asked P'u Yi why he went to Manchuria and why he accepted the position as Manchukuo's head of government. "I had a double motive," P'u Yi replied with equal directness.

P'u Yi explained that the Manchu Dynasty had abdicated with the avowed intention of restoring sovereignty to the people. But the power relinquished by the dynasty had passed into the hands of ambitious and grasping warlords who plunged China into incessant civil war. The welfare of the people was disregarded. Moreover, P'u Yi continued, he was actuated by "personal motives." The Articles of Favorable Treatment were violated, the allowance paid to him canceled, and his private property confiscated. The republic had treated him with disrespect and defiled the sanctity of his ancestor's tombs. It was natural, therefore, that when trouble erupted in Manchuria he should follow developments with attention and try "to improve the condition of his ancestral province."

Woodhead then brought up another much-discussed question:

> "Then the story that you were kidnapped and sent to Port Arthur under Japanese escort on a destroyer is not true?" he asked. According to Woodhead, P'u Yi threw back his head and roared with laughter. "Kidnapped?" he said, "Kidnapped? No! No!"

The League of Nations' Lytton Commission, investigating the Mukden Incident, asked similar questions when they arrived at Hsinking. By indirection, in a courteous, diplomatic fashion they asked P'u Yi the "manner" of his arrival in Manchuria and the "manner" in which Manchukuo was founded. "I came to Manchuria after being chosen by the Manchurian masses," P'u Yi recited. "My country is completely independent." Itagaki, who was present at the Lytton interview, smiled. When the members of the commission departed, he told P'u Yi, "Your Excellency's manner was perfect—you spoke beautifully."

The parade of visitors during that first year in office also included "independent" Japanese observers, among them, K. K. Kawakami, the Washington correspondent of *Hochi Shimbun*. He was visibly impressed with P'u Yi's informality during an interview. On being ushered into the Chief Executive's drawing room, he found that "Mr. P'u Yi was standing and extended his hand to me." Kawakami was taken aback. "I had heard of his plebeian manners," he wrote, "but the woolen vest of pullover which he wore under his sackcoat rather surprised me. Was this unconventional attire an affectation or an expression of his genuine desire to be 'democratic'?" Kawakami was obviously embarrassed; he had arrived in the then regular habiliment of the diplomatic correspondent, morning coat and striped trousers.

After a half-hour conversation—("what we talked about was immaterial")—"the Chief Executive came to the door of the room and cordially shook my hand," Kawakami wrote. "Surely a new era had dawned upon the Manchu house."

Only a generation earlier all foreigners in the presence of a Manchu emperor had to kowtow, a humiliation which once made an indignant American minister to Peking blurt out, "I *kowtow* only to God and women." Now the last of the Manchu line behaved like an English squire. Was this Johnston's influence?

Manchukuo's existence in its first months was tenuous. No nation other than Japan recognized the new state and even Tokyo waited seven months before doing so. The delay reflected the continuing debate within Japan over the course of action in Manchuria.

As Admiral Okada, who served as navy minister in the 1927 Tanaka and 1932 Saito cabinets and was named premier in 1934, explained to Allied interrogators in 1946, "After the occupation of Manchuria, the Kwantung army was the real government in

Manchuria." P'u Yi's regime, he testified, was "completely dominated and controlled by the Kwantung army. . . . The government
of Japan had no way of learning what the plans and activities of the
Kwantung army were in those years."

Not only did the former prime minister brand Manchukuo an
invention, but so did his war minister, Sadao Araki, with whom
Okada was at odds. Araki, who stood trial after World War II with
Doihara and Itagaki and was sentenced to life imprisonment, told
Allied interrogators that the decision to create Manchukuo was
made by the Okada cabinet at the request of the Kwantung army,
which also suggested that it was "advisable to set up Henry P'u Yi as
head of the Manchukuo government."

As war minister, Araki had the power to reject the Kwantung
army's proposal, but, he said, that would have been "irresponsible"
unless he came up with an alternate solution to the Mukden Incident
and its aftermath. "I thought," he said, "that the request of the
Kwantung army would settle the Manchurian matter to the interest
of all parties concerned." Thus, he finally proposed to the cabinet
that Japan recognize "Henry P'u Yi as governor [sic] of Manchukuo." The cabinet concurred; the need at the moment was to
establish unity at home in the face of hostility abroad. The cabinet
was probably influenced by sly army pressure. The militarists
circulated rumors that the Kwantung army would declare itself
independent of Tokyo if the cabinet refused its request, an action
which conceivably could precipitate war in Japan.

By 1933, however, it was already clear that the creation of
Manchukuo and the installation of P'u Yi as Chief Executive had
solved nothing. Indeed, the failure of P'u Yi to assume the title of
emperor generated disappointment among the Manchu and Mongol
minority communities of Manchuria. P'u Yi himself discreetly raised
the question of his investiture as emperor during his first year in
office as chief executive, but he did not press the matter nor did he
carry out his threat to resign in view of the tense situation in Japan
and the failure of the world at large to recognize his new state.

Gradually, however, Tokyo tilted toward establishing a monarchy for Manchukuo. There were several reasons. One was the need to win over the Manchu and Mongols which became important as popular Chinese resistance to the Japanese military occupation spread and clashes between Japanese army patrols and Chinese "bandits" began to occur regularly. Now the Manchu and Mongols considered their "Chief Executive" only a quasi-civil-service officer who could be easily removed if the Japanese decided to annex Manchukuo. Another reason arose from the fact that the Kwantung army needed Mongol and Manchu support if it intended to press south of the Great Wall. Finally, proponents of monarchy argued that the creation of an emperor would commit Japan, a monarchy itself, more firmly to the maintenance of Manchukuo; neither the world at large nor the Manchurians themselves could then fail to be convinced of Manchukuo's permanence.

In the autumn of 1933, as the *kaoliang*, a sort of sorghum, the principal crop of Manchuria, was harvested, the Kwantung army conveyed to P'u Yi the glad tidings that Tokyo was prepared to recognize him as emperor of Manchukuo.

P'u Yi, in his own words, "went wild with joy."

His joy might have been tempered if he had had access to the secret minutes of the Japanese cabinet session of December 22, 1933, at which the plan for restoration was adopted. On that occasion the cabinet expressed concern about rising apprehensions among the Manchurians and concluded that the "apprehensions are based upon the form of government." Such fears would dissipate, the cabinet agreed, with the establishment of a monarchy. But P'u Yi's elevation to the throne may be attended by "evils." The evils were not defined, but they are not difficult to unravel. In the Japanese perspective, there was only one genuine claimant to the title Son of Heaven: Hirohito. P'u Yi's restoration could be wrongly interpreted as a restoration of the Great Ch'ing Dynasty. After all, P'u Yi himself still considered the Violet Enclosure his own. Furled away in homes and shops in Peking were dragon flags awaiting the reappearance of the Son of Heaven. Rather than run the political risk of a dynastic revival in China, however remote, and rather than confuse the minds of the Japanese people, who had been raised to believe that Hirohito was the true Son of Heaven, the cabinet endorsed a monarchy in Manchukuo but only with this proviso: "It must be made clear that the enforcement of monarchy is not a restoration of the Great Ch'ing Dynasty, but the creation of a new monarchy for Manchukuo alone." Even with the establishment of a monarchy, the cabinet decided, "there will be no change in the policy or spirit of directing Manchukuo." In effect, whether P'u Yi was Chief Executive or emperor, Japan and/or the Kwantung army would continue to pull the puppet's strings.

P'u Yi did not wait to discern the broad outlines of policy. Informed officially that Tokyo approved his investiture as emperor of Manchukuo, his first thought was to send to Peking for the wardrobe of the previous Emperor Kuang Hsu which the High Consort Jung Hui had secretly been keeping in good condition since the 1912 abdication. When couriers returned with the imperial robes, embroidered with five-toed dragons, P'u Yi's eyes glistened with fierce pride and desire. "I gazed with emotion at the dragon robes preserved for twenty-two years," he said. During those years he had endlessly dreamed of putting them on. By his donning the robes, he felt the Great Ch'ing Dynasty would be resurrected, as he reascended the throne.

But the Kwantung army objected to the symbolism and pointedly observed that Japan recognized him as emperor of Manchukuo, not as the Great Ch'ing Emperor of China. At his investiture, the army insisted, he must wear the full dress uniform of the commander-in-chief of the Manchukuo armed forces, a glorified version of the republican general's uniform he had worn for fun as a child.

P'u Yi balked. "What will the members of the Aisin-Gioro clan think if they see me ascend the throne in a foreign-style uniform?" he asked.

A row ensued, a portent of things to come. The conflict was settled by compromise. P'u Yi would wear the dragon robes to perform the ceremony of announcing his accession to heaven and he would appear in military uniform at the enthronement.

In the early morning hours of March 1, 1934, while the crust of the Manchurian plain was still frozen, P'u Yi, attired in his imperial dragon robes, performed a sacrifice before the Altar of Heaven, a hastily arranged ceremony at a nearby Buddhist temple. Driven to the site in a bullet-proof limousine, he wore a fur-trimmed, pearl-studded hat adorned with a red tassel, and a blue gown with dark red sleeves richly brocaded with five-clawed yellow dragons, the robes worn by all the Manchu emperors of China at their ascension.

As a spirit offering, P'u Yi reverently lifted toward heaven a jade amulet, a bolt of yellow silk, and three goblets of rice wine. Then he was handed the jade seal of state, the third set of seals he had acquired in the twenty-eight years since his birth: the interlocking eight pieces of jade of the Manchu Dynasty which he had accepted in 1908 and again in 1917, the gold seal he received in 1932 as Chief Executive, and now the jade seal as emperor of Manchutikuo, as it was now called in official documents though nowhere else, the "ti" signifying the fact that it was a monarchy.

As P'u Yi prayed to the spirits of his ancestors, did he envision a return to the sacred Dragon Throne in Peking? More than likely; for, on that morning all the agonies and torments of his adolescence and youthful maturity were compensated 10,000-fold. He had pacified the perturbed spirits of his forefathers. His own spirit, confined to a dynastic purgatory from the age of six, soared upward. If emperorship of Manchukuo was so exhilarating, how much more ecstatic would the moment be when he once again gazed on the glistening yellow roofs of the Forbidden City!

The high priests sacrificed a snow-white bull, and, as P'u Yi prayed, an altar fire was lit and a thin column of gray smoke rose skyward, symbolizing the transmission of his prayers to the spirits of the dead. P'u Yi now publicly adopted the *nien hao*, or reign title, of K'ang Teh (Tranquillity and Virtue). The first character for tranquillity, *k'ang*, in Confucian philosophy, suggests an interlude or preparatory period of "advancing peace" before the emergence of universal happiness and brotherhood; in effect, Manchutikuo would become a model state, the first stage of a two-stage design which would eventually return him to Peking.

Precisely on the twelfth stroke of noon, the coach turned into a pumpkin and the Emperor K'ang Teh reappeared for his formal investiture attired in a field marshal's uniform, resplendent with oversized epaulettes, badges, medals, and ribbons. The Salt Monopoly Building of Hsinking, a huge, squat, ugly structure, had been renamed and redecorated to serve as the Hall of Ceremony. As P'u Yi entered the building, he walked slowly along a crimson runner and methodically climbed the steps leading to the jade throne. The ceremony of the seal was reenacted and his acceptance of the inscribed block of jade signified his formal coronation. P'u Yi held the seal firmly in his slender fingers, then pressed it against his first imperial rescript. Written in black ink on a yellow scroll, the rescript proclaimed the beginning of an era of tranquillity and virtue for Manchuria. The audience, which listened attentively, was a colorful mix of Manchu bannermen, Mongol clansmen, Chinese Confucianists and monarchists, and Japanese field grade officers and diplomats. His clansmen bent the knee three times and performed the ninefold kowtow. For P'u Yi, it was like old times.

As the ceremony unfolded, one hundred cannons roared a salute to the new emperor. The buildings of Hsinking shook as the earth beneath them trembled. Planes flew overhead and dropped tens of thousands of proclamations. Fifteen thousand guests gathered at the municipal garden to pay their respects to the new sovereign, and for two hours a procession snaked through the main thoroughfares of the capital. Incongruous as it may seem, the procession, which featured a pageant of floats, most of them in the shape of dragons, was led by White Russian police and Japanese gendarmes. That night Roman candles and rockets lit up the heavens. A foreign correspondent dryly observed that the most spectacular fireworks display was inadvertently ignited "when the fireworks of a group of streethawkers accidentally exploded." In many ways, perhaps, Manchukuo itself was inadvertent. P'u Yi's Empress Elizabeth, accompanied by her father and a brother, and by various members of P'u Yi's family, had traveled to Hsinking for the coronation under Japanese protection. On the night of his escape from Tientsin, P'u Yi had left a letter behind to be delivered to the Japanese consul-general informing him of his departure and asking him to afford adequate protection to the empress and her entourage, who remained at his residence in the Japanese concession. She and her party eventually traveled to Manchukuo in an ordinary steamer where P'u Yi greeted them. But at the coronation, other than putting in a gracious appearance at a garden party, there was no ceremonial role for Elizabeth. For P'u Yi, a high point of his first year on the throne came when he was visited several months later by his aged father, Prince Ch'un, who had cuddled him in his arms when he first ascended the throne. The prince made the trip unmolested from Peking where he had continued to live an apolitical existence in his weathered mansion, rarely leaving his own court-yard to tour the rapidly changing Chinese world around him. When Prince Ch'un's motor car arrived at the new palace, P'u Yi saluted him, and Wan Jung, attired in Manchu court dress, knelt before him. P'u Yi then accompanied his father into a sitting room where no one else was present. In his memoirs P'u Yi revealed what occurred between the two, prince and emperor, father and son. "I knelt before him," P'u Yi confided, "and greeted him in the old style."

On the occasion of his father's visit, a sumptuous Western-style banquet was held in honor of the visitor from the center of the universe. And as the champagne glasses were filled, the emperor's younger brother, P'u Chieh, raised a glass and delivered a toast, "Long live His Majesty, the Emperor!"

These were happy days, perhaps the happiest of P'u Yi's majority. But the days were short. The reality of the present soon crushed the illusions of the past.

CHAPTER 19

The Paper Emperor

In his new role P'u Yi, now the Emperor K'ang Teh, lived in a manner befitting the title. His residence, a compound of several buildings enclosed by a high wall, was lavishly redecorated and renamed the Emperor's Palace; the term Imperial Palace was conspicuously avoided because that was the name of Hirohito's domicile in Tokyo. As in Peking, however, P'u Yi's throne faced south and, with pride in their voices, his clansmen again referred to him as He Who Always Faces South. As court business was conducted, palace officials in mandarin gowns and jackets and imperial guards in Manchu dress flanked the throne. In many other respects the new court faintly resembled the Forbidden City. P'u Yi's imperial bodyguard numbered 300 men. A budget of 3 million yen ($1.5 million) was set aside for the imperial family; 800,000 yen was earmarked as P'u Yi's personal "pocket money." In addition, the Manchukuo government set aside 5 million yen in bonds in the imperial family's name. The interest on these bonds amounted to 150,000 yen annually and was an extra source of personal income, raising the emperor's annual expense account to almost 1 million yen. As of old, P'u Yi purchased lavish gifts—jewelry and fine clothes. He also amassed a large collection of mechanical toys. Toys had fascinated him since his childhood and his choice of such a hobby was in keeping with his make-believe world. Like P'u Yi himself, the toys possessed an inherent, incongruous make-believe reality. An impressive table of viands was prepared daily. The kowtow was reintroduced, the bamboo rod reinstated. Servants were whipped on their bare buttocks, a form of punishment which continued to excite and exhilarate the Lord of Ten Thousand Years. Only the yellow, five-toed dragons of the Great Ch'ing Dynasty were absent and, of course, the authority of a Manchu emperor beyond the walls of his palace.

When P'u Yi went for a spin in the countryside, a convoy was organized. Traveling at high speed to avoid a sniper's bullet, his motorcade resembled a Gobi desert storm, throwing up columns of dust. His bullet-proof, bomb-proof limousine, a Lincoln, was conspicuous. The car was specially fitted in Detroit with steel floors and sides, the body painted bright vermilion, the roof and running boards trimmed in gold. Golden orchids, P'u Yi's new crest, adorned the radiator cap and decorated the doors.

Twice a year the emperor made extensive journeys through his 380,000-square-mile realm. He inspected fisheries along the Amur and Ussuri rivers, which formed disputed frontiers with the Soviet Union. He visited the forests on the bank of the Yalu, which delimited the border with Korea. He toured the great Fushun colliery which boasted the broadest coal seams in the world, upward of 480 feet thick, perhaps the most important coal deposit outside the United States. He inspected the steel works at Anshan, the largest in East Asia after Japan's, and the third largest producer of rolled steel and steel ingots in the Far East, the "Asian Pittsburgh." He journeyed also to the agricultural experimental station at Kungchu-ling, in the heart of the country where imported Merino sheep and Berkshire hogs were interbred with tough Manchurian varieties.

Four times a year P'u Yi performed public religious ceremonies, sacrificing to heaven, at temples: the Temple of the Loyal Souls

Who Founded the Empire, the White Pagoda, the Shrine for Epitaph, and the Temple of the Corner Mountain. Annually, he visited Kwantung army headquarters to extend congratulations on Hirohito's birthday. He worshipped at the Dragon Fountain Temple, nestling among the Thousand Ridge mountains, and he prayed at the eleventh-century Buddhist temple at Tienshan.

As an emperor, he busied himself initially with banquets and receptions. The pomp and circumstance intoxicated him. "The splendor satisfied my vanity," he said later. "It blinded me to reality." The first anniversary of his accession to the jade throne was observed in 1935 with military parades, formal dinners, and grand balls. Yet the police in Hsinking were strongly reinforced for the occasions "to forestall demonstrations," as the local press explained.

Johnston reappeared in his life that year but this time only briefly. Ostensibly on a visit to Mukden to study the Manchu archives, he visited with P'u Yi at the Emperor's Palace. Did Johnston finally come to realize that P'u Yi represented a lost cause? Or was Johnston also intoxicated by the pomp and circumstance? He left no clues. In a sentimental biographic sketch published after his death, his English friend, R. Soame Jenys, wrote, "The results of his researches were never published [and], as was his wish, all his unpublished papers were destroyed at his death."

Beyond question, however, Johnston's loyalty to P'u Yi remained undiluted. Following his last journey to the Far East, he retired to the small island of Eilean Righ, in Loch Craignish, Argyll, and from the rooftop of his home flew the Manchukuo flag. Three years after his retirement, on March 6, 1938, he died at the age of sixty-four. Johnston had been a warm and stimulating figure and even his Chinese adversaries respected and admired his integrity, his sympathy for, and his fidelity to, China's imperial past.

Pat a dog's head, the Chinese say, and up goes his tail. So it was with P'u Yi who was accorded the greatest honor since his arrival in Manchuria when he received an invitation from the Chrysanthemum Throne to visit Japan. P'u Yi seized on the opportunity to make the trip to establish a personal link to Hirohito as political leverage against the Kwantung army.

The empress did not accompany him on his journey to Japan. The *Japan Times*, quoting palace sources, ascribed Elizabeth's failure to make the trip to "ill health." But the reason went far deeper.

By now P'u Yi's domestic scene resembled a disaster area. An emperor with one empress and no consorts, he and Wan Jung ruled in name only. A pasteboard empress with real authority in the hands of the Japanese, Elizabeth lived like P'u Yi, under unofficial house arrest. Compounding the situation, her relationship with him was cold. In his own mind, P'u Yi felt that Wan Jung was responsible for driving out his other wife, Wen Hsiu. After Tientsin, he and the empress dwelt in separate worlds while living under the same roof; they rarely met and spoke to one another, either civilly or in anger.

Reasonably vigorous and healthy, suffocating in jejune Hsinking, confined to the palace compound, married to a "eunuch," the empress drifted into a relationship with a member of the imperial guard. P'u Yi was livid when he learned of the affair. "She behaved in a way that I could not tolerate," he said. She was confined to her quarters thereafter. In her despair and melancholy, Wan Jung turned to opium. Addicted, she fell apart mentally and physically, withdrew from reality, and passed phase by phase through the terrifying stages of physical and social deterioration associated with heroin: loss of appetite and weight, sleeplessness, fits of desperation and anxiety commingled with moments of euphoria. The unraveling of her mind, body, and soul cannot be pinpointed accurately in time, but it appears to have started in 1935.

Thus, P'u Yi prepared for the journey to Japan alone. With a view to impressing him and the foreign powers, Tokyo dispatched a 30,000-ton battleship, *Hie Maru*, 640 feet long and mounting twelve 14-inch guns, to bear him to Japan. En route, in the middle of the Japan Sea, a fleet of seventy Japanese warships greeted his arrival with thunderous ceremonial broadsides. The welcome so moved him that he took brush in hand, and in the imperial tradition, composed a short poem in the classical style:

The journey is not only
to admire mountains and waters
but to make our alliance shine
like sun and moon.

P'u Yi anchored on the west coast of Honshu and traveled by rail to Tokyo, where Hirohito personally greeted him at the station, an extraordinary honor. In an age before summitry, their meeting marked the first visit in the history of the Far East between two sovereigns, not petty monarchs but the last descendant of a Chinese dynasty and a Japanese emperor claiming an uninterrupted lineage of 2,595 years. In P'u Yi's subtle Manchu phrase, it was a meeting of "sun and moon."

Although it was overshadowed by the fanfare, there were the profound dissimilarities in the political traditions represented by the two emperors. Hirohito—high-strung, bird-like in his movements, short in stature—had been taught from the cradle that an emperor reigned but did not rule, that he was inviolable, that he stood above the maddening scene. By contrast, the tall and slender P'u Yi, who moved with aplomb and assurance, was taught that an emperor both reigned and ruled. An incompetent emperor, therefore, was in danger of losing the mandate of heaven, if not his head. In Japan, deposing the emperor was unthinkable. Both P'u Yi and Hirohito did share the isolation and loneliness of their thrones, however. Both were prisoners of forces over which they exercised little or no control.

For eight glorious days, P'u Yi was treated like the emperor he was destined not to be, and in the process he enchanted the Japanese. When, for example, he visited Hirohito's mother and strolled with her through the imperial garden, he graciously extended his arm to the dowager empress as they encountered a slight incline along their path. The incident caused a sensation among the impressionable Japanese.

P'u Yi's visit was more ceremonial than political, although a state visit, by its very nature, sweeps along on a political undercurrent. During the visit, for example, P'u Yi held a private audience for twenty Japanese who rendered him "service" in the creation of Manchukuo. Seventeen of them were senior military officers and one of the three civilians was the controversial Mitsuru Toyama, the founder of the Black Dragon Society and a leading theoretician among the radical ultranationalists. The closest Hirohito came to talking politics was at a state banquet during which, reading from a prepared script, he referred to the "inseparable relations between our two countries." Perhaps the most significant moment of the visit, not appreciated by P'u Yi at the time but greatly rued later, occurred when he visited the Meiji Shrine, one of the holiest centers of pilgrimage in Japan. Built in pure Shinto style, the shrine housed several relics of Shintoism, including two sacred swords and two sacred mirrors. By performing obeisance at the shrine, which was tied directly to Japan's traditional emperor worship, he was being drawn deeper and deeper into the Japanese web.

On his departure from Japan, P'u Yi described himself as "deeply moved by the magnificent reception given me by the Japanese imperial family." Boarding his warship for the homeward journey, he broke into tears and asked his escort, Baron Hayashi—whom he had first met in 1932 when, as grand master of ceremonies of the Japanese Imperial Household Department, the baron accompanied a Japanese prince on a visit to Manchukuo—to convey his thanks to the emperor and his mother. The gesture so touched the baron that it moved him to cry. Was this a put-on by P'u Yi? Perhaps, but during the visit, for the first time since his childhood, he was accorded the respect and attention he felt due him as emperor. How could he help but be moved?

In Hsinking, P'u Yi promptly brought his newly acquired leverage into play against the Kwantung army. Summoning the privy council and the Kwantung army's staff, including its new commander, General Jiro Minami, he remonstrated: "The friendship between Japan and Manchukuo has led me to the firm belief that if any Japanese acts against the interests of Manchukuo he is guilty of disloyalty to his majesty the emperor of Japan, and that if

209

any Manchurian acts against the interests of Japan he is being disloyal to the emperor of Manchukuo." By equating himself with the Japanese emperor, P'u Yi hoped to neutralize the influence of the army and become more independent. But his hope quickly foundered.

Just how little chance there was of his asserting his independence is shown by the files of the Manchurian General Affairs Office and by crates of documents marked, "Confidential Records Concerning Manchurian Affairs," seized by Allied forces in Tokyo in 1945. A study of these documents melts the pretense that an independent Manchukuo ever existed as rapidly as spring snow.

As early as November 3, 1932, the Kwantung army drafted a secret policy paper which outlined the rules for "guiding Manchukuo." In plain language, it stated, "Officials of Manchukuoan lineage [e.g., P'u Yi] shall outwardly assume charge of the administration as much as possible while officials of Japanese lineage must satisfy themselves by controlling its substance." Nothing could be more blunt unless it was the Japanese adage that only a fool, if he has power, displays it.

P'u Yi was completely powerless. When he was installed as Chief Executive, Japanese advisers were attached to all Manchukuo departments. With his elevation as emperor, these advisers became official members of the Manchukuo government. Thus, each Manchukuo minister had a Japanese vice minister at his elbow. Even so, the fanatical Kwantung army did not trust its own nationals, and all Japanese officials in the P'u Yi government were placed under the army's jurisdiction. This was necessary, the secret directive explained, in the event that these Japanese "in the future might be absorbed" by their Manchurian counterparts. Just as the Manchu had feared that the Chinese, with their superior culture and numbers, would swallow them after the conquest of China, as they had all other invaders, the Japanese feared the same fate; they feared that even in the twentieth century, no foreign power or foreign ideology could persevere in China without acquiring a Chinese coloration.

Another secret instruction declared that the people of Manchu-kuo would have no voice in government affairs. "Political parties and political bodies shall not be permitted to exist and we do not welcome the rise of political ideas among the people," the directive said. "Rather, we shall lead the general situation skillfully in accordance with the principle of 'let the people follow blindly.' "

To ensure that the people followed, the Japanese installed in Manchukuo a *pao chia* system of block associations, a method of thought control which the militarists later perfected in Japan and which exists today in China as it did in imperial times. As a safety valve, however, in view of P'u Yi's distaste for political parties, an association, the Concordia Association, was established in Manchu-kuo "to organize the masses" and "to cultivate a spirit for the rites and glad acceptance of heavenly commands."

P'u Yi's government hardly enjoyed popular backing, however; it received its principal support only from the racial and linguistic minorities inhabiting Manchuria—Manchu, Mongols, Koreans, and White Russians, minorities that had been displaced by massive waves of Chinese immigration. But the overwhelming majority of the people of Chinese racial origin were hostile or indifferent, generally pro-Chinese and anti-Japanese. In its thirteen-year history, Manchukuo never enjoyed "the goodwill and wholehearted cooperation" of its Chinese inhabitants, nor did P'u Yi.

Politically sterile, Manchukuo did not even maintain a flimsy pretense at economic independence. The satellite state became a testing ground for the socialist theories of Japan's radical nationalists. The economic blueprint for the regime, contained in a secret document entitled, "Economic Construction Program for Manchu-kuo," dictated a program that would avoid "the evils of an uncontrolled capitalist economy." Virtually the whole economy was brought under state control: wireless, telephone, telegraph and broadcasting facilities; the railway system; the oil industry; steel mills; coal mines; the textile, tobacco, and cement industries; sugar refining; even beer production. Five-year-plans, on the Soviet model, were introduced. With an eye to a future energy crisis, the directive observed that since Manchukuo was endowed with an almost inexhaustible supply of coal, attention should be focused on the liquefaction of coal "in view of the rapidly increasing domestic demand for liquid fuel and the dearth of petroleum resources."

For good measure, a joint economic committee was established to deal with economic and financial questions. It was composed of eight members, four from Manchukuo and four from Japan, including, of course, the commander of the Kwantung army. Three of the four Manchukuo representatives were cabinet ministers under Japanese control, and the fourth was director of the General Affairs Office, a post "forever" occupied by a Japanese.

Foreign policy was also controlled. A secret Japanese policy directive held that Manchukuo must submit all diplomatic problems to the Japanese ambassador for "thorough and unreserved deliberation" before adopting a course of its own. The Japanese ambassador, perhaps needless to observe, was also the commander-in-chief of the Kwantung army. Concurrently, he held the post of governor of the Liaotung Leased Territory, including control over the major naval base at Port Arthur. In truth, he was the chief of government of Manchukuo. The directive on foreign policy was unnecessary, however, since the Manchukuo Foreign Affairs Ministry was instructed at the outset that "the foreign policy of Manchuria is founded on the foreign policy of our [Japanese] empire."

Secret instructions aside, formal treaties were entered into which made a mockery of Manchukuo's independence. The army, for example, set up an official Manchurian Development Corporation to engage in migration and land development as a cover for the Japanese colonization of Manchukuo. And a Japanese-Manchukuo defense treaty was signed which reduced Manchukuo to the status of a military base.

In his 1964 autobiography, P'u Yi gives an elaborate account of how he came to sign the defense treaty. His story claims that Cheng Hsiao-hsu, then the premier of Manchukuo, slipped the document into a pile of state papers one day and in a casual tone said, "This is the agreement your subject has made with the Kwantung army commander-in-chief, General Honjo." The following dialogue, according to P'u Yi, ensued:

"Will your imperial majesty please approve it?"

P'u Yi looked at the agreement and was furious. "Who told you to sign this?"

"These are the conditions Itagaki laid down," the premier said. "Itagaki told your imperial majesty about them."

"Nonsense," P'u Yi replied. "He never told me, and even if he had done so, you still have no right to sign before consulting me."

"I did it on Itagaki's instructions."

"Who is in charge here?" P'u Yi inquired, his voice rising. "You or I?"

"Your subject would not dare to presume. The agreement is a temporary measure. How can your imperial majesty refuse to sign if you want the help of the Japanese? All that is conceded in it is what the Japanese already have in fact."

As P'u Yi observed in his memoirs, Cheng was right. All that Cheng had conceded was what the Japanese already had.

By the treaty's terms, Manchukuo turned over to Japan complete control of the "defense and security" of Manchukuo and permitted Japan to "maintain troops" in Manchuria. The Japanese army was also empowered to administer railways, communications, harbors, waterways, and airways, and to expand these facilities as it saw fit with Manchukuo providing supplies and equipment as required. Thus, P'u Yi was compelled to provide the hempen coil for his own hangman. But, in truth, despite P'u Yi's account of the signing of one treaty, he had secretly signed a similar letter of agreement on March 6, 1932, before the formal establishment of Manchukuo. This came to light in the unpublished semiofficial diary of the Mukden Incident prepared by an assistant to Itagaki and entitled, "A Secret Diary of the Manchurian Affair." By the terms of the letter, control of Manchukuo was put into the hands of the Kwantung army and out of reach of the Japanese government. A copy of the letter came to light in Tokyo in 1946. It consisted of five articles and provided the Kwantung army with the right to garrison troops in Manchukuo, to appoint state councillors and to control railways, harbors, waterways, and air routes. The document was approved by P'u Yi before his inauguration as Chief Executive and it bore his seal as the Emperor Hsüan Tung and a notation of acceptance in his own handwriting. The date, March 10, 1932, was affixed the day after his inauguration. Thus, P'u Yi's recollection of how he came to sign the agreement is for the most part a fabrication.

Through these various secret directives, private agreements and public treaties, Manchukuo was converted into a formidable Kwantung army bastion. Seaports were expanded, airfields and barracks enlarged, new ammunition and fuel dumps built, and the border areas facing the Soviet Union and the Mongolian People's Republic—Russia's "Manchukuo"—fortified. Manchukuo served as a pivot from which the Kwantung army could strike with equal swiftness at either China, the Soviet Union, or Mongolia. Stalin, Chiang Kai-shek and Mao Tse-tung were acutely aware of the developing situation and considered P'u Yi's Manchukuo a screen for Japanese expansion on the Asian mainland. As P'u Yi's ancestor Nurhachu had observed in the seventeenth century when he established his capital at Mukden, "It is a position from which the Chinese frontier can be readily reached in the event of trouble . . . and Mongolia is within two days striking distance."

When P'u Yi came to Manchuria, the military barracks in the country had a billeting capacity for 100,000 men. By 1937 the region's billeting capacity rose to 12 divisions, with about half of the new barracks built adjacent to the Soviet and Mongolian borders. Between 1937 and 1941, the number of barracks in Manchuria trebled and Manchukuo billeted 39 infantry divisions, or about 800,000 men. When P'u Yi arrived in Manchuria there were only five airfields in the country, and no air base. Thereafter, the Kwantung army undertook a rapid expansion of air facilities to accommodate a build-up of the imperial Japanese air force for operations against China, Mongolia, and Russia. The number of air bases, airfields, and landing fields rose from 5 in 1931 to 150 in 1937 to 287 at the time of Pearl Harbor. Harbor facilities were also expanded. Port Arthur, Dairen and Fusan became the funnels through which millions of Japanese soldiers passed on their journey of conquest south of the Great Wall.

Stalin, who justifiably feared a two-front war—Hitler was then in ascendancy on his western flank—responded to the Manchukuo build-up by double-tracking the Trans-Siberian railway, expanding the Red army's arterial highways in the Soviet Union's maritime province, erecting new munitions plants in Siberia and ordering a counterbuild-up of the Red air force at Vladivostok, a major naval base astride the Sea of Japan and Russia's only deep-water port with access to the Pacific.

Within Japan itself, as the Kwantung army strengthened its position in Manchuria, the moderates made a last ditch effort to block Japan's slide toward total war. They fought the good fight between 1931 and 1936, and failed.

Several months after the Mukden Incident, the premier of Japan, seventy-five-year-old Tsuyoshi Inukai, recommended to Hirohito that the emperor issue an imperial rescript ordering the army to withdraw from Manchuria. Not surprisingly, nothing came of this simplistic solution. Inukai also dispatched a secret mission to China to confer with Chiang Kai-shek in the hope of resolving the Manchurian affair peacefully. Inukai's envoy communicated with the Japanese premier by code, but the army intercepted the messages and broke the code. Finally, on May 8, 1932, in desperation, only a few weeks after P'u Yi was installed as Manchukuo's Chief Executive, Inukai delivered an antimilitaristic speech. A week later he was shot and killed at his official residence.

Inukai's murder placed the radical nationalists and military socialists on a collision course with the moderates. The struggle ended in 1936, a year after P'u Yi's state visit to Japan, when assassins attacked Premier Okada, and five other leading Japanese moderates. Okada survived but three of the moderates were killed. The attack was inspired by the fact that the moderates had won in parliamentary elections a few days earlier. The self-appointed saviors of Japan, the messianic radicals, would not permit the ballots of the Japanese people to interfere with their world mission of *Pax Japonica*.

Shortly after his inauguration as *Chien Ching*, or Chief Executive, P'u Yi requested American recognition of Manchukuo. But Secretary of State Henry Stimson had formulated a doctrine of nonrecognition toward Manchuria on January 7, 1932, and the United States declined to revise it. Although the United States was not in the League of Nations, the world organization followed the American lead and refused to recognize Manchukuo's existence. Nonrecognition of Manchukuo was carried to absurd lengths, and in many respects it proved impractical.

On August 1, 1932, for example, Manchukuo issued its first regular series of postage stamps, seven of which bore the familiar formal picture of P'u Yi, attired in upturned white collar and black tie, his shoe-polish-black hair matted down like a wet bathroom towel, his face expressionless, his eyes peering out from behind thick lenses like the protruding eyes of a goldfish staring through an aquarium tank.

China notified the Universal Postal Union that it would hold these "puppet stamps" invalid and Chiang Kai-shek insisted that all European mail to the Far East—which was usually carried by railway across Russia and Manchuria—be rerouted through the Suez Canal, a line of communication which would add a month and more to mail delivery. This was clearly impractical—airmail was still in its infancy—and the world body was forced to a retreat from the doctrine of nonrecognition. The League agreed that mail would continue to be moved across Manchuria, bearing Manchukuo postmarks and Manchukuo postage due stamps and so forth, but that *de facto* philatelic recognition of Manchukuo did not imply *de jure* or legal recognition of Manchukuo's existence as a state. "In all the foregoing there is," a diplomatic historian of the period wrote, "a large element of fiction." Yet as a result of this subterfuge, P'u Yi's portrait entered the world's households. Stamp collecting was then at the height of its popularity and P'u Yi's picture turned up in millions of stamp albums, from Bronxville to Brisbane. An empty face peering through oversized, horn-rimmed spectacles, on brown or purple Manchukuo stamps—that is how "Mr. Henry P'u Yi" is still best remembered today by the generation raised in the 1930s.

The need to fictionalize Manchukuo's existence was carried over into more serious diplomatic work.

"We in the American consulate general at Mukden made believe that Manchuria was still part of China," John Davies, Jr., a consular official who later became General Joseph Stilwell's political adviser in China during the war, recently wrote in his memoirs. "When we had to write the word Manchukuo, the rule was to enclose it in quotation marks—'Manchukuo.' At the same time we were expected to maintain informal contact with the Manchukuo foreign office. This entailed occasional trips to the capital, Hsinking, on which we pretended to be not American officials but private citizens.

"The Manchukuo foreign office went along with the petty dissembling," Davies continued. "The vice minister with whom we dealt was himself a bit of an official fraud. He was not a Manchurian, but a Japanese." Unknown to Davies, the fraud he was dealing with came under the jurisdiction of the Kwantung army and not the Japanese Foreign Office. In a sense, the vice minister was a fraud within a fraud.

Thus, the world was presented with the farce of fictionalizing the existence of a fictitious state and, of course, a fictitious emperor, P'u Yi.

CHAPTER 20

King to Pawn

For a cardboard emperor in a glittering capital such as Peking, life was entertaining at least. But in shabby, forlorn Hsinking, where the old Salt Monopoly Building, now the imperial palace, was the most impressive structure, P'u Yi and his consorts found themselves entrapped in a dull, colorless existence. Within the Forbidden City, the ghosts of the past and exciting prospects for restoration kept their adrenalin flowing. Tientsin, of course, was alive and stimulating with its diplomatic and social whirl, its curio shops and red light district, the visits of foreign warships and the throb of industry. By contrast, Hsinking was a backwater, a nondescript Manchurian town whose solitary attraction was the railway depot, the only escape route from the humdrum.

After settling into Hsinking, P'u Yi arranged, through the Japanese, for his relatives in Peking and Tientsin to join him. All of his seven sisters and four brothers accepted the invitation, except for his fourth brother and his sixth and seventh sisters. The three exceptions, all students, preferred to remain in Peking with their father, the aging Prince Ch'un. By now the republicans, under

218

Chiang Kai-shek, had shifted the capital of China to Nanking in an effort to escape from Peking's pervasive past history. The Nationalists did not deem the Forbidden City the proper administrative center of a republic. In Peking, Prince Ch'un and the children who remained at his side lived unmolested. From the republic's standpoint, it was still useful to maintain an open channel of communication to P'u Yi through his family should the occasion arise.

As the Emperor K'ang Teh of Manchukuo, P'u Yi centered his social life almost exclusively on his family. One of his sisters he married to a grandson of the premier of the new Manchurian nation, Cheng Hsiao-hsu. Another sister married into Elizabeth's family and she and her husband also settled at Hsinking. Still another sister married into Manchu nobility and another married Chang Hsun, the warlord who had put P'u Yi on the Dragon Throne for a second time in 1917.

Aside from the Japanese, the new capital was virtually off limits to foreigners. Occasionally, a minor diplomat assigned to Nanking or an itinerant foreign correspondent visited P'u Yi's capital. But P'u Yi was completely out of touch with the diplomatic community in which he and Elizabeth had thrived in Peking and Tientsin. After Japan's recognition of Manchukuo, five years passed before the Germans and Italians followed the lead of their Axis partner and recognized Manchukuo. In the end, they were joined only by a mixed bag of states: Hungary, El Salvador, Poland, the Soviet Union, Thailand, and the Vatican, some of whom accorded the new state *de jure* and others *de facto* recognition.

After settling in Manchuria, P'u Yi had arranged for his horse, "Mr. Ponto," to be shipped to Hsinking in anticipation of some good polo matches. But he quickly discovered that, aside from a few bannermen and Japanese cavalry officers, there was nobody with whom to play the game. He was also forced to put away his well-worn golf clubs; Hsinking had no golf course. He had a tennis court built on the palace grounds and, attired in white slacks and jumper and white sneakers, he frequently played General Tung, the chief of his bodyguards, but that was the extent of his physical activity. The rest of his spare time, which was ample, especially during the long Manchurian winters, was devoted to bridge and *wei-ch'i*—a Chinese game of strategy—or to playing with his toys. He spent hours with his electric trains—Lionel and American Flyer sets made in America. Like a child's, his imagination soared as the crack express and the long freight traveled to and fro atop an elaborately constructed beaverboard. He also amused himself with his extensive collection of mechanical toys, most of them imported from Germany and Japan. He was especially fascinated by a toy tractor equipped with rubber treads which could climb over cardboard boxes. When the marriages of his various sisters, over the years, produced offspring, P'u Yi brought out all his toys and played the role of dutiful, doting uncle.

During these years P'u Yi lost what little appetite he did have. He had never been a big eater. The Manchukuo palace still maintained a lavish kitchen though, largely for the benefit of his relatives and visiting Japanese dignitaries. Its staff was capable of producing both Chinese and Western dishes (Japanese food appeared to be taboo) and turkey, American style, was one of the family favorites. The palace wine cellar was always well stocked, but P'u Yi was never more than a social drinker, as ceremonial occasions dictated.

With the Japanese running the administration—or more accurately, with the Kwantung army running Manchukuo—P'u Yi found his job a sinecure. It required little more than the signing of edicts, decrees, proclamations, and the like. Except on Tuesday, his busiest day, he partook in no direct political activity. Tuesday was set aside for a weekly meeting with his cabinet and his ministers' Japanese advisers. Despite his limited political role, he voraciously read the papers each morning for clues to the drift in world affairs and hints about Japanese policy. Except for discussing their contents daily with his intimate Manchu and Chinese advisers, such as Cheng Hsiao-hsu, he was in no position to act in his own or Manchukuo's interest. In time, a sense of deepening political frustration mounted within him. His empress, of course, had found release from their confined life in drugs, but this P'u Yi staunchly refused to do. That was perhaps the only modicum of self-respect he would eventually possess.

As the Japanese pulled the strings on Manchukuo's political, economic and military straitjacket, the faithful band of Manchu, Mongols, and Chinese who had rallied around P'u Yi grew increasingly disenchanted. Among them was Cheng Hsiao-hsu, the premier and now the emperor's brother-in-law, a man who had been instrumental in counseling P'u Yi to accept Japanese assistance for the "great enterprise."

Within a month of P'u Yi's return from his visit to Japan, General Minami, the new Kwantung army commander, informed the emperor that the premier "wishes to retire as he is exhausted by his efforts." P'u Yi had heard that Japan was dissatisfied with Cheng Hsiao-hsu and took the hint. He was also anxious to bring into play what he believed was his new found leverage with Hirohito. Agreeing at once to Cheng's dismissal, he proposed a successor. "To my surprise," P'u Yi wrote, "I ran straight into a brick wall." General Minami shook his head and told the emperor he need not trouble himself with the problem because the army had already selected the new premier and that "all will be well if you choose Chang Ching-hui for the job." Chang, Manchukuo's defense minister, was a pint-sized figure with a short mustache who had a reputation, at least on the surface, for being an enthusiastic supporter of Japanese policies.

Having squeezed Cheng Hsiao-hsu dry, the Japanese discarded him. The venerable Confucian scholar, broken in health by the realization that he and his emperor had been deceived by the Japanese, was forbidden to leave the capital, his bank account was frozen and he was placed under twenty-four-hour surveillance by the *kempeitai*, who were now under the command of a newly arrived radical militarist from Tokyo, a fifty-one-year-old colonel with a Samurai background, Hideki Tojo. Tojo soon became chief

221

of staff of the Kwantung army, then war minister, and finally premier of Japan, an ultranationalist who led Japan into the dead end of Pearl Harbor.

After "running into the brick wall," P'u Yi should have recognized that if the Japanese militarists treated Hirohito with disdain as a mere figurehead despite their vaunted patriotism, they would be bound to treat him with contempt. But P'u Yi tripped over his own ego. He was at this time still infatuated with his own importance following his visit to Japan. "I was too intoxicated to come to my senses," he later wrote. But incident after incident sobered him and gradually brought about the realization that he was a paper emperor whom the army manipulated at will, not unlike Hirohito himself.

P'u Yi's other advisers soon followed Cheng Hsiao-hsu into limbo. Some voluntarily resigned, others were dismissed, imprisoned, or executed. Secretly, some worked for the Chinese and others for the Russians. One of them, Ling Sheng, the son of the former Chinese imperial governor of the Manchukuo province of Hsingan, felt betrayed by Itagaki, who had induced him into joining P'u Yi in Manchukuo. The Japanese had promised to recognize a genuinely independent Manchukuo but failed to do so. Ling Sheng established secret links with the Soviet puppet government of Mongolia, and through the Mongolians with the Russians. The Japanese found out, arrested him, and formally charged him and his private secretary with passing military information to a Soviet and to two Mongolian espionage agents. He was sentenced to death.

P'u Yi was shocked. He had sufficient cause. Ling Sheng's son was engaged to another of P'u Yi's sisters. Clearly, P'u Yi could trust no one. In his autobiography, mixing truth and fiction as he was prone to do, P'u Yi referred to Ling Sheng's arrest for "anti-Manchukuo, anti-Japanese activities," but did not cite his involvement with Soviet intelligence. He also claimed that the governor had been beheaded. Actually, Ling Sheng was shot and, for good measure, so were several members of his official family.

Whatever the case, one by one, like Agatha Christie's ten little Indians, P'u Yi's stalwart supporters fell by the wayside.

The Japanese also selected an adviser to replace the dismissed Cheng Hsiao-hsu. Their choice was a Kwantung army officer, Yasunori Yoshioka, who possessed a mustache which seemed larger than his frame. Yoshioka had befriended P'u Yi in Tientsin and his military career thereafter was meteoric, from lieutenant colonel to lieutenant general within a decade. Officially, he now served in a dual capacity as a Kwantung army staff officer and as attaché to the Manchukuo imperial household. He was forever at the emperor's side and P'u Yi felt under surveillance. But Yoshioka inwardly respected P'u Yi and considered him unique, and he was drawn to him as the emperor of China. In his own peculiar way, P'u Yi exercised this sort of charisma on many of the people who came into contact with him: Chen Pao-shen, Reginald Johnston, Cheng Hsiao-hsu, Yoshioka. In one degree or other, they were awed by his presence. It was not P'u Yi the individual who attracted them—he was personally unattractive—but the sense of history which enveloped him. Through their association with him, they brushed China's imperial past.

Shrewd, alert, ever mindful of the slightest shift in the political breeze, P'u Yi seized on Yoshioka's friendship to continue to try to develop a Tokyo counterweight to the Kwantung army. Whenever Yoshioka returned home on a visit, P'u Yi exploited him as a courier and drafted personal messages to the Japanese emperor sending along small gifts for Hirohito's mother, the empress dowager. As for Yoshioka, he thought of Hirohito, his own Son of Heaven, as a divine father; he sought to impress on P'u Yi that the "empress dowager is the equivalent of your imperial majesty's mother, and I am therefore almost a relation of yours." "I feel," he frequently added, "very honored by this."

P'u Yi's working relationship with his custodian aside, the polluted, pestilential atmosphere continued to deepen within the Hsinking palace.

Prince Te, a Mongol nobleman who had financially supported P'u Yi at Tientsin, was among those who grumbled increasingly about the overbearing behavior of the Japanese. One day P'u Yi and the prince held a private talk in P'u Yi's sitting room and the following afternoon Yoshioka—"with a grim expression on his face," P'u Yi remembered—inquired about the nature of their conversation. Did the prince express dissatisfaction with Japan? "My heart pounded," P'u Yi said. "I knew that I could either make a firm denial, or better, 'retreat by advancing.' " P'u Yi's dilemma was that he did not know whether the Japanese had bugged his palace or whether Prince Te had told the Japanese everything, perhaps under duress. Preoccupied solely with survival, a preoccupation which dominated his thoughts as he matured, he exhibited a mental gymnastic ability which he gradually developed into a polished art form. "Prince Te must have been lying," he replied ambiguously, leaving the matter there. Yoshioka fortunately did not press the questioning further. In P'u Yi's memoirs, the prince's ultimate fate is not discussed, and there is no mention of his fate in the Manchukuo press.

Several days later, however, as a result of the incident, the Kwantung army informed P'u Yi that henceforth the attaché to the imperial Manchukuo household must be present whenever he conferred with anyone from outside the palace precinct. Furthermore, from this period on his incoming mail would be screened—for his own security, of course. Thus, as in the Forbidden City, in his youth, when he planned his Tom Sawyer escapade, P'u Yi again came to use his younger brother P'u Chieh—William—as a go-between. Traveling between Manchukuo and Japan, where he attended cadet school, P'u Chieh kept him informed of developments in the "outside world." Some of the reports chilled him. One day, P'u Chieh reported that P'u Yi's former English interpreter, a youthful Manchurian who had been assigned to the Manchukuo embassy in Tokyo, had "disappeared" in Japan. Observed in contact with Americans, the interpreter was detained by the *kempeitai* and was never seen again.

In time, the Japanese also shut off P'u Chieh as a conduit, and they did so ingeniously. On his return from Japan in 1936, after he graduated from the military academy, his Japanese friends suggested he wed a Japanese woman. At first P'u Chieh, who had married a young Manchu, Tang Shih-hsia, about the same time that Henry and Elizabeth wed, took the suggestion lightly. So did P'u Yi. But a year later Yosioka proposed to P'u Yi that his brother marry a Japanese for political reasons, to strengthen the "friendship between our two countries." And, he added, the army had a lovely candidate, a distant relative of Hirohito.

P'u Yi was alarmed. His fear, like Janus, had two surfaces. A Japanese wife within the imperial family circle would place the palace under unending surveillance. Of greater import, however, was the question of the succession. If P'u Chieh married a Japanese princess future Manchu emperors might be part Japanese. P'u Yi was childless, and the likelihood was that he would remain so. In the organic law of Manchukuo, officially published in the *Manchukuo Government Bulletin* of March 1, 1934, the first article stated that "the Manchu empire shall be reigned over and governed by an emperor. The succession to the imperial throne shall be determined separately." But a law of succession was not promulgated until 1937 and then only as laid down by the Japanese.

With his empress an opium addict, the Kwantung army dangling a Japanese spouse before his brother, and the law of succession still unresolved, P'u Yi decided to acquire a new consort. The bride he chose was Yu-ling, or Jade Years, a seventeen-year-old Manchu woman known to her admirers as "the girl with the willow waist." They were married on March 25, 1937, a little more than a month after his thirty-first birthday. By this marriage the emperor felt he had outwitted the Japanese, who had been hinting that perhaps he, too, should consider acquiring a Japanese consort. But the Japanese in turn outmaneuvered him. They recognized P'u Yi's homosexual tendencies and were not overly concerned about his latest, face-saving marriage. Nonetheless, on the eve of the marriage ceremony the Japanese promulgated, through their hireling Manchukuo cabinet, a law of succession which provided that if P'u Yi died without male issue, P'u Chieh or his male offspring would succeed to the jade throne.

The newly married P'u Yi had fresh cause for concern. P'u Chieh, under incessant Japanese badgering, had consented to take a Japanese wife, Hiro Saga, the daughter of Marquis Saga, a girl whose striking features were brought out by her flowing *kimono* and brightly colored *obi*, or sash. In 1974 P'u Chieh's Manchu wife, in a memoir about her life in the Forbidden City, claimed "he was forced" by the Japanese to sign papers divorcing her. After the divorce, Princess Tang managed to make her way to Hong Kong where she has lived unobtrusively most of the time since; she has never seen William again.

P'u Yi's fear that with the passage of time an emperor of Japanese blood would sit on the Manchu throne was heightened when P'u Chieh and Hiro were wed on April 3, nine days after P'u Yi's third marriage. It was now a race between the two brothers to see who would be the first to beget a son. For the first time, in his memoirs, P'u Yi suggested that he attempted heterosexual relations. Clearly, the desire for survival drove him to extremes. "I was even worried about what would happen if I had a son," he said, "as the Kwantung army made me sign a document saying that I would send any son of mine to Japan when he was five years old to be brought up by a nominee of theirs." There is no evidence, however, that such a document ever existed, and it is unlikely that it ever did.

When Hiro announced later that year that she was pregnant, P'u Yi foresaw still another danger. "I was deeply concerned for my own safety and even [sic] for my brother's," he wrote, "as the Kwantung army seemed quite capable of killing both of us for the sake of getting an emperor of Japanese descent."

Both brothers relaxed when Hiro gave birth to a girl, Princess P'u Hui-sheng, the first of two daughters.

In 1959 P'u Chieh's Japanese wife published her memoirs in Tokyo under the title *Ruten No Ohi*, which incorporated scenes as wild as any in Edgar Allan Poe. The princess's account of her first meeting with P'u Yi and the royal family is terrifying. At a Western-style banquet in honor of the newly married couple, P'u Yi presented his new sister-in-law with a wristwatch inlaid with sapphires and diamonds. Elizabeth was present, the first time she appeared in "public" since the discovery of her love affair with the imperial guard almost two-and-a-half years earlier. The dinner moved along routinely as many family occasions do. Elizabeth was in superb control of herself until the main course was served, roast turkey *à la Americain*. As a palace servant offered her a serving from a huge yellow porcelain platter, the empress seized a piece of turkey in both hands, tore it into bits, and gnawed it like a caged animal, exhibiting symptoms of lycanthropic seizure. Seconds turned into hours as the stillness of the imperial dining hall was broken only by the crushing of bones and munching of meat. Hiro was mortified. In an effort to pass over the embarrassment lightly, the empress's brother banged the table, laughed heartily and grabbed a piece of turkey for himself, emulating his mentally deranged sister. The other guests followed suit. It was a moment of horror that lived with Hiro for the remainder of her life.

In her memoirs, Hiro also brought to light a situation within the royal household which had been rumored over the years in Peking, Tientsin, and Hsinking. Demurely, she wrote that she had heard of "such things" in Japanese as well as Chinese history, but that she never fully believed that "such things" ever existed. Hiro discovered that the emperor possessed an "unnatural love" for a pageboy. Within the inner circle, the sheared sleeve and shared peach was not hidden from view; on the contrary, the pageboy's role in the emperor's life was fully recognized and he was addressed as the male concubine. Hiro, incidentally, sympathized with Wan Jung, as did Nora Waln before her, and suggested that it was the presence of the male concubine which drove her to opium.

In his memoirs, P'u Yi refers to his various wives but makes no mention of the male concubine. However, he devoted several paragraphs to the pageboys and described them as "the most wretched victims of my rule." They were usually drawn from a

Hsinking orphanage and were selected intermittently for "service" in the palace, usually at the age of seventeen or eighteen. P'u Yi refers by name to only one of them, a youth by the name of Sun Po-yuan. According to P'u Yi, "he found life in the palace intolerable and tried to escape." After being recaptured on his first attempt, he was badly beaten with a bamboo rod on his bare bottom. But he found palace life so disquieting that he made a second escape, through a duct in the central heating system. After crawling around for two days in the labryinth, suffering from hunger and thirst, he emerged and was captured. In the spirit of the Empress Dowager Tzu Hsi, P'u Yi ordered: "Give him a good lesson." He was whipped with the bamboo rod until he was nearly dead. Out of compassion, and fear that if the boy died his spirit would return to haunt his tormentor, P'u Yi summoned a physician to save his life. It was too late. Thereafter P'u Yi spent several days kowtowing and reciting scriptures in front of a Buddhist altar, praying for the boy's soul to cross safely to the next world. Was this young man the male concubine? Did he reject P'u Yi's affection? Was P'u Yi's compassion that of an emperor empowered to decree life or death, or was his compassion that of a lover?

To absolve himself of culpability in the youth's death, P'u Yi also ordered the assistants who had beaten the boy to strike the palms of their own hands with bamboo rods every day for six months as a penance.

During the six years of their marriage, his female concubine, Jade Years, like Wan Jung and Wen-Hsiu before her, bore P'u Yi no child. The marriage was mysteriously cut short by her death in 1943; P'u Yi suspected that the Japanese poisoned her because she was outspoken in her dislike of them and in her pro-China sentiments, and he made this charge publicly three years later.

Upon her death, Yoshioka again urged the emperor to acquire a Japanese wife. But P'u Yi continued to resist, and finally, in exasperation, the Kwantung army presented him with the photographs of several Manchurian girls attending a Japanese school at

Mukden. Although P'u Yi realized that the girls were hopelessly indoctrinated, he felt compelled to make a choice. In what now appeared to be a developing case of pedophilia, which is found in homosexuals as well as heterosexuals, he selected a fourteen-year-old girl, Yu-Ch'in, or Jade Lute. "I chose a girl who was young and not highly educated," he explained in 1946, "thinking that I would be able to deal with her even if she had been trained by the Japanese."

During these years he plumbed the depths of his nature, always thinking he had located bottom only to find, to his dread, that he could sink lower, and that the lower depths were infinite.

According to Hiro, although there is no evidence to support it, after the death of Jade Years and before P'u Yi's marriage to Jade Lute, a twelve-year-old girl was brought into the palace to serve as his secondary consort. After three days, the story goes, she fled in terror. The tale may have a tincture of truth since young girls were occasionally introduced at court as menials, and for P'u Yi's amusement. Given a set of household chores, each girl ultimately erred in some detail, and would have her buttocks bared for a thrashing at the emperor's pleasure.

Never for a moment during its thirteen-year existence did either Manchukuo or its emperor enjoy the "tranquillity and virtue" P'u Yi solemnly proclaimed at his investiture. For that matter, neither did the imperial family. Hiro Saga was no exception.

At the end of World War II she and her two daughters returned unscathed, via Shanghai, to Japan to settle in Tokyo. One of P'u Yi's half-Japanese nieces, P'u Hui-sheng, developed into a comely beauty and at the age of nineteen fell passionately in love with the nineteen-year-old son of an official of Japan's Northern Railway. As in a *kabuki* drama, Hiro frowned on the relationship between a princess of the royal blood and a commoner. On December 10, 1957, the two lovers joined in a suicide pact. In a mountain glen, the boy shot the princess, cradled her head in his arms and then shot himself. In the Japanese tradition, they left behind, in a twist of paper, locks of hair and fingernail cuttings. The affair made the front pages in Japan. The ashes of the two lovers were mingled and interred in the same urn. The tragedy reads like a footnote out of P'u Yi's poetic, imperial past.

CHAPTER 21

The Way of the Gods

As P'u Yi sat on the jade throne, he not only faced south but, like his ancestors, three centuries earlier, he also faced the Great Wall. With great expectations, despite his distaste for the Japanese he watched in fascination as the Japanese army, on one pretext or another, began to push south and undertake the piecemeal conquest of China. The painless occupation of Manchuria had whetted the appetite of the radical nationalists and Japan was swept up by an irresistible war psychology. "The Japanese army is determined to break China to its will," the United States ambassador to China cabled Washington in 1935, "whatever the consequences may be."

For Chinese of all political hues, from Nationalist to Communist, the Japanese invasion recalled a familiar historical pattern. All the great invasions of China had come from the north.

By 1937 the Japanese drive had blossomed into full-scale war as Japanese and Chinese troops clashed at Wanping, a small town of narrow streets situated a few miles southwest of Peking at the eastern end of the Marco Polo Bridge. The overcrowded Chinese mainland thereafter was turned into a charnel house, the setting for an appalling slaughter which ended, with grotesque irony, in the great firestorms over Hiroshima and Nagasaki. To cite one example, which was multiplied almost endlessly: When the Japanese army entered Nanking, it unloosed what a surviving eyewitness described as "hell on earth"; 260,000 hapless, unarmed civilians were butchered. Like the Manchus before them, the Japanese were overwhelmed by the sheer size of the Chinese population with which they had to deal, and they sought to bend that mass by calculated terror.

Each time Yoshioka, like a music coach in the prompter's box, reported another Japanese "victory" in China, P'u Yi dutifully joined him in bowing in the direction of the battlefield to honor Japan's war dead. When Japanese newsreels were shown in the palace, P'u Yi and his cabinet ministers stood at attention whenever Hirohito's picture flashed on the screen and they applauded scenes showing Japanese troops in victorious combat against the Chinese. As one of P'u Yi's ministers said after the war, "We did so because the film projectionists were Japanese." After the fall of the three cities where the opening scene of the Revolution of 1911 had unfolded, Yoshioka suggested, P'u Yi said, that "I should write a congratulatory letter to the butcher Okamura who had taken the city and that I should send a telegram to Hirohito." Whether P'u Yi acquiesced in these matters willingly or not is debatable. But he must surely have been aware of the flood of rumors south of the Great Wall claiming that the Japanese were again toying with the idea of restoring him to the Forbidden City.

With the Japanese in Peking, Doihara maneuvered openly, in the words of an Associated Press dispatch, "to prepare the way for the return to Peking of Henry P'u Yi." Indeed, Doihara complained to the news agency's correspondent that "I have come to China in a spirit of friendliness but this does not always meet with a friendly response in China." Inside Japan, there were reports that "some of the more extreme Japanese military leaders look forward to the day when P'u Yi will mount the Dragon Throne of his imperial ancestors in Peking." And in a confidential dispatch to Washington, the astute American ambassador in Tokyo, Joseph C. Grew, cabled as early as 1935 his suspicion that Japan might incorporate North China into P'u Yi's Manchukuo as "a vast Manchuria-North China empire."

But the same old concern arose in Japan over the advisability of reestablishing a rival claimant to the title of Son of Heaven, and nothing came of these rumors and reports. Instead, the Japanese set up for occupied territories in China a series of puppet provisional administrations which were poured from a Manchukuo mold.

As Japan's army pushed further into China with final victory always elusive, Manchukuo provided grain, manpower, and war supplies for the Japanese war effort. In a speech from the throne, P'u Yi called on the people of Manchukuo to carry out their duties patriotically "to support the holy war." The Chinese detested him, formally denounced him as a war criminal and in 1940 served a death notice on him. That year Wu Chi-lun, a prominent Chinese attorney, married P'u Yi's youngest sister and settled in Japanese-occupied Shanghai. On March 4, three days after P'u Yi celebrated the sixth anniversary of his ascension to the Manchukuo throne, a black-clad gunman entered the young couple's private residence and shot Wu Chi-lun to death. The Shanghai press dryly observed, "A political motive is suspected."

Heady with success, the Japanese militant and radical nationalists were not content with the occupation of Manchuria and large sections of China. They also entertained very definite ideas about the desirability of adding the Soviet maritime province, including Vladivostok, and the northern half of Sakhalin, to Japan's burgeoning empire. This would give the Japanese complete control of the Japan Sea. They also developed an appetite for Mongolia, the territory west of Manchukuo which the Russians kept hermetically sealed from the rest of the world.

Fearful of being squeezed between the Japanese militants in the East and Hitler in the West, Stalin accorded P'u Yi and Manchukuo *de facto* recognition and adopted a passive, noninterventionist policy in the Sino-Japanese War. To further assuage the Japanese, he sold

Russia's financial interest in the Chinese Eastern Railway to the P'u Yi government. But the Japanese militarists interpreted appeasement as weakness. "Border incidents" flared along the Soviet-Manchukuo and Mongolian-Manchukuo frontiers. By 1938 the Kwantung army officially reported more than 2,400 "incidents." On one occasion, in an effort to avoid a confrontation, Stalin demilitarized two islands in the Amur River, the first and only time Moscow voluntarily evacuated territory in Asia which it claimed as its own.

The Kwantung army was merely waiting for Hitler to divert Stalin's attention before it launched a general offensive. Neither the Japanese nor P'u Yi had long to wait. On February 21, 1938, in the most militant speech of his career until then, Hitler demanded the right of self-determination for Germans in Austria and Czechoslovakia, both countries on Stalin's western flank. As the capitals of Europe trembled and clung to the hope that Hitler could be appeased, they were too preoccupied to pay attention to a significant paragraph in Hitler's fiery peroration. "I believe a Japanese defeat in the Far East," he said, ". . . would exclusively benefit Soviet Russia." Accordingly, the Führer declared, "Germany will recognize Manchukuo." "I have decided on this step," Hitler said, "in order to draw the line of finality between the policy of fantastic lack of understanding and the policy of sober respect for the facts of reality."

P'u Yi's elation over recognition by one of the great powers was partly offset by the realization that Hitler's speech was a signal to Japan to attack the Soviet Union. P'u Yi's interest did not extend beyond the Black Dragon River. An attack on the Soviet Union, involving Manchukuoan troops, he felt, would divert Japanese attention from their military effort south of the Great Wall where his real interests lay. As P'u Yi feared, the Japanese six months later launched a "feeler operation" against the Russians on the heights of Changkufeng, near the junction of the Manchukuoan, Korean and Russian borders, a triangular area near Posiet Bay where the Russians had begun construction of a submarine and air base. The Kwantung army drove two-and-a-half miles into Soviet territory, their attack spearheaded by tanks and supported by heavy artillery and aircraft. Stalin now declared that Russia would "defend every inch of Soviet soil." *Pravda*, the official Communist Party daily, specifically accused the "Kwantung army of attempting to drag Japan into a war with the Union of Soviet Socialist Republics." Moscow warned Japan that the "Far East is not so far . . . our Red pilots will remind you it is much further from Tokyo to Moscow than Moscow to Tokyo." The Soviet air fleet at Vladivostok was poised to strike at Japan if the Changkufeng incident developed into a general war as had the "incidents" at Mukden and the Marco Polo Bridge.

Changkufeng's passage-at-arms was short and bloody. Three thousand were killed or wounded, three-fourths of them Japanese. The Japanese were burned badly. A fortnight later they signed a truce. P'u Yi was relieved. An all-out struggle between Russia and Japan, which might turn Manchukuo into a battlefield, had been avoided. For the first time pressure in Tokyo had brought the Kwantung army to its senses, momentarily.

But the army was determined to probe Soviet defenses elsewhere along the frontier and to avenge its losses. In the summer of the following year, as war clouds gathered over Europe, heavy fighting erupted between Russian and Japanese armies at Nomonhan along the Mongolian-Manchukuoan border. Only that spring, on May 31, 1939, Stalin had entered into a "mutual assistance" treaty with his Mongolian satellite and declared that Russia would defend Mongolia "just as vigorously as we shall defend our own borders."

P'u Yi viewed the Mongolian fighting with special interest. He was convinced that the Mongolian clans, if provided the opportunity, would rally around him as they had rallied in the salad days of the Manchu-Mongol alliance under the Great Ch'ing Dynasty. But he never had the opportunity to find out. The Japanese assault was poorly timed; it coincided with the Stalin-Hitler nonaggression pact, which came as a stunning surprise to the Kwantung army. It felt betrayed by Hitler.

Freed from pressure in the west, Stalin turned on the Japanese with a vengeance. The Russians met Japanese force with greater force and put on a dazzling display of mechanized warfare. The fighting was the bloodiest between the two countries since the Russo-Japanese War of 1905. More than 20,000 men were killed at Nomonhan, largely Japanese and Manchukuoan support troops. Double-crossed by Hitler, their putative ally, the Japanese somersaulted the following year and entered into a nonaggression pact of their own with Stalin. *Pravda* hailed the accord as a "historic reversal in Japanese-Soviet relations." And the Japanese foreign minister, the diabolical Yosuke Matsuoka, a radical nationalist and champion of Japanese expansionism, confided to Stalin that the Japanese radical nationalists and militarists were spiritually Communists. "We are moral Communists," Matsuoka said, "although we do not believe in political and economic communism." Stalin beamed. Under the terms of the nonaggression pact, Stalin pledged the Soviet Union "to respect the territorial integrity and inviolability of Manchukuo" and the Japanese, for their part, "pledged to respect the territorial integrity of the Mongolian People's Republic." In effect, Russia and Japan, pursuing their centuries-old strategy, each recognized the other's new sphere of influence in territory claimed by China.

As for the Chinese, Chiang Kai-shek rejected the Russian-Mongolian-Japanese-Manchukuo détente. He declared that the "northeastern provinces [Manchuria] and Outer Mongolia [the People's Republic of Mongolia] are integral parts of the republic of China. They will always remain Chinese territory." Significantly, Mao Tse-tung felt the same way, and made this plain in the course of Edgar Snow's interview with him in 1936.

With his personal relations with the Japanese deteriorating, and his Manchukuo empire embroiled in border disputes, P'u Yi's dream of returning to the Forbidden City waned. "When the Marco Polo Bridge fighting broke out and led to the Japanese occupation of Peking," he said, "some princes and old-timers in Peking were eager for a revival of the old order, but by now I knew that this was impossible." Instead, his principal concern was his own security.

The historic forces over which he exercised no control had reduced his "great enterprise" to the most common denominator of all men, the struggle for survival. "My only remaining [concern] was to how to preserve my own safety," he said. And just as he had gone to any length to restore the dynasty and avenge the spirits of his ancestors, he now went to any length to preserve himself. In the process he came to hate himself.

One day early in 1940, Yoshioka lingered in his office after a meeting about official matters. "As he had not gone," P'u Yi said, "I guessed that he had some other important business on his mind." In a corner of the room was a statue of Buddha, the face radiating the virtue and tranquillity which P'u Yi had promised Manchuria. Yoshioka strode over to the Buddha. "Buddhism came from abroad," he said, hesitatingly. "A foreign religion. As Japan and Manchukuo share the same spirit they should share the same beliefs, yes?"

P'u Yi stirred uneasily. He sensed that the Kwantung army was obliquely telegraphing its punch, and he was puzzled.

Several days later Yoshioka returned to the theme and proposed that for the sake of the friendship and spirit of unity between Manchukuo and Japan, "there should be a religious identity between the two countries." As he left, he remarked, "I trust your imperial majesty will think it over."

P'u Yi was more perplexed than before. "This time I did not know what to do," he wrote in his memoirs. From childhood, whenever he was confronted with a problem, he turned to his advisers for counsel. But the Japanese had stripped him of counselors. In his bewilderment, he longed for a Chen Pao-shen, a Reginald Johnston, a Cheng Hsiao-hsu. "I had to think the problem out for myself," he confessed.

Suddenly, he recalled that the Japanese planned to observe that year the 2,600th anniversary of the founding of their empire by the Emperor Jimmu-Tenno (Divinely Brave Emperor), the fifth descendant from Amaterasu-Omikami, the Sun Goddess, or, more precisely, the Heaven Shining Bright Deity. Every Japanese emperor was a reincarnation of the Sun God, and Japanese who died

237

for the emperor became godly themselves. This concept was at the core of the Japanese cult of Shintoism, the Way of the Gods.

At the beginning, Shintoism possessed neither a system of theology nor ethics. But in the fifth century Confucianism and Buddhism entered Japan by way of China and Shintoism absorbed part of their teaching. In the eighteenth century, when the Manchu Dynasty was at the zenith of its power, the Shinto cult was recognized in Japan by the state, not as a religion but as a "public institution" enjoining the people to cultivate ancestor worship and emperor worship. Shintoism blended with Buddhism, a true religion, and with *bushido,* the code of chivalry of the Samurai, or warrior class. Its form of worship consisted of obeisance, offerings, and prayers—the offerings primarily food and drink and strips of paper, representing cloth, attached to a wand and placed on an altar. With the reemergence of the Samurai class in modern dress, Shintoism became a vehicle which the militarists and radical nationalists could ride in their creation of a totalitarian state.

P'u Yi realized that, by indirection, Yoshioka had proposed that he convert to Shintoism. P'u Yi trembled at the suggestion. After his first visit to Mukden, where he prayed before the tomb of Nurhachu, the Exalted Founder of the Great Ch'ing Dynasty, the Japanese assiduously refused him permission to revisit the Manchu tombs. P'u Yi surmised that they sought to make a distinction between the Great Ch'ing Dynasty and the new Manchukuo Dynasty. But the Japanese had another reason: they did not want him to sacrifice publicly in the Chinese Buddhist manner, and thereby strengthen Buddhism in Manchukuo. They wanted to detach Manchuria from the Chinese sphere completely, temporally and spiritually.

"Now I was being called upon to acknowledge myself as a descendant of a foreign line," P'u Yi exclaimed in disgust. But he could no longer claim his soul his own. "I had to agree to this proposal," he said, "to preserve my life and safety."

Actually, the Japanese themselves were divided on the policy of imposing Shintoism on Manchukuo through the barrel of a gun.

Some Japanese, particularly those with experience in China, thought that such a policy would antagonize the Chinese, arouse fierce opposition, and further isolate Japan. But the militarists and radical nationalists, heady with triumph, won the day. Shintoism was foisted upon P'u Yi and Manchukuo. The cult proved unpopular among the Manchu, Mongol, and Chinese officials of the régime, and even more unpalatable to the people.

On June 26, 1940, P'u Yi returned to Japan for his second and last visit as the Emperor K'ang Teh, travelling aboard the battle cruiser *Hyuga Maru*. During the ensuing eight-day sojourn, the Japanese press reported gleefully that P'u Yi visited Japanese shrines and "worshipped like a devout Japanese." Unreported was the most humiliating experience in his humiliating thirty-four years. During a private audience with Hirohito, P'u Yi, playing out a scenario prepared by the Kwantung army, requested permission to worship the Japanese Sun Goddess in the Shinto manner, for the sake of "indivisible unity in heart and virtue" between Japan and Manchukuo. Whether or not the Japanese emperor was primed for the request is uncertain. P'u Yi implied that Hirohito was startled. "If that is your imperial majesty's will," Hirohito said, "I must comply with your wish."

Hirohito then showed his guest three objects: a sword, a bronze mirror, and a curved piece of jade, the three sacred objects which represented the Sun Goddess. Six years later, under Allied interrogation, P'u Yi bitingly said, "As he explained them to me, I thought I was in an antique shop." Were these objects sacred? Did they represent the spirits of his new ancestors? "I burst into tears on the drive back," he said.

He had always felt that the destruction of the tombs of his ancestors was the most traumatic experience in his lifetime. No longer. "I found this even more difficult to stomach," he said in 1946. But stomach it he did. By doing so, he betrayed his ancestors, just as he had betrayed China and Manchuria. Until 1940, P'u Yi found comfort in the rationalization that all his acts were filial deeds done in the name of his ancestors for the sole, and honorable, purpose of restoring the Great Ch'ing Dynasty. Throughout, he expected the spirits of his ancestors to understand his plight and protect him. Now he could no longer use his ancestors as an excuse. Nevertheless, even in converting to Shintoism, he retreated deeper within himself to find a justification for his behavior. He planned to sacrifice to his forebears in private, as usual, while acknowledging his new Japanese ancestors in public.

Thus, on his return from Tokyo in July of that year, he openly prayed before a shrine of the Sun Goddess which the Kwantung army had erected in the courtyard of his palace. He prayed for the welfare and happiness of the Manchurian people. "This act," observed Hugh Byas, the veteran Japan correspondent of *The New York Times*, "might be called a conversion." Byas reported that, according to the Japanese, P'u Yi had converted "out of appreciation for Japan's establishment of the Manchukuo Empire."

Shinto shrines popped up throughout the countryside and everyone walking past a shrine was compelled to bow at the waist "on pain of being punished for disrespect." Invariably, the punishment was a savage beating by Japanese gendarmes.

P'u Yi also issued an imperial rescript which children were compelled to memorize and recite at school. "On the occasion of our happy return to our own country we have respectfully established the national foundation shrine in which to make offerings to the Heaven Shining Bright Deity," the rescript said. "We shall pray in our person and with the deepest reverence for the prosperity of the nation; and we shall make this an eternal example that our sons and grandsons for ten thousand generations shall follow it without end. Thus, may the basis of the nation be consolidated by venerating Shintoism."

"Let all our subjects understand our meaning," he concluded. "By the command of the emperor!" In the hallways of history, one could hear the echo of the Old Buddha, "Hear and obey!"

On closer inspection, of course, the rescript was little more than a put on. If the spread of Shintoism depended on *his* sons and grandsons, it would not spread very far.

To inform the world of the latest development, the Manchukuo postal administration, as part of the celebration to commemorate the 2,600th anniversary of the founding of the Japanese empire, issued 20 million commemorative stamps. Millions of children around the world dutifully pasted them into their stamp albums.

Defeated on all sides in the temporal world, his spiritual world collapsing, P'u Yi escaped in the only way a prisoner can escape—by turning inward. He became a devout Buddhist, recited the holy scriptures daily and prayed before the image of Lord Buddha. Taking the Buddhist scriptures to heart, he became a nominal vegetarian since Buddhism admonished against the taking of animal life. His retreat sometimes went to extremes. "I did not allow my staff to kill flies, insisting that they drive them away instead," he said. "And when I saw a cat catching a mouse, I had the whole staff chase the cat away to save the mouse's life."

Visions of hell crowded his dreams. He became an insomniac. He rose at 11:00 A.M., took breakfast at noon, dined at 11:00 P.M. and retired at 3:00 A.M., more often than not, to struggle in hellish dreams until he fell asleep exhausted with the approach of dawn.

In this period, he also returned to one of the old practices of the Forbidden City: consulting oracles. He repeated divinations, usually by burning bones and reading their ashes, over and over again until he received a "good omen." His fear of death deepened. He found himself surrounded by spies. He trusted no one. He did not touch his food until someone first tasted each dish. Clearly, he was breaking under the strain.

The term "brainwashing" did not come into vogue until Mao Tse-tung occupied the Forbidden City at the end of 1949. But in the 1930s, the Japanese employed a term which was synonymous, "thought control." Either phrase is useful in describing the period through which P'u Yi passed during these years. His staff also felt the strain and waited patiently for him either to commit suicide or turn in a burst of fury upon his Japanese tormentors. He did neither. Instead, he crept more deeply into himself, and his nightmares became more vivid. One day he went outside for a bit of exercise

241

within the compound. He was shaken by a line scrawled in chalk on a palace wall: "Haven't you had enough humiliation . . . ?"

"I was terrified," he said.

CHAPTER 22

The Eagle and the Bear

Irresistibly, the Japanese slid toward total war. Willingly or unwillingly, P'u Yi was swept along with them.

In 1941 Japan set up a committee to prepare for the celebration of the tenth anniversary of the founding of Manchukuo. Tojo, then war minister and actively planning the attack on Pearl Harbor, spared precious moments to head the program. He did so, as the *Japan Times Weekly and Trans-Pacific* observed, to "leave the world in no doubt that [the Japanese] are invincibly convinced that the fate of their country is bound up with that of the new state." Of course, it was really the other way around.

By now, the Japanese were mired down in China proper. The militarists had boasted in 1937 that they would bring China to her knees in three months. But the months turned into years as millions of men were poured into the conquest of China, regular divisions, newly organized divisions, enlarged divisions, reorganized divisions, mixed brigades, and home and independent garrisons. All for naught.

As long as the Japanese were preoccupied with China,

243

however, P'u Yi was reasonaly secure. His overriding fear, after the border wars of 1938–1939 with the Soviet Union, was that the Japanese, still convinced of their invincibility, might pivot in Manchuria and attack the Soviet Union on a massive scale while the struggle for China was still unresolved. He was heartened in 1941, therefore, when Stalin entered into his neutrality pact with Japan, especially since in it the Kremlin guaranteed Manchukuo's frontiers. Some of P'u Yi's old confidence returned. He interpreted the neutrality pact as meaning that Japan was free to press the war in China without looking over her shoulder. But P'u Yi did not know the Japanese; he never did.

Just as Stalin's pact with Germany freed Hitler to strike against the West, Stalin's pact with Japan did the same. Japan now attacked in the Pacific and in Southeast Asia. The circle of war closed. The conflicts in Orient and Occident joined, a chain reaction which had started in Manchuria in 1931. "The course of aggression there embarked upon was followed by successive aggressions in Asia, Africa and Europe," Secretary of State Cordell Hull said in 1942 in an overview of the war, "and has led step by step to the present world conflict."

On December 8, Manchukuo time, Yoshioka broke the news of Pearl Harbor to a stunned and perplexed P'u Yi. At the Kwantung army's suggestion, P'u Yi issued an imperial rescript that same day which pledged Manchukuo's support for Japan's war effort. By custom, imperial rescripts were made public by the State Council. On this occasion, however, at Yoshioka's urging, P'u Yi broke precedent and personally read the rescript over the Manchukuo radio network. It was the first time a Manchu emperor had ever spoken on the air; perforce, it was the first time his subjects heard the reedy, high-pitched voice of a descendant of the Exalted Founder, of a former Chinese emperor. The rescript, "On the Current Situation," expressed Manchukuo's determination to live or die with Japan "united in heart and virtue."

A year to the month after the war ended, P'u Yi, under interrogation, conceded that the rescript bore his name as the

Emperor K'ang Teh; but he shifted the responsibility for drafting it wholly onto the six Japanese vice ministers in the Manchukuo cabinet. "In our hearts," he said, he and his people opposed the rescript. "But under the oppression of the Japanese," he said imploringly, "what else could we do?"

Whatever the political merits of the Japanese administration in Manchuria, it was clear that in the first decade of Manchukuo's existence, the Japanese had performed an economic miracle. Under their tutelage, Manchukuo was transformed, to become the greatest concentration of industrial, mining and railway development on the Asian mainland. Manchuria fulfilled its potential as a Ruhr of the East. In its factories, armaments, electrical components, ball bearings, heavy industrial equipment, and machine tools were manufactured. In its mines the production of iron ore, coal, gold, lead, zinc and molybdenum soared. Coal output alone tells the story. Production rose from 8.9 million tons at the time of the Mukden Incident in 1931 to 20.7 million tons by the time of Pearl Harbor.

As viewed from P'u Yi's jade throne, Manchukuo was a bystander during the war. No imperial rescript ever declared war on the Allies. Legally, Manchukuo was neutral. Of course, a neutral Manchukuo ideally served the Japanese war effort—as a buffer against the Soviet Union; as a rest and rehabilitation camp for Japan's expeditionary corps in China; as a training ground for new Japanese recruits; and as an industrial haven which was, for a time at least, out-of-bounds to American bombers.

But if Manchukuo and its emperor were a fiction, so was their neutrality.

Manchukuo became Japan's principal granary and arsenal outside the home islands. The country was so valuable to the Japanese war machine, that a few months after Pearl Harbor Tojo, now premier, made a personal on-the-spot tour through it to exhort greater industrial output. In the course of his visit, P'u Yi greeted him with the comforting declaration, widely published in the Japanese press, that Japan "may rest assured that I shall devote the full resources of my empire to support the holy war of Japan, our parental country." Tojo, who perpetually perspired, mopped the dome of his head and beamed appreciatively.

But as the war lengthened, the conflict had its baleful effect on Manchuria. For the first time, the region suffered food shortages, as bumper crops were diverted to Japan. Youths between the ages of nineteen and twenty-three were conscripted for military duty, and those from twenty-six to forty-eight were organized into labor gangs to boost industrial production. In 1944, 15,000 laborers were recruited for military construction projects and working conditions were so bad that one-third of them died. Shipping between Manchukuo and Japan was heavily attacked by Allied aircraft. Manchukuo's contribution to the Japanese war effort was so significant that the third daylight raid undertaken in the Pacific theater by the big new Flying Superfortresses, the B–29s, was flown against P'u Yi's empire on July 30, 1944. The attack was carried out by two groups from the 20th Bomber Command, United States Air Force. The B–29s bombed the Showa steel works at Anshan and the port of Dairen, near Port Arthur. "Results were good," an Allied communiqué announced the next day, "and our losses extremely light." The Americans lost one of their planes to intense Japanese and Manchukuoan antiaircraft fire.

P'u Yi's foreign office (read: the Japanese) lodged a strong protest against United States "aggression" and Domei, the official Japanese news agency, emphasized that "Manchukuo has not declared war on the Anglo-Americans." It accused Washington of perpetrating the raid "for propaganda purposes," whatever that was supposed to mean. The United States rejected the protests outright; under the Stimson Doctrine, the United States did not recognize the legitimacy of P'u Yi's government and considered Manchuria Chinese territory under enemy occupation.

Among P'u Yi's courtiers, raids against Manchukuo, however, were a fair indication of Japan's deteriorating military position. The war closed in on Hsinking as well as Tokyo. Japan's situation grew desperate. Yoshioka begged P'u Yi to set an example and donate personal articles to the war effort, especially metal. P'u Yi generously surrendered some jewelry—rings, earrings and the like—and ordered the palace carpets removed and presented to Japan as a gift. These acts of loyalty and confidence in Japan made the front pages in Japan and Manchukuo.

But while P'u Yi went through the motions of fervently supporting Japan, the Manchurian people became increasingly restive. Resistance to the Japanese spread and industrial production slowed. Premier Chang Ching-hui, with P'u Yi's blessing, ordered a "drastic reorganization of the home front" in 1943 and, in a nationwide broadcast, indirectly, gave the resistance heart. "In the production field," the premier said, "there is some evidence of lack of cooperation." His statement was the first official confirmation that resistance, both active and passive, was developing inside Manchuria. Chungking, China's wartime capital, monitored the broadcast and recognized the implications. With the war nearing an end, a new struggle for postwar control of the rich Manchurian hinterland was in the offing.

In 1931, 1937, and again in 1941, Chiang Kai-shek publicly declared that China would never rest until it recovered its three northeastern provinces. To emphasize the point, on September 18, 1942, on the occasion of the eleventh anniversary of the Mukden Incident, a group of thirty-two Manchurian-born academicians who had taken refuge in Free China, sent a joint message to Britain, the United States, and the Soviet Union which declared that victory over Japan would not be complete "until and unless the last Japanese soldier is driven from these provinces." Since neither Britain nor the United States entertained any special interest in Manchuria, the broadside was obviously addressed to Moscow.

The Chinese had cause for concern. Shortly thereafter, the Institute of Pacific Relations, an influential, academically inclined study group in the West, founded in 1925 as "an unofficial and nonpolitical organization" and sometimes exploited by the left to loft trial balloons, held a conference in Quebec at which one of those balloons was released. A suggestion was advanced that Manchuria should not be returned to China; perhaps the Soviet Union should occupy Manchuria; as compensation, the Chinese should occupy Indochina which before the war had been under French control. Chungking was dismayed and so were many Far Eastern specialists. "China does not want Indochina," *Ta Kung Pao,* the most respected Chinese daily of the period declared from Chungking. "We want Manchuria and we won't stop fighting until it is returned."

Much to the relief of the Chinese—and to P'u Yi's horror—the Allies declared in 1943, at the Cairo Conference, attended by Chiang, Roosevelt, and Churchill, that they harbored "no thought of territorial expansion." They agreed that "all the territories Japan has stolen from the Chinese, such as Manchuria," should be restored to China. In effect, P'u Yi was told that his reign was temporary. Stalin was advised to abandon any dream of replacing the Japanese in Manchukuo. Of greater significance, however, in the light of postwar developments, was the fact that Chiang's position was endorsed by Mao.

Thus, on September 19, 1943, in his first public address as the president of China, the Generalissimo pledged to recover Manchuria. "We are more confident than ever of our ability to regain all lost territories in the northeast as well as to spare no sacrifice that the consummation of this task may entail." The 240-member People's Political Council, which included representatives from Manchuria and from the Chinese Communist Party, gave Chiang a standing ovation. Mao sent Tung Pi-wu as his delegate; this was the same Tung whom Mao chose as acting president in 1972 following the mysterious death of Lin Piao who was later accused of plotting a coup against Mao. In 1974 Peking began to refer to him as acting chairman. *

Chiang, and doubtessly Mao too, were aware of P'u Yi's ambiguous position in Manchuria. The Generalissimo recognized that the former emperor was a feeble, malleable puppet, but that in the event of Japan's sudden surrender, he and his premier, Chang

---

* In 1945 I interviewed him and, in line with Stalin's "right strategy" at the time, Tung espoused "pro-American" sentiments.

Ching-hui, could play a useful role in reasserting Chinese sovereignty in the territory and, naturally, the authority of the Nationalist government.

Within a month, as a follow-up to the Cairo Conference amid evidence of growing resistence in Manchuria to the Japanese, the Chungking government-controlled daily *Yi Shih Pao*, extended this offer to P'u Yi and Wang Ching-wei, the head of the Japanese puppet regime in occupied China proper:

> If the traitors are willing to turn over a new leaf, we will forgive the past and allow them to reform. If P'u Yi or Wang Ching-wei broke away from the Japanese and served their country at a later stage, we would allow them once again to be Chinese, and even give them freedom of assembly and speech for publication and for forming associations.

At a *later* stage, that is, at the war's end. Once again there surfaced the indestructible political value of the last Manchu emperor. Given the continued existence of Manchu and Mongolian clans in the sensitive Sino-Russian border areas, P'u Yi was a cipher in the great power equation. In math, a cipher is defined as a naught, a zero. But it is far more than that, obviously. The same may be said of the role of the cipher in politics. Just as the concept of zero is of infinite value in mathematics, so is the human cipher in power politics. Sometimes the ciphers are employed as heads of state, as in the case of Hirohito. And sometimes the ciphers are employed as buffers surrounded by those who really wield the power.

Be that as it may, the Nationalists' public offer, at a time of Chinese patriotic fervor and stringent wartime censorship, lent credence to persistent rumors that Chungking had established a clandestine link with Hsinking. P'u Yi's behavior at the time of the Japanese surrender, and that of his premier, strengthens this suspicion.

While the jockeying for postwar control of Manchuria intensified, the Americans completed plans for the invasion of Japan. With General MacArthur's concurrence, the United States joint chiefs of staff actively pressed for a Russian invasion of Manchuria to neutralize the Kwantung army. American intelligence was faulty however. By 1944 the Kwantung army existed largely on paper. In October of that year the Japanese high command had withdrawn about 750,000 troops from Manchuria to guard the home islands against the approaching American onslaught.

Given the accuracy of Soviet intelligence in Manchuria between 1931 and 1941, as revealed after the war, the Russians must have been aware that the Kwantung army was as formidable as, to borrow Maoist metaphor, a paper tiger. In character, the Russians bluffed, and, also in character, they drove a hard bargain. With their trial balloon at Quebec having been shot down over Cairo, Stalin moved skillfully to reestablish the foothold the Czars had held in P'u Yi's ancestral homeland.

On February 11, 1945, at Yalta, a Russian beach resort astride the Black Sea, Stalin extracted from his Anglo-American Allies secret guarantees that in the postwar settlement the Manchurian railway system would be jointly operated by a Sino-Soviet company which would safeguard "the preeminent interests of the Soviet Union" in the region; that Port Arthur would revert to Russia under a leasing arrangement for use as a naval base; that Dairen would become an international port, ostensibly with Russia first among equals; and that the Mongolian People's Republic would be "preserved," that is, win Chinese recognition.

The Yalta agreement made no pretense of hiding Moscow's Czarist objectives. On the contrary, it openly restated them. The document declared that "the former rights of Russia violated by the treacherous attack of Japan in 1904 shall be restored." Nothing, of course, was said of Chinese rights; and nothing of Manchu rights, if there were still any.

For his part, as the *quid pro quo,* Stalin pledged to attack Manchukuo "within two or three months" after Hitler's defeat and to conclude a "treaty of friendship" with Chiang Kai-shek; in effect, to keep hands off China in the event of a recrudescence of the

Chinese civil war. The Chinese were not informed of the Yalta accord until the war ended, six months later.

The fallout after publication of the accord was considerable. The Chinese felt humiliated and many Americans felt that the United States had betrayed her ally. Yet, in a sense, Yalta put a lid on Russian aggrandizement. When the Russians entered the war against Japan, as they most probably would, Stalin could, in any case, have seized the territories in question and even considerably more land, without consulting his Chinese and American Allies. Thus, for example, a minute attached to the Yalta covenant recorded Stalin's pledge that the invading Red army would pull out of Manchuria "within three months after Japan's surrender."

If the Chinese were in the dark about Stalin's Manchurian strategy, so were P'u Yi and the Japanese. P'u Yi was badly shaken when, on April 5, 1945, Yoshioka privately informed him that the Russians had renounced their five-year neutrality pact with Japan. This meant that the Kremlin was no longer committed "to respect the territorial integrity and inviolability of Manchukuo." Thereafter the emperor's sleepless nights increased. He resumed the old habit of pacing endlessly back and forth across the room breaking unlit cigarettes in his fingers.

Ever since Pearl Harbor, P'u Yi's palace had been alive with speculation that the Russians might eventually join the war against Japan by attacking Manchukuo. As early as 1942 Radio Tokyo refuted these rumors, branding them "incorrect" and citing the Soviet-Japanese Neutrality Treaty as an earnest reflection of Stalin's intentions. Even so, Tokyo repeatedly accused the Allies of "inciting" Russia to attack Manchukuo. Now Tokyo could no longer point to the nonaggression pact with Moscow as a safeguard against a Soviet assault. Clearly, P'u Yi felt, a Russian attack could be expected at any time after April 13, 1946, when the Soviet-Japanese Neutrality Treaty expired. Inwardly, P'u Yi's great hope was that the Pacific war would end before then without completely enveloping Manchukuo. But what then? Japan was in ashes,

American bombers ranged over his realm, the Allies refused to recognize the legitimacy of his state, Chinese armies—Nationalist and Communist—were primed to move into Manchuria with the collapse of Japan, and in the background was the specter of Russia. Relentlessly swept into such a political vortex, how could P'u Yi survive?

The emperor pondered his options. In polite terms, they were slender. There was one detestable avenue of escape: Chiang Kai-shek, the man whom P'u Yi, rightly or not, held responsible for the "cultural revolution" of 1928 that had despoiled the Manchu tombs. At least Chungking had alerted him to stand by to support China and the Nationalists at "a later date." The date was near at hand. But before he could decide his next course of action, P'u Yi's artificial world disintegrated.

On August 2, at Potsdam, the United States called on Japan to surrender and hinted at the development of a secret weapon. The Americans observed that the force converging on Japan was "immeasurably greater" than the force that had just toppled Hitler. This was Japan's moment of truth; but like a boxer clinging to the ropes, the dazed Japanese neither fought nor went down. Four days later as the very earth of Hiroshima shook to its core, Stalin must have felt Manchuria slipping from his grasp. On August 8, eight months *before* the expiration of the Soviet-Japanese Neutrality Treaty, and forty-eight hours after the atomic bomb fell on Hiroshima, the Russians invaded Manchuria.

"For forty years have we men of the older generation waited for this generation, waited for this day," Stalin said jubilantly. "And now this day has come." In a far different context, P'u Yi might well have echoed Stalin's conclusion: "And now this day has come."

CHAPTER 23

Stalin's House Guest

Manchuria juts into the Soviet Union almost as if it were a large peninsula surrounded by a Russian sea, and Stalin's August 9 invasion of Manchukuo was a model of coordinated peninsular strategy. Doubtlessly, it is studied and restudied today in the staff schools of the Chinese People's Liberation army. The Russians attacked Manchuria simultaneously from three sides. From Vladivostok, General Meritskov knifed into eastern Manchuria. From across the Amur River, General Purkayev struck south. From the west the main force, under Marshal Malinovsky, plunged into Manchuria's western reaches, its right flank reinforced by a Golden Horde in modern dress, a division of Mongolian cavalry, 80,000 strong.

Russian soldiers, fanning out in Manchuria, must have been pleasantly startled to discover manifold traces of Russian influence in the territory—wooden houses in a Russian style commonly found in Siberia and the Soviet maritime province; a scattering of Greek Orthodox churches with their distinctive onion-shaped domes; hotels and restaurants serving, along with traditional Chinese dishes, such Russian specialties as borscht and ice cream floating in coffee; and the ability of a surprising number of Manchurians to address them in Russian.

By all rights, this was the world's first "Six Day War." Japan surrendered on August 15. But Moscow ignored the surrender and pressed the offensive. Indeed, two days after making peace, the Japanese appealed to General Douglas MacArthur, the Supreme Commander for the Allied Powers, to take steps to effect an immediate halt to the Soviet offensive. The Japanese reported that Moscow's behavior complicated the Kwantung army's desire to implement Hirohito's acceptance of the terms of surrender that had been offered to Japan at Potsdam. Despite their surrender, the Japanese complained, "the Soviet forces are still carrying on the offensive."

On the morning of the invasion, Yoshioka, accompanied by the commander of the Kwantung army, hurried to P'u Yi's palace to break the news that the Red army had crossed the frontier. P'u Yi was numb. No sooner had they completed their report when Hsinking's air-raid sirens sounded and Soviet bombers, bright red stars on their wings glistening in the sunlight, appeared from over the northern horizon. P'u Yi, his brother P'u Chieh, members of their respective families, Yoshioka and others, fled to the newly constructed air-raid shelter in the palace courtyard. P'u Yi may have felt a sense of déjà vu. Twenty-seven years earlier he had heard the first bombs fall on China when the Forbidden City was attacked. Then, as now, he felt he was the target.

Somewhat melodramatically, from August 9 onward, P'u Yi had been keeping a loaded pistol on his person—melodramatically, because it raised the question of what he planned to do with it. Did the last Manchu emperor plan to shoot it out with the Russians before being taken prisoner? The fate of the Romanovs was probably not too far removed from his mind. Yet resistance on his part seemed unlikely. At no time previously had he ever displayed physical valor. Political heart, sometimes; physical courage, never. Or did he mistrust his Manchurian camp followers and fear one of them might seek to take revenge on him at the last moment as a wartime collaborator? Perhaps. For that matter, did he fear that the Japanese might try to do away with him, like a piece of incriminating evidence, before he fell into the hands of the Allies? Or, having lost the mandate of heaven, did he arm himself against heaven? Did he plan, like the last Ming emperor, whom the Manchu displaced, to take his own life to escape outrageous fortune? Conceivably. But with a pistol? This was hardly in keeping with his cultural heritage. Poison or a yellow silken cord might do, but a gun could not. Whatever the reason for arming himself, the possession of a loaded revolver gave him a sense of courage, however false. The handgun comforted him and acted as a tranquillizer. Clearly, he was by now an unstable man and, with a gun, a potentially dangerous one.

On August 10, with the Japanese in retreat on all fronts, he was informed of the Kwantung army's plan to fall back on the Great Wall, whose psychological formidability obviously outweighed its military value. P'u Yi was instructed to gather up a few belongings and get ready to move to T'unghua, a small town locked away in the mountains along the wild Korean border. There a temporary capital would be set up pending the completion of preparations for his flight to Japan. But P'u Yi stalled. Strenuously, he objected to leaving Manchuria.

"If your imperial majesty does not go," Yoshioka warned him, "you will be the first to be murdered by the Soviet troops." There is no reason to doubt Yoshioka's sincerity, given his attachment to P'u Yi as the Emperor Hsüan Tung. But P'u Yi reasoned, he claimed later, that if the Japanese thought the Allies wanted his head, might not the Japanese also want it? As a witness, he could implicate any number of Japanese in war crimes.

In 1946, with the war over, he publicly claimed that the Japanese "wanted to kill all of us in order to silence us." And a decade later, as a Chinese captive, in his first interview with Westerners—David Chip of Reuters and Lucian Bodard, a French writer—he reasserted that the Japanese planned to murder him. "I had not dared to show that I did not want to go to Japan for fear that the Japanese would kill me," he said. "I had served them for fourteen years and knew too much about their record and cruelties." Yet there is an element of disbelief in these statements. If the Japanese wanted to put him aside, the Korean border region was a convenient setting, certainly easier than Japan itself. More than likely, mindful of the Chungking offer, he sought to remain behind and work out a deal with the Nationalists. This is something he could not admit to in 1946 when he was Stalin's prisoner, nor ten years later when he was Mao's.

In an effort to assuage the Japanese, however, he resorted to what had become common practice for him. On August 11, he summoned his premier, Chang Ching-hui, and the latter's Japanese alter ego, Takebe Rokuzo, then director of the General Affairs Office and the real civilian authority in Manchukuo, together with several Kwantung army staff officers. "We must support the holy war of our parental country with all our strength," he assured them, "and we must resist the Soviet army to the end, to the very end." By this statement, he told Chip and Bodard later, he hoped to allay Japanese suspicions that he might turn against them.

That same day realizing that he had not eaten since the previous evening, because the train of events had been so hectic, he directed his personal attendant and bodyguard, Ta Li, Big Li, a man of large athletic build and a master at the art of *kung fu,* to fetch him food. Big Li returned with a few biscuits and reported that the cooks had fled. The rats were abandoning the ship.

Warily, P'u Yi retired to his suite and, with P'u Chieh's assistance, filled an attaché case with an emperor's ransom of jewels and uncut gems. From among his 200 personal seals he chose one and stuffed it into his pocket—the chop of the Emperor Hsüan Tung, the seal fashioned from the wondrous eight interlocking pieces of jade whose possession was tangible evidence of his legitimacy as the Celestial Emperor, the ruler of a fourth of mankind.

Two nights later, on August 13, the imperial family arrived at

Talitzkou, a small coal mining town near the Korean border whose beauty, P'u Yi confessed later, "I was too terrified to appreciate." By this time, the royal family and entourage had grown to formidable numbers. In the confusion of the period, there is no exact accounting of who the passengers were but the group was known to include: Elizabeth, along with her opium pipe, her father, and brother; P'u Yi's brother P'u Chieh, his Japanese wife, Hiro, and their daughters; his young concubine, Jade Lute (Yu-Ch'in); several nephews and nieces; P'u Yi's personal physician; and Big Li, his bodyguard. They went no further. Here on the fateful fifteenth Yoshioka, drawn and subdued, announced Hirohito's decision to endure the unendurable and suffer the insufferable—surrender. In his memoirs, P'u Yi said that he bent the knee and kowtowed to heaven, intoning, "I thank heaven for protecting his imperial majesty." The passage was written within the context of his cringing, obsequious behavior in the presence of the Japanese but the incident has a ring of authenticity for a reason he did not mention. When, on August 15, Hirohito addressed his people by radio, for the first time on the air, and ordered a cessation of hostilities, the Japanese emperor had a word for P'u Yi and other collaborators in Japan's lost cause. In the surrender rescript, the Japanese emperor, without naming names, expressed "the deepest sense of regret" to the P'u Yis of the war who "cooperated with the empire toward the emancipation of East Asia." Yoshioka read out this particular passage to P'u Yi. In the circumstances, it is reasonable to assume that in Hirohito, P'u Yi recognized himself: the isolated man who symbolized power but was powerless. P'u Yi's gesture in kowtowing to heaven may have been a heartfelt gesture and not the sham he later intimated that it was.

After reporting on the surrender, Yoshioka told him that Tokyo expected him to carry through with the plan to fly the Manchu emperor to Japan. "But his imperial majesty cannot assume unconditional responsibility for your imperial majesty's safety," he said, referring to Hirohito. "This will be in the hands of the Allies."

P'u Yi, who possessed a low fear threshold, paled. He had

visions of himself in Allied hands, in the dock as an enemy collaborator.

At 1:00 A.M. the following morning, in the imperial Chinese tradition, when "all great diplomatic measures and dark deeds are transacted by the emperor between midnight and daylight," P'u Yi put his seal as the Emperor K'ang Teh to an abdication rescript, the third time in thirty-three years that he had stepped down from a throne. Yoshioka, Chang Ching-hui and Takebe Rokuzo witnessed the solemn act. In it, P'u Yi told his people that he had given up the empire "out of concern for your welfare and happiness." Like the abdication rescript of 1917, it was never published or broadcast. A year later, under Allied questioning, he offered this matter-of-fact version of his abdication: "General Yoshioka, together with other Japanese ministers, came to see me," he said. "Then they showed me a piece of a paper and explained to me that this is the paper by which I will announce I will voluntarily renounce, that I will voluntarily give up, the throne."

The business at hand finished, Chang left for Hsinking, which now reverted to its old name of Changch'un, ostensibly to await the arrival of the Russians. Instead, he established radio contact with Chungking and announced the establishment of a "Committee for the Preservation of Public Order." Chang apparently had been Chiang Kai-shek's contact inside the P'u Yi régime; more than likely, he was responsible for the graffiti P'u Yi had seen on the palace wall: "Haven't you had enough humiliation?" The following day fighting broke out in the former Manchukuo capital between the Kwantung army and P'u Yi's imperial guard.

As these events unfolded, on August 14, on the eve of the Japanese surrender, China and the Soviet Union signed a "Treaty of Friendship and Alliance." By its terms, the Chinese accepted the concession Stalin won at Yalta, and conceded Mongolia to Russia in return for a Soviet reaffirmation of "respect for China's full sovereignty over the three eastern provinces" and recognition of "their territorial and administrative integrity." China was forced by circumstance to sign the treaty. Stalin had seventy divisions inside

Manchuria. A protocol on Manchuria was appended to the treaty. It stated that the Soviet armed forces in Manchuria were under the jurisdiction of the Soviet field commander, while "all Chinese nationals, both civilian and military, shall be under Chinese jurisdiction," and "this jurisdiction shall also extend to the civilian population on Chinese territory, even in the event of crimes and offenses against the Soviet armed forces with the exception of crimes and offenses committed in the zone of hostilities which are subject to jurisdiction of the Soviet commander-in-chief." Thus, with Japan's collapse, and Manchukuo's dissolution, P'u Yi was, by Sino-Soviet agreement, destined to become a Chinese prisoner.

Three days after the treaty was signed, with the Russian armies converging on Harbin, Yoshioka notified P'u Yi that a small transport plane was ready to fly him to Tokyo but that he could select only eight members from his entourage. Without hesitation, he chose his brother P'u Chieh, two brothers-in-law, three nephews, a physician, and Big Li, his personal attendant. He abandoned all the women in his party—empress, concubine, sisters, sister-in-law, and nieces. Elizabeth was in no condition to travel, he explained, and the women's responsibility was to remain at the side of the empress. War, he continued, was a man's business and the next stage of the journey was dangerous. Jade Lute pleaded to go along but he assured her that arrangements had been made for them to follow him to Japan and "in three days, at the most, you and the empress will see me again." There were, in truth, no arrangements, nor could there be. In point of fact, he never saw any of them again, except Jade Lute and, then, only briefly.

As he boarded the Nakajima transport plane, P'u Yi realized that for the first time since his childhood among the fawning foxes of the Violet Enclosure, he was free of all the women in his life, from the Old Buddha, the dowager empress, through Elizabeth, Wen Hsiu, Jade Years, and Jade Lute. His attitude toward women had always been confused. He feared them and felt insecure in their presence. Yet fear did not breed respect; on the contrary, he was contemptuous of them. Always he preferred the company of men.

Shortly before dawn, the single engine plane took off for Mukden, the ancient seat of Manchu power, where he and his party were to transfer to a twin-engine transport for the flight to Japan—and into American hands.

As the party sat idly in the modernistic lounge of the Mukden Municipal Airport, waiting for an 11:00 A.M. take-off, the field suddenly reverberated to the sound of a flight of planes as a squadron of Soviet twin-engine PS–84s, a Russian version of the American Dakota, built with the aid of the Douglas Aircraft Company, touched down, disgorged airborne troops and seized the airdrome without firing a shot.

A Soviet officer, accompanied by a platoon of Red army soldiers, their submachine guns at the ready, descended on the lounge. P'u Yi and his party rose to their feet as they entered. The officer surveyed the motley group. His eyes settled on the last Chinese emperor who, even in this awkward, tense moment, stood apart from the others. Like a life-sized billboard poster, the officer immediately recognized the expressionless face, the black-rimmed glasses, the slender ascetic frame. Intently, the Russian studied his face as if he were recalling the silhouette charts which identify friendly and unfriendly aircraft. "Mr. P'u Yi," he said, extending a hand. P'u Yi shook hands, mechanically. The officer relieved him of his sidearm. "You will have no need for this," he said in broken English. Among the 594,000 prisoners the Russians captured during their Manchurian-Korean campaign, he was the biggest prize. A year later, almost to the date of his capture, P'u Yi described his detention quaintly. "I was asked to stay behind in Soviet Russia," he explained with a characteristic straight face.

P'u Yi and his party, including Yoshioka, and several other Japanese, were escorted to a Soviet transport plane and flown to Tungliao, a Mongolian airstrip where the party alighted to stretch their legs while the aircraft refueled. During the interlude, P'u Yi, as he told interviewers after the war, "signaled to the Russians to separate us from Yoshioka and the other Japanese." When the prisoners reboarded the plane, they were divided into two groups, Manchurian and Japanese.

Then they flew to Chita, a Siberian *oblast* town, originally a Cossack fort which had served as a trading post between the Russians and the Manchu, Mongols and Chinese. In 1920 Chita proclaimed itself the capital of the Far Eastern Republic and appealed to the Bolsheviks for military assistance. Lenin sent in the Red army, which never left the town. Two years later the Republic was dissolved and incorporated into the Soviet Union.

After deplaning at dusk, the Japanese party was led to a prisoner-of-war camp. P'u Yi never saw Yoshioka again. Clutching his attaché case, he and the members of his group were marched off to a waiting Russian convoy. In the dark, the convoy rolled out of Chita and headed across the Siberian wasteland. His Russian army escorts were grim and spoke not a word to him. Their silence unnerved him. After an hour of driving, he was terrified. As the convoy approached a wood, the line of vehicles suddenly halted and the incident described in the prologue took place. Petrified, P'u Yi expected to be ordered from the limousine, stood up against a tree and shot. When a Russian officer, holding a machine gun, ordered him out and pointed to a tree, P'u Yi froze. But when it developed that the Russians thought this was simply a good spot to relieve themselves, he alighted, stood up against a tree, and urinated. Relieved, both mentally and physically, the emperor resumed his journey. For P'u Yi, it was a journey to nowhere.

Another hour slipped by. They entered a mountain gorge and drew up before a large, handsome building which had the outward appearance of an oversized hunting lodge. The officer leading the party pointed to the structure and said, "Hotel." Suddenly, P'u Yi's spirits soared, the color returned to his face, the tenseness evaporated. He smiled for the first time since his capture. At the lodge he was met by a group of Red army officers, including the general in command of the Chita *oblast*, and a Soviet civilian, a member of the NKVD, the People's Commissariat of Internal Affairs, the dreaded secret police. The police agent addressed himself to the last emperor of China. "You will be detained here in the name of the Union of Soviet Socialist Republics," he said, "until your case is decided." His words were ominous, but his tone friendly.

In Manchuria, meanwhile, the war rolled on. Having been the first battlefield of World War II, Manchuria was also the last. On August 20 Soviet armies, driving toward each other from different directions, linked up at Harbin and drove south to occupy Mukden. Two days later Port Arthur and Dairen were overrun. That same day, with the campaign at an end, Radio Moscow announced for the first time that P'u Yi had been taken prisoner. He is interned in "a safe place," the announcement reported. The location was not identified.

Had the name of the place been disclosed, it probably would have been met with disbelief. P'u Yi's lodge was a sanatorium known for its mineral springs and was frequented as a health resort by prominent Red army officers and high Communist Party functionaries. P'u Yi was provided a private room with a panoramic view. No effort was made to divest him of his attaché case. Big Li continued to wait on him. He was also provided with a hastily organized, poorly tailored wardrobe; at the time of his capture, he was attired in slacks, a soft weave jacket and white sport shirt.

His table was superior, although he had to acquire a taste for some of the dishes. Meals were served three times daily with a Russian tea in the late afternoon; the tea was accompanied by *zakuski*, alternating hot and cold hors d'oeuvres. The regular menu ranged from *staschi* (cabbage soup) to *sosiski* (sausage) to Siberian *pelemeni* (savory dumplings), which reminded him of Chinese *chiao tzu*. The caviar, fresh from the Caspian, was plentiful, as was the vodka, although P'u Yi was little more than a social drinker. His only complaint was that the water tasted queerly but after a few months he developed a fondness for mineral water.

The Russians—medical staff, patients, and guards—showed him every consideration. Addressed as "your excellency," accompanied by an armed guard, he took frequent walks in the countryside.

A Red army colonel, a military interrogator by the name of Rudziavtsev, was assigned to him as a Chinese-Russian interpreter. The library was well stocked, in Russian, of course, but he had no interest in reading, not even in looking at pictures. Provided with a radio, he had no interest in music. He was overtaken by lassitude and disinterest, and at the same time by a vague sense of satisfaction and relief. The king's pawn had been captured and put aside.

For him, not only was the war over, but all those wild dreams of restoration, of gazing once again on the Forbidden City. So too were the fleeting thoughts of flight abroad alternating with the compulsion to seek revenge and placate the perturbed spirits of his ancestors. The mental kaleidoscope which had kept him awake night after night had given way to a strange sensation, peace of mind.

Removed from the polluted palace atmosphere of Hsinking, released from the nightmare that was the Kwantung army and Manchukuo, freed from the burdens of office, real and perceived, he suddenly found himself relaxed, at ease with the world. The worst had come, he had lost everything, and yet he had survived, almost miraculously. In the last years of his counterfeit monarchy, he had verged on a nervous breakdown. Now his detention at the Siberian lodge proved to be fortunate for him. Here he regained his composure and self-assurance. His Russian confinement, as it developed, was just what the doctor ordered.

In autumn, he began to receive regularly a Chinese-language newspaper, *Shih Hua Pao*. The paper was published daily by the Red army at Lüshun, a minor port near Dairen, which the Russians now called by its Czarist name, Dalny. Judging by the paper, the Russians had replaced the Japanese in Manchuria. And judging by its contents, the Chinese were at it again—locked in civil war, in a terminal struggle for control of Manchuria. But just as he shunned books and music, he found himself, the innate political animal, disinterested in politics, almost apolitical. "I took no interest in the war as I felt it made no difference to me who won—the Communists and Nationalists both wanted my head," he later wrote. His only desire was never to return to China.

Occasionally, however, he received intimidating news. One day an NKVD officer casually remarked, "Remember Semenov?" How could P'u Yi forget the Cossack terrorist who was later deported from America as a mass murderer and whom he, P'u Yi, had enlisted in Tientsin to raise a private army for him in the Manchurian border regions. "Well," the officer continued, "he was taken prisoner and sent to Moscow." P'u Yi nodded, his face a blank. "Thought you'd like to know," the NKVD man said. "I just learned he was hanged." And on April 30, 1946, in *Shih Hua Pao*, he read that many of his former Japanese associates—Tojo, for example, Doihara, and Itagaki—had been indicted as class A war criminals and were to be tried by a military tribunal for "crimes against peace, conventional war crimes, and crimes against humanity." Among the charges against them and eleven others out of the twenty-nine indicted was the charge of murder in connection with the planning and execution of Manchukuo's undeclared war against the Soviet Union in 1938–1939, a war over which he had presided as the Emperor K'ang Teh.

Suddenly, the Chita idyll was interrupted. In the spring of 1946, he was informed that he was about to be flown to Japan. For a moment, he thought that perhaps the Americans had arranged a barter for him. But this made no sense. What would the Americans want with him? Then he was told he would be flown to Tokyo to testify as a witness for the prosecution at the International Military Tribunal for the Far East, Nuremberg's opposite number, the so-called Tojo Trial. P'u Yi greeted the news with a mixture of relief and anxiety, relief that he would go to Tokyo as a witness, not as a defendant, and anxiety that his appearance before the tribunal would thrust him back into the limelight, into the great power arena. The Chinese, then, might demand his extradition to stand trial as a wartime collaborator; indeed, he was surprised that they had not done so already. Once again he had the sinking feeling that he could not escape history, not even as a prisoner of war, that—against the rules of the game—the pawn was being returned to the chess board.

But, then, he should have realized that in the great game in which he had been involved throughout his life there were no rules.

Shortly thereafter, he was flown to a fashionable villa outside Khabarovsk, or Poli, as the Chinese call the Russian town built along the right bank of the Amur River, just below the confluence of the Ussuri. Dominated by a dilapidated Russian Orthodox church, its tulip-bulb dome out of place in the landscape, Khabarovsk itself was like any cosmopolitan Manchurian city—Mukden, Harbin, or Port Arthur—inhabited by Russians, Koreans and Chinese with a dash of Manchu, Mongols, and other border peoples.

At the villa, he was treated with continued deference. The villa itself was well appointed; in one respect, it reminded him of the sanatorium that he had just left. The portrait of his benefactor Stalin smiled pleasantly down from a wall in each room. He often thought about Stalin. How could he avoid doing so under those circumstances? There was something unreal, even bizarre, about the hospitality he was receiving from his host. Stalin had entertained literally millions of house guests in Siberia. Few had survived. Why, then, should the greatest mass murderer of the twentieth century treat him with such courtesy? Clearly, he was not being treated as an ordinary prisoner or as a political prisoner or a war prisoner. He was being accorded the respect due to a head of state. So unique a prisoner would not be treated in such fashion without the benefactor's knowledge, and approval. But why? So that he would testify as a friendly witness at Tokyo? This was ludicrous. He would gladly testify against the Japanese. There had to be a deeper reason. But P'u Yi had no way of finding out what it was.

CHAPTER 24

MacArthur's Custody

In the company of an NKVD detail, on August 9, 1946, P'u Yi flew into Tokyo's Atsugi Airport. For the occasion he wore a dark, poorly cut, ill-fitting double-breasted blue serge suit, baggy in the cuffs in the Russian manner, and a black Russian workingman's cap, the kind popularized by Lenin in the 1920s. Exhibiting the familiar black-rimmed spectacles—his trademark—he stepped, with a bounce and wide grin, from an American lend-lease, Soviet-marked Catalina flying boat, as though he were a tourist on holiday. Clearly, during the past year the great burden of guilt which had driven him to the edge of nervous collapse as the emperor of Manchukuo had been lifted. His confinement as Stalin's "house guest," astonishingly, had had therapeutic value, and some of the old assurance, confidence and authority revived within him.

As soon as he and his armed escorts, several in uniform and several in mufti, disembarked, he passed through the formality of being screened by members of the United States Army Counter-intelligence Corps. Although the Russian prosecutor had arranged for P'u Yi's appearance at the trial, it was on condition that upon completion of his testimony, he would be returned to Soviet authorities and flown back to Russia. Even so, the moment P'u Yi placed his foot on Japanese soil, he came under the jurisdiction of SCAP (Supreme Commander for the Allied Powers). Legally, once he stepped from the aircraft, he was in General Douglas MacArthur's custody.

But he was unwanted by SCAP; indeed, he was an embarrassment. To ensure the smooth functioning of the occupation and to speed Japan's postwar recovery, MacArthur had vigorously resisted Stalin's demand that Hirohito be indicted as a war criminal. Stalin was anxious to try Hirohito for political reasons, with a view to creating instability within Japan, the kind of social turmoil the surfacing Japanese Communists could exploit. For emotional rather than political reasons, the British Commonwealth countries also pressed for the emperor's indictment. In the last resort, they held Hirohito responsible, as legal head of state during the war years, for the Japanese army's barbaric treatment of the Commonwealth's war prisoners and civilians in the Japanese-occupied territories of Burma, Hong Kong, Singapore, Brunei, Malaya, and other British possessions. In his memoirs, MacArthur freely admitted that he had "stoutly resisted" these demands. And Solis Horowitz, a member of the prosecuting team who had studied Japanese during the war at the United States Army's Military Intelligence Service School, observed in a postmortem of the Tokyo trial, "A study of the governmental machinery from both the point of view of theory and of operation showed the emperor's role to be that of a figurehead"— in sum, Hirohito was another P'u Yi.

Nonetheless, MacArthur's command feared that P'u Yi's presence in the witness box would incite new demands for Hirohito's indictment. If not his indictment, then at least his calling as a witness like P'u Yi.

Although the Russians had instructed P'u Yi as early as June to prepare for the trip to Tokyo, the non-Russian members of the tribunal's international prosecution section were, as an American attorney expressed it, "unable to get a line on him" when they announced their intention to subpoena him. Among the prosecutors, of course, there was general recognition of the fact that World War II, in part, had its origins in the Mukden Incident and that P'u Yi was a central figure in that event. As late as July 27, 1946, the chief of the Russian counsel, Associate Prosecutor S. A. Golunsky, whom I interviewed at the time, claimed that he possessed no information on P'u Yi, not even his whereabouts. The denial was widely published in a United Press dispatch. Golunsky, who possessed a credibly good command of English, had received the degree of doctor of law in Moscow in 1938, in the midst of the great Stalin purge during which, according to Roy A. Medvedev, the dissident Soviet historian, Stalin was executing in one day as many people as the Czarist secret police did in one year.

Golunsky's denial may have been prompted by security reasons; for, two weeks later, P'u Yi landed in Tokyo and ten days after that, on August 16, accompanied by his NKVD security detail, he entered the witness box at the Tojo Trial. For all practical purposes, this was P'u Yi's international debut.

Only minutes by jeep from Hirohito's palace, the tribunal was located in the former War Ministry building from whose subterranean chambers the Japanese high command had directed the war. The cavernous courtroom was furnished in brown—the walls creamy brown with dark brown molding, the chairs some deep brown and some a light brown, that was almost the color of the uniforms of the generals in the dock. Eight square boxes, suspended from the ceiling, each containing a battery of four klieg lights, illuminated the scene below. In an age before television, each moment of the two-and-a-half-year-long trial was recorded by a cluster of United States Army motion picture cameras, an imperishable celluloid record of the proceedings, actions and behavior of the defendants, witnesses and court, complete with soundtrack. The president of the tribunal, Australia's Sir William Webb, who had investigated Japanese army atrocities in New Guinea as Australia's war crime commissioner, was flanked by judges representing the other victor powers: the Philippines, New Zealand, France, the

Soviet Union, China, the United States, Great Britain, Canada, The Netherlands, and India. Of these judges, attired in black robes or military uniforms, one represented a colony (India) and four others represented Asian colonial powers (Britain, Soviet Russia, France, and The Netherlands, the latter two already engaged in colonial wars in Vietnam and Indonesia).

Closely guarded by manicured American military police whose white helmets shone under the arc lights, twenty-six of the original defendants were still in the dock (two had died natural deaths and one was found mentally-unfit to stand trial). The spectators, almost exclusively Japanese, with a smattering of GIs, crowded the public gallery in the balcony. Beneath the gallery, at armchair desks, sat the press (including this author), like a group of Chinese scribes. Each seat in the tribunal was equipped with a headset and a panel of switches for the simultaneous translation of the proceedings into Japanese, Chinese, English, and Russian, a system not unlike that currently employed at the United Nations. To the right of the defendants, sat the translators enclosed in glass like a collection of exotic butterflies.

When the forty-year-old former Celestial Emperor entered the courtroom, all eyes turned in his direction. The face was instantly recognizable with an assist from postage stamps, Sunday supplements, and the newsreels: vacuous, expressionless, the inevitable horn-rimmed glasses obscuring the high cheekbones. In real life, standing free, he seemed slightly heavier than he appeared from his photographs, perhaps as a result of his Russian diet, and much taller, about five feet ten inches. Like a stage manager, giving the scene just the right touch, he held a white ivory fan in his right hand. Like New York, Tokyo in August is hot and humid, at times stifling.

Of all the witnesses during the trial, none possessed so special a relationship to the defendants and none could, unless Hirohito himself were to be placed in the box. P'u Yi had been associated, in one way or another, with twenty-two of the twenty-nine original defendants. Doihara, Itagaki, Minami, and Tojo, all of whom have been mentioned earlier, were there. So were General Yoshiro

Umezu, the former Kwantung army commander and ambassador to P'u Yi's Manchukuo court; General Shunroku Hata, war minister when P'u Yi visited Hirohito in 1940; Koki Hirota, the former premier who negotiated Japan's alliance with Hitler and whom P'u Yi awarded in 1938 the First Order of the Chrysanthemum; General Heitaro Kimura, who directed the Manchurian Land Development Corporation and later commanded the Japanese army in Burma; General Kuniaki Koiso, the former Kwantung army chief of staff, a racist who succeeded Tojo as premier; Okinori Kaya, the former counselor of the Manchurian Affairs Bureau to whom P'u Yi had awarded the First Order of Merit with the Pillar of the State; General Sadao Araki, army minister at the time P'u Yi was installed as Chief Executive of Manchukuo; Naoki Hoshino, the man who ran Manchukuo's finances as chief of the General Affairs Office and later served in Tojo's cabinet; Shigenori Togo, Japan's ambassador to Hitler and Stalin, whose career started in Japan's Mukden consulate; General Kenryo Sato, war minister who was secretary of the Manchurian Affairs Bureau at the time of Pearl Harbor; General Akira Muto, a Kwantung army staff officer who later commanded Japanese forces in the Dutch East Indies (Indonesia) and the Philippines; Takasumi Oka, secretary of the Manchurian Affairs Bureau; Mamoru Shigemitsu, diplomatic troubleshooter who had gone on special cabinet missions to Manchukuo in 1936 and 1942, and signed the Japanese instrument of surrender aboard the U.S.S. *Missouri* in Tokyo Bay in 1945.

From the dock, the defendants followed each of P'u Yi's steps as he approached the witness box. They watched with anticipation; Itagaki's face was wreathed in smiles, as though welcoming an old friend to the party. The judges, prosecution and defense staffs, the Japanese and Allied press, the pages and the spectators, all followed the light footfalls of the last emperor of China. Only the trained American military police, unmoved, stared rigidly ahead.

For a few seconds, though it seemed much longer, the tribunal was transfixed, ensnared by history. Abruptly, Sir William Webb brought the court back to reality.

President of the Tribunal: Mr. Chief Prosecutor.
Chief Prosecutor: We call as the next witness, Henry P'u Yi.
Marshal of the Court: Mr. President, the witness is in the court and
will now be sworn.

For the next eleven days, P'u Yi was the center of the world, the focus for which he was destined from the moment he entered the Forbidden City. He alternately dazzled and infuriated the tribunal with a pyrotechnical display of cunning, guile, and downright deceit. His performance belied the caricature, disseminated by the pop-news weeklies, that behind the empty face was an empty head. In the jargon of the boxing world, P'u Yi floated like a butterfly and stung like a bee. His performance was all the more impressive since the ring was a sandbox which provided no footing.

He was also, in the words of the tribunal's president, "a most unusual witness." From the outset, it was clear that he was on trial. He entered the courtroom as the prisoner of one nation sitting in judgment, the Soviet Union, and formally branded a traitor by another, China. The chief counsel for the prosecution, Joseph B. Keenan, a political crony of Franklin D. Roosevelt and a former member of the Justice Department, openly conceded that the witness was "brought into court under somewhat unusual conditions."

Clearly, his presence was controversial. Since 1931 he had willingly or unwillingly allied himself to Japan, served as Manchukuo's head of state during the undeclared war with the Soviet Union, and exhorted the Manchurians to support Japan's "holy war" against China. For the record, however, the president of the tribunal repeatedly observed that the witness was not a defendant. When the defense, during cross-examination, insisted that P'u Yi was a willing puppet, Sir William Webb admonished: "It is beside the question of whether he was a willing or unwilling puppet." Then he added: "We are not trying the witness." But it was clear to everyone that P'u Yi was testifying with threat of his own indictment himself as a war criminal hanging over him.

271

In this peculiar situation, P'u Yi adopted his familiar strategy of "retreat by advancing." As many in the courtroom strained to listen to his natural voice with one ear, while turning up the volume on their headsets for translations coming into the other ear, he softly recounted how Itagaki pressed him to collaborate with Japan in Manchuria and that his "desire then was to refuse" but that he had no option. "If I refused," P'u Yi said, "my life was threatened." Then he turned to the judges. "At that time the democratic nations were not trying to resist the Japanese militarists," he said icily. "I alone as an individual was hardly able to resist them."

But didn't he ever ask the Japanese to make him an emperor? No, he lied. Didn't he believe that he had a heavenly mission to retain the Forbidden City? No, he lied again. Over and over again, he stressed that all his acts since 1931 were committed under duress. With a measure of truth, he said, "I was not a free man." He then went into detail about how he was forced to convert to Shintoism, describing it as "the worst humiliation that I have ever faced."

Unlike Hirohito, who was prepared at the end of the war to bear sole responsibility for every military and political decision of his people, and told MacArthur so at their initial meeting, the last Manchu emperor, as decadent as the court which reared him, not only shunned responsibility but also betrayed his advisers and blamed them for his own behavior. He also, of course, blamed the Japanese, whose protection he had sought first in Peking, then in Tientsin.

Always it was others who were responsible for his actions. "My desire then was to refuse them but under the 'threat' of military force and the advice of my advisers, I had to accept to save my own life," he repeated.

As for the revival of the Great Ch'ing Dynasty, he disclaimed "any intention of a restoration." This, too, was the hope of his counselors, who possessed "old minds" and were accustomed to "working under former monarchs." "Whatever they thought cannot be considered as representative of my point of view," he said. "Their ideas were very different from mine."

What about Johnston? Didn't he write that P'u Yi planned a dynastic restoration? "Ridiculous," P'u Yi said. The Japanese "compelled" him to go to Manchuria. As for Johnston, he sloughed him off. "Johnston wrote this book with a commercial end in view," he said. "He wanted to sell his book for money. I should not be held responsible for what Johnston wrote."

Thus, out of cowardice, out of a distorted view of his own value as the sole survivor of a great dynasty, he betrayed everyone around him.

The flinty president of the tribunal grew exasperated. "I hate to make this observation," Sir William Webb said, going on to make it. "We are not trying the witness, of course, but we are concerned about his credit. Now, danger to life, fear of death, does not excuse cowardice or desertion on the battlefield; neither does it excuse treason anywhere. All morning we have been listening to excuses by this man as to why he collaborated with the Japanese. I think we have heard enough."

But P'u Yi was only warming up for the testimony to come. Unctuously, he adopted a pro-Russian and pro-Chinese posture. The Soviet Union never entertained aggressive designs on Manchuria, only Japan. He himself was a Chinese "patriot" who secretly, unilaterally played a double game. He accepted a central role in Manchuria only in the hope of maintaining a Chinese presence in the region until Japan was defeated and driven out covertly. Thus, he claimed a hand in the Allied victory. "We have succeeded in dragging along the situation until the Japanese surrender," he said, adding, "Manchuria is part and parcel of Chinese territory and the Manchurian people are a part of the Chinese people"—a position espoused by all Chinese to this day, from Taipei to Peking, and, admittedly, a position which required an undercoat of courage on the part of a Soviet prisoner in view of Stalin's postwar presence in Manchuria.

In his new-found role of Chinese patriot, he described Sun Yat-sen, the man who more than any other was instrumental in bringing down the Great Ch'ing Dynasty, as a "great man," told of his love for the republic, and concocted a story about Jade Years, his third wife and number two consort. "My wife, my late wife," he repeated softly, "was deeply in love with me. She was twenty-three years of age when she contracted a kind of disease. At the time she was a very patriotic Chinese. She always comforted me by saying that I had to be patient for a time, then we can retaliate [against the Japanese] in the future."

Then he threw the tribunal into an uproar with the accusation that after brief treatment by a Japanese physician she was poisoned. Who poisoned her? "It was General Yoshioka," P'u Yi said. "A month later General Yoshioka proposed to me that I should marry a Japanese girl, and he showed me a number of pictures of Japanese girls. At that time I was in a dilemma. On the surface I could not refuse. So I told him that if you want me to marry I can only marry a girl whom I really love. . . . Later on I married a young Chinese [sic] girl."

The young Manchu girl was the fourteen-year-old Jade Lute. Hastily, he explained that he selected her because "being young, she could be educated in the way I liked and not be assimilated or educated in the Japanese way."

Elizabeth's name—the name of Wan Jung—never arose in the testimony.

As he testified, day after day, one week into the next, the familiar names of the men in the dock cropped up. Throughout his testimony, Doihara, "the master murderer," stared into space; Umezu looked askance; Muto, thoughtful; Minami, annoyed; and Hoshino, upset. Itagaki, alone, seemed to enjoy the spectacle.

Under intense cross-examination, the defense tore into P'u Yi's credibility. Major Ben Bruce Blakeney, one of the few American defense attorneys who spoke fluent Japanese, a man who had spent the war as chief of the Japanese section of the Prisoner of War Intelligence Division of the United States Air Force, was disparaging. "We have here a witness who willingly testified that in the past on numerous occasions, under threat of force, he has distorted the truth," he said. "I intend to impeach him."

The defense battered him, but the result was like a wave breaking against a rock jetty. "When you walked into this tribunal for the first time were two Soviet guards with you?" the defense asked. The prosecution objected to the question and Sir William sustained the objection. "Do the Chinese plan to try you as a war criminal?" The prosecution objected, and again Sir William sustained them.

The main line of the defense's assault was generated by P'u Yi's earlier assertion that he had one regret. "I regret that I didn't tell Lord Lytton and his commission the whole truth," he said, adding, as he slipped unconsciously into the royal first person plural, "if we had told Lord Lytton and his commission the truth then, we would have been killed long ago." This statement threw into question all his testimony, as it did his autobiography eighteen years later in which he also claimed that he deliberately lied to Lord Lytton because Itagaki was present at their interview.

At this point it is noteworthy that in his three-volume autobiography, written under Communist surveillance in Peking, he devoted only four paragraphs to his role at the Tojo Trial, although this was one of the highlights of his career. Manifestly, an analysis of his testimony at Tokyo showed that from the Lord Lytton interview onward, P'u Yi was never free to disclose his true thoughts: He was always a prisoner, in the custody of either Japanese, Russians, Americans, or Chinese.

P'u Yi's situation at the International Military Tribunal for the Far East was therefore not unlike the position in which he found himself with the Lytton Commission eighteen years earlier. On the tribunal sat Stalin's judge, Major General I. M. Zaryanov, at his right a Chinese justice, Mei Ju-ao, the representative of Chiang Kai-shek's government. On the international prosecution staff were Golunsky and Justice Hsiang Chi-chung, the chief prosecutor of the Shanghai High Court, who had formerly served as prosecutor of the Supreme Court of China. At the door were two Soviet armed guards. The building itself was covered by American security patrols. What could P'u Yi be expected to testify to under these circumstances?

Yet P'u Yi handled himself so deftly that within a few days he had the tribunal in turmoil.

At first, like a spring bather putting a toe into the water before wading in, P'u Yi was contrite and recondite. He portrayed himself circumspectly with humility. Gradually, the power and authority instilled into him in childhood gave rise to confidence and, stunningly, P'u Yi took charge of the tribunal and turned the show into his day in court. Once again the representatives of the barbarian and semibarbarian nations beyond the borders of the Middle Kingdom listened attentively to the voice of the Celestial Emperor.

He dominated the court. "I have not completed my answer to your previous question yet," he frequently said when interrupted in the course of a soliloquy. "You don't have to ask me all these questions," he barked on one occasion. And on another, he shouted: "I don't think it advisable to waste any more time on this." Still later, in reference to some notes he was asked to produce, he replied after the noontime recess, "During the lunch hour I was rather busy; I didn't have enough time to locate them." This was brazen. Each day, during the lunch recess he was confined to the "birdcage," as the room for prisoner-witnesses was called because of the chicken wire nailed across the windows. Except on one occasion when, through the connivance of his American guards and with the permission of his NKVD detail, he was interviewed by United Press, the only interview he gave during his Japan sojourn, he spent the noontime recess idly waiting to resume his testimony. After each day's session, he was driven under guard to the Soviet embassy whose spacious grounds were surrounded by a high wall and were patrolled by regular Red army soldiers. Within the Russian compound, he was held incommunicado.

The questions directed to him during the trial were often pointed: Do you believe that you have a heavenly mission to regain the Forbidden City? Did you ever ask the Japanese to help you restore the throne? Did you leave Tientsin for Manchuria voluntarily? Did you enter into a secret written agreement with the Kwantung army before you ascended a Manchukuo throne? On December 8, 1941 (Pearl Harbor, Pacific Time), did you issue an imperial rescript declaring full support for Japan? Did you discuss with the Russians the testimony you have given this tribunal? Has your only concern over the years been to save your own life?

His vague answers and imperious behavior annoyed the Japanese defense. "The witness has taken over counsel and the answer he is giving now is not responsive to the question which was asked," a defense attorney remarked at one juncture. On another occasion, the defense angrily charged, "It is obvious that the witness does not wish to answer any question at all."

Judging from the manner in which he replied under cross-examination, it appeared that P'u Yi often understood a question in English before it was translated into Chinese, a distinct advantage for a prosecution witness who might one day find himself in the dock. "By the way," a defense attorney casually asked, "do you speak English . . . Mr. P'u Yi?"

"Some of [the questions] I understand," he replied evenly, "and some, not."

Deviously, he often replied to a question above the head of the tribunal. To talk continually about his plans for a restoration of the monarchy in Manchuria, he said, "sounds queer to me." The reason? "There was never any monarchy *restored*," he pointed out. Technically, he was correct. The old Manchu Dynasty was never restored; when he was installed as the Emperor K'ang Teh, he established a new monarchy.

For days P'u Yi and the defense squabbled over written documents, the secret agreement he signed with the Kwantung army *before* his investiture as Manchukuo head of government, for example, and other hard evidence of his complicity with the Japanese. Like Dickens's artful dodger, he skirted responsibility for private papers bearing his seal, the "chop" of the emperor of China, Hsüan Tung, and even more for those bearing the seal of the emperor of Manchukuo, K'ang Teh.

277

In one instance, the defense produced a letter P'u Yi sent Itagaki in 1931 in which he indicated a willingness to accept a Manchurian throne under Japanese patronage. "Was this letter written by you or under your direction, bearing your seal as the Emperor Hsüan Tung?" he was asked. P'u Yi glanced at the paper and suddenly jumped to his feet. The tribunal's military police intuitively flexed their muscles, as did the Soviet security guard. Sir William ordered from the bench: "Keep your seat!"

In a rising voice, P'u Yi confronted the defense. "They should be found guilty of counterfeiting this document!" he cried out.

Toward the conclusion of the cross-examination, an exasperated defense attorney told the tribunal, "I should like to direct the attention of the tribunal that, from the beginning of this witness's testimony until the conclusion at the present time, concerning discussion of his notes and memoranda, he has palpably and willfully lied to the tribunal."

P'u Yi answered these assaults by the defense with his own attack. "I don't blame you, being counsel for the defense," he said, imperiously. "Of course, you would like me to distort the truth. . . . But facts are facts."

The daily cross-examination, intended to wear down the witness, instead wore down the judges, translators, prosecution and defense. At times members of the tribunal squabbled with each other, largely over what the witness did or did not say as relayed by the translators, the subtlety of P'u Yi's Chinese presenting the translation section with a formidable problem. P'u Yi rarely replied to a question with a simple "yes" or "no," even when instructed to do so.

Harassed, the language arbiter, Major Moore, a United States Army linguist, protested on one occasion directly to Sir William. "Mr. President," he said, "since my qualifications have been called into question, I hope the tribunal will indulge me in saying that I have had thirty years of experience in Oriental question and answer, and it is an established fact that an Oriental, when pressed, will dodge the issue."

Sir William was aghast at the racial implications of the remark. "Well, now, Major Moore, you have said a thing which you should not have said," the president of the tribunal said sternly. "It is quite beyond your province to comment on the nature of evidence given by Orientals, and I ask you to withdraw that comment."

Visibly strained, Moore apologized. "I was pressed," he replied.

The Chinese prosecutors were outraged. "I think it is quite a gratuitous charge against Oriental people," Judge Hsiang shouted. And Keenan, a grass roots American politician, decried "the notion that Orientals have the invariable habit of dodging the issue."

"I think, I can safely say on behalf of every member of the court," Sir William Webb said in an effort to close the matter, "that we do not share Major Moore's view." But the Japanese defense got in the last word. "As an Oriental, Mr. President," Dr. T. Okamoto said, "I appreciate your remarks."

Throughout this byplay, P'u Yi sat motionless in the box with an expression on his face of cool innocence, if not wry amusement. And this was the hapless figure commonly portrayed by journalists and historians of the period as the marionette of marionettes, physically and mentally deficient.

In the wake of his appearance before the tribunal, the welter of confused testimony was such that when the Japanese historian Sadako Ogata undertook to write a definitive work on the Mukden Incident a decade ago, from a Japanese perspective, she concluded, "The degree of his willingness to assume the leading role [in Manchukuo] remains unclarified."

On August 27, eleven days after P'u Yi first took the stand, Sir William Webb terminated the cross-examination.

"The witness has taken up a certain stand that he was wholly under the direction of the Japanese," Sir William said. "It is a simple stand. No amount of cross-examination is going to dislodge him from it. That is obvious. If we terminate cross-examination, it does not necessarily follow that it will be because we believe the witness. We may have open minds about that. It will be because we think further cross-examination is utterly useless. And we do not question the ability of the cross-examiners. That has nothing to do with it."

The defense requested that "this witness be held in Tokyo." At a later stage, they planned to introduce handwriting experts and recall P'u Yi to the stand. But Sir William cut them short. "We see no reason whatever why this man should be kept in Tokyo," the president of the tribunal said. P'u Yi was remanded to the custody of the Soviet authorities and flown back to Vladivostok. If the tribunal was relieved to see him depart, so was MacArthur. The SCAP, who sent his bombers aloft against P'u Yi's Manchukuo, made no request of the Russians to detain him for wartime collaboration, although MacArthur was empowered to do so. The initial American policy issued September 22, 1945, twenty days after Japan's formal surrender, held that persons charged with being war criminals should be arrested, tried and, if convicted, punished. "Those wanted by another of the United Nations for offences against its nationals," the policy declaration added, "if not wanted for trial or as witnesses or otherwise by the Supreme Commander, shall be turned over to the custody of such other nations." Clearly, the United States did not want to retain him for trial or as a witness. Legally, he was already in Allied custody—Soviet captivity. Privately, the Americans advised the Chinese to raise the matter of his extradition to China through their Moscow embassy, if they were interested in bringing him to trial in China. The Americans were simply not going to become involved in the ultimate fate of the last Chinese emperor.

In retrospect, as I look back on the testimony which I listened to daily throughout P'u Yi's appearance in the box, as I heard the Celestial Emperor parrying the questions of his interrogators, ever mindful of his own personal safety and aware that the Russians and Chinese were not yet done with him, four of his statements stand out from among the hundreds he made—from the flotsam and jetsam littering the sea across which he was swept by the tides of history. They were:

> Now that I have failed and all my dreams have not been realized, I am most regretful.

In the past ten years or more the suffering I have experienced and the oppression imposed on me are beyond ordinary people's imagination.

To me, the word "freedom" has lost its meaning.

I can do nothing but weep.

These simple truths sum up the life and times of the last Manchu emperor. Any one of them would serve as his epitaph. But his epitaph would not be written for another twenty-one years, almost another generation.

CHAPTER 25

With Love to Mao

In the first months of P'u Yi's Russian internment, Manchuria was caught up in a reign of lawlessness which surpassed that of the Chang Tso-lin and Japanese periods. The Red army stripped the countryside like locusts in a millet field, plundering the region of $2 billion worth of goods, from heavy industrial equipment down to P'u Yi's collection of mechanical toys. Machines which could not be dismantled and removed were cannibalized for spare parts, or smashed. With plunder rode other horsemen, rape and murder. Women were unsafe on the streets of Mukden and Harbin. Behind locked doors, people lived in terror. Longing for liberation from Japanese rule, the Manchurians discovered, as Robert P. Martin, a *New York Post* correspondent reported from Mukden on March 4, 1946, that "six months of Russian occupation has been worse than fourteen years of Jap [sic] occupation." A Chinese, for example, who had the courage to talk to Martin and other Western correspondents after he had been twice warned by the Russians not to see them was shot dead in the street in broad daylight.

In May, as the Soviet army withdrew, President Truman dispatched a mission to Manchuria, headed by Edwin W. Pauley, to "prove or disprove" the stories emanating from the country. In Mukden, Pauley's mission found the situation "appalling." The Red army had systematically confiscated food and other stockpiles. It had dismantled machinery and equipment, power generators, electric motors, transformers, laboratories, and even hospitals. In the process, buildings were damaged, mines flooded. "After the removals," Pauley reported, "the Soviet forces permitted and even encouraged Chinese mobs to pillage, taking official movies in some instances." Coal production was reduced to a trickle and the people passed a bitter winter huddled around *kangs* whose heat could not be maintained. Pauley accused the Russians of promoting "chaos" and of reducing "the populace to hunger, cold and unrest."

The Russians did not deny that they had plundered Manchuria but they claimed the region's industrial assets as "war booty." Major General Andrei Kovtou-Stankevitch, the Red army's Mukden commander, held that his troops expropriated the equipment in accordance with a Big Three agreement reached "either at Yalta or Berlin—I'm not sure off-hand." Both London and Washington denounced his claim as an outright fabrication.

Stalin's claim to "war booty" was only part of the story. Early in 1946, in an *aide-mémoire* to Chiang Kai-shek, the Russians not only claimed all Japanese enterprises of the former state of Manchukuo as booty but also proposed that remaining enterprises— coal mines, power plants, steel mills, chemical industries, cement factories—"be jointly operated by China and the Soviet Union." The Nationalists were livid. "China has found it impossible to agree to this Soviet proposal," Chiang Kai-shek replied.

Yet stripping Manchuria was only a facet of Russian policy. The Russians also blocked Manchuria's seaports and railroads to the entry of Nationalist troops while providing the local Chinese Communist forces with access to Japanese arsenals. In short, under Field Marshal Lin Piao, who had trained in Moscow, the Chinese

Communists swarmed across Manchuria and established the spring-board from which they later marched south, in the historic pattern, to conquer all of China.

Lin was joined in the northeastern provinces by Li Li-san, a rival of Mao who had broken with him and fled to the Soviet Union in 1930 and who now turned up as political adviser to a self-styled Manchurian "autonomous local government." Stalin had cultivated Li Li-san in his political hothouse for fifteen years, awaiting the opportunity to bring him into play. Since neither Lin Piao nor Li Li-san were then members of the Politburo of Mao's Chinese Communist Party, their presence in Manchuria, together with that of the Red army, gave rise to the suspicion that Stalin sought to promote the creation of a Communist government in Manchuria free of Mao's control. This was the tentative conclusion of many prominent observers of Chinese affairs, including John K. Fairbank. Others felt that since China had been forced to recognize the Mongolian People's Republic, Mongolia might assert a sphere of influence in Manchuria since western Manchuria had almost as many Mongols as Mongolia itself and old maps showed that Mongolia once extended eastward nearly as far as Harbin. More-over, unlike the Manchu who were largely culturally assimilated by the Chinese, the Mongol tribes continued to retain their own language and cultural traditions. Oxford's F. D. Jones belonged to this school of thought. "It would suit the Soviet Union's interests," he wrote, "if northern Manchuria became independent of China since such a development would, in view of the . . . Mongolian People's Republic in Outer Mongolia, complete a belt of buffer states between the east Siberian possessions of the Soviet Union and China."

Thus, Stalin pursued a three-ply policy in Manchuria. First, he sought to destroy Manchuria's industrial-military complex. Second, he sought to delay the Chinese Nationalist reoccupation of the territory, pending a Chinese Communist takeover, and, third, as a hedge against the outcome of the Chinese civil war, he sought to encourage creation of a satellite Communist Manchuria independent of Mao. Stalin's strategy therefore is crucial to an understanding of why the Kremlin, in striking contrast to its barbaric behavior inside Manchuria, treated P'u Yi with courtesy and civility.

Stalin's behavior was explicable because, like Lenin and the Czars before him, he implemented a basic policy of ringing Russia's Chinese frontier with buffer states, a series of "Manchukuos." The Czarist policy was crude and obvious, dictated at gunpoint; Lenin's policy, subtle and sophisticated; and Stalin's, a blend of both. Thus, for example, in his touted 1919 declaration in which Moscow renounced the treaties and special privileges of the Czars in China, Lenin included a significant qualification with reference to Manchuria. "The Soviet government renounces the conquests made by Czarist governments which deprived China of Manchuria and other areas," the declaration said. "Let the people living in those areas themselves decide within the frontier of which state they wish to dwell, and what form they wish to establish in their own *countries*" (author's italics). In a fair plebiscite, the border peoples—Manchu, Mongols, and others—would probably opt for independence and thereby emerge as buffers between Moscow and Peking. In an unfair plebiscite, the buffers would be annexed or reduced to satellite status. Stalin's blend of Czarist and Leninist policies was manifest in the treaty he forced China to sign in the closing hours of World War II. In the Czarist tradition, the Russians shot their way across Manchuria and forcibly reacquired their special rights in the territory. In the Leninist mold, China was compelled to recognize Mongolia's independence if "a plebiscite of the people of Outer Mongolia confirms that they desire [independence]." With the Red army in Manchuria, on October 20, 1945, a "plebiscite" was conducted in Mongolia. The outcome was a foregone conclusion. The Mongolians opted, without a single dissenting vote, for the Soviet satellite state of the Mongolian People's Republic. It should be noted, however, that after casting a ballot, each Mongolian voter was required to sign his name to it, this, in a police state on the Stalinist pattern.

In the same period, Stalin annexed Tanna Tuva, an area about the size of Britain which Chiang Kai-shek, in his memoirs, described as "part of China's territory in Outer Mongolia." With China weakened by civil war, Stalin promoted a separatist movement in Sinkiang which proclaimed an independent East Turkestan Republic.

Thus, piece by piece, Stalin sought to cushion the Sino-Soviet border, at China's expense, with buffer states in Sinkiang, Mongolia, and Manchuria.

But the stakes in Manchuria were the highest, in terms of people, area, raw materials, and industrial potential; as a result, the situation there was also the most roiled as three armies operated within the territory, Stalin's Red army, Chiang's Nationalist army and Mao's People's Liberation army. In this situation, P'u Yi entered Stalin's calculations.

The last Manchu emperor of China was a man without a country. Yet he still retained a certain legitimacy as the last occupant of the Dragon Throne, the acknowledged liege of the Manchu, the only border people with an historic right to Manchuria. Better still, from Stalin's viewpoint, P'u Yi was malleable. Chinese monarchists, warlords and republicans, White Russians and Japanese had all used him. Given the opportunity, the Chinese Nationalists and Communists alike would use him too. Why, then, shouldn't Stalin profit by him if the occasion arose? For Stalin, P'u Yi was a wild card in his Manchurian game plan.

Thus, Stalin treated P'u Yi with deference, as a house guest. P'u Yi often pondered the reason for Stalin's benign treatment. If he suspected Stalin's game, he never let on either in his memoirs, in interviews, or from the witness box at Tokyo. In his memoirs, for example, P'u Yi attributed the humane treatment he received from Stalin to the fact that Moscow was constrained in its treatment of him by some sort of agreement among the Allies on the treatment of prisoners.

On his return from Tokyo in the summer of 1946, and for the next four years, while the struggle for Manchuria and for China was resolved in the Communists' favor, P'u Yi was confined to his villa at Khabarovsk. Its spacious grounds were turned into a semi-permanent detention camp not only for him but also for other high officials of Manchukuo who had been swept up in the Soviet invasion of Manchuria. His brother William, P'u Chieh, was there; so were his brothers-in-law, and several members of the Manchukuo State Council and Big Li, his personal servant. Although his fellow internees did not dare address him as "your imperial majesty," given the circumstances of their confinement, he was referred to by the code word *shang*, or above, a corruption of *shang ti*, supreme ruler or emperor.

During this Russian interlude, P'u Yi continued to enjoy the relative luxury of private quarters. The Russians permitted him, unlike other prisoners, to dine alone. Occasionally, when he condescended to do so, he joined his fellow prisoners at supper and they deferred to him. The Russians provided him with a set of *ma chiang*, a game which was first developed in China under the Manchu and which, after World War I, at about the time of P'u Yi's abortive, second ascension to the Dragon Throne, was popularized in the West under the patented, commercial name of Mah-Jongg.

The Russians also assigned him a small vegetable plot and he spent his idle mornings gardening. Horticulture fascinated him. "This was a new experience for me," he remarked in an interview later. For the first time at the age of forty-one, the emperor of China dirtied his hands. For the first time, he came into contact with the real world, not the elaborate superstructure man has erected on it. For the first time, as he pointed out in his memoirs, he acquired insight into the nature of that real world, into the intangible relationship between man and his Creator, an insight which transcended the rites of revealed religion. Reginald Johnston would have beamed approvingly if he had seen P'u Yi puttering among his plants.

When he was not tending his seed beds or playing *ma chiang*, the last emperor of China sat pensively by the window in his private, upper floor room, gazing out across the rugged hills of the Outer Palisades Country and wondering about his ultimate fate.

The Russians brought little political pressure to bear against him. For a time they sought to indoctrinate him, but the effort was half-hearted, almost casual. They introduced him to the Chinese editions of Marx, Engels, Lenin, and Stalin, including such obscurant tomes as *Problems of Leninism*. These political tracts bored him. "I found the books depressing," he confided later, "and irrelevant."

At the villa, he continued to receive the Red army paper, *Shih Hua Pao,* now published at Dairen. But as before, his interest in politics was aroused only occasionally. The civil war raged on in China, and the fickle mandate of heaven appeared to shift in the Communists' favor. As far as he was concerned, his only hope for survival lay in interminable Chinese civil conflict, a stalemate in which neither side won and in which the Russians played the role of fulcrum. Oddly enough, he and Stalin shared this mutual interest. Sometimes the news rattled him, not only the reports of spectacular Chinese Communist victories, but such items as a dispatch of December 23, 1948, that seven of the men against whom he had testified at Tokyo were hanged as war criminals—among them Doihara, Itagaki, and Tojo.

In 1949 the news was consistently bad. The Nationalists collapsed, Chiang Kai-shek fled to Taiwan, and Mao Tse-tung entered Peking. In triumph, Mao's armies streamed through the main gate of the Forbidden City, the gate reserved for emperors, and occupied the Violet Enclosure of P'u Yi's youth.

Then on September 21 Peking's ancient cannons roared and red pennants flew from the battlements of the Sacred City as Mao proclaimed, on behalf of a quarter of mankind, "We announce the establishment of the People's Republic of China!" Ten days later, the New China was formally inaugurated as a quarter of a million troops paraded across *Tien An Meng,* Heavenly Peace Square, with the fifty-six-year-old Mao in the reviewing stand, savoring the greatest moment of his life. The festivities continued daily through Double Ten, October 10, the thirty-eighth anniversary of the revolution which had toppled P'u Yi from the Celestial Throne.

If P'u Yi entertained misgivings about the future, his uneasiness probably verged on panic when he learned on February 1, 1950, in the midst of a Stalin-Mao meeting at Moscow, that the Soviet Union formally proposed to the United States the creation of "a special international military court to try as a war criminal the emperor of Japan" on the charge that he planned "germ warfare" against the Soviet Union and Mongolia in 1939 and against China the following year. (In retrospect, this was a curious charge in the light of Communist charges during the Korean War, which broke out four months later, that the United States was engaging in "germ warfare.") Moscow also announced that the newly established People's Republic of China had joined the Soviet Union in the demand for Hirohito's head. Nothing was said of the former emperor of China and Manchukuo.

The United States rejected the Soviet demand.

Mao had left for Moscow in December, his first journey into the non-Chinese world, to attend Stalin's seventieth birthday celebration, to negotiate a new treaty between China and Russia and to discuss "other questions." Was the extradition of P'u Yi among the "other questions"? However small a point on the agenda at the Communist summit, it was a matter of life and death to the last Manchu emperor.

Mao journeyed to Moscow by special train via Manchuria and the Trans-Siberian railway. His conference with Stalin was extraordinary; it lasted two months. On February 14, 1950, beneath the crystal chandeliers in the grand ballroom of the Czars, the two Communist leaders jointly toasted the signing of a new thirty-year treaty to replace the Stalin-Chiang accord. They also toasted their "interminable, unbreakable unity."

Stalin's behavior must have disappointed Mao. "It is the immediate task of China to regain all our lost territories, not merely to defend our sovereignty below the Great Wall," Mao had told

Edgar Snow in 1936. "This means that Manchuria must be regained." And with a Communist triumph in China, Mao added, Mongolia will "automatically" revert to China.

Be that as it may, by the terms of the Stalin-Mao pact, the Russians clung to Mongolia and delayed their exodus from Manchuria. The Russians remained in joint control of Manchuria's ports and railways until the end of 1952. Ostensibly, the Russian sphere of influence there was maintained as a trip wire against a Japanese-American attack on China, a rather flimsy excuse. As it developed, although the railways were returned in 1952, the Russians continued to occupy the big naval base of Port Arthur until 1955, two years after Stalin's death, using as a pretext the Korean War.

But while Mao was eventually able to push his ally out of Manchuria, he, like Chiang Kai-shek before him, lost Mongolia when he was forced to accept the results of the "plebiscite" in the territory. Even so, as Francis Watson pointed out in his brilliant *The Frontiers of China*, Mao gained the somewhat fine point of recognizing the "independent status" rather than the "independence" of the Mongolian People's Republic. A reading of the new treaty gave rise to the conclusion that from the standpoint of Russia's long-term interests in Manchuria and elsewhere along the Sino-Soviet border—as well as those of P'u Yi—Chiang Kai-shek's triumph in the civil war in 1949 would have been preferable to Mao's. Only after Sinkiang and Manchuria joined Mongolia in the fold as buffer states recognized by China, would it serve the Kremlin's interest to welcome China into the Communist camp. But China held on to Manchuria and Sinkiang. The Chinese civil war did not work out according to Stalin's game plan. Mao's victory was premature.

Although the details are lacking, during the Moscow talks, Mao requested P'u Yi's extradition. For Stalin, P'u Yi had lost all value now, even his value as a ventriloquist's dummy, and the Soviet dictator readily agreed.

At the end of June, 1950, a few days after North Korea invaded the South, a development which surprised P'u Yi as much as it probably surprised Mao Tse-tung, P'u Yi's Russian hosts told him to prepare for the journey "home." The emperor paled, and his stomach knotted. The following month he and a contingent of other Manchukuo "war criminals," including his brother P'u Chieh, were placed aboard a prison train for the 450-mile trip to the nearest Sino-Soviet rail junction, a rather ludicrous exercise since he need only cross the Amur, which flowed past Khabarovsk, to be in Chinese territory. On board he was separated from the others and placed in a special carriage with a group of Red army officers. The officers, in high spirits, observed P'u Yi's distraught appearance, and sought to cheer him up. The Russians plied him with beer and sweets and, in the course of the journey, told him uproarious stories about barracks life. "But for all this," P'u Yi later said, "I felt that they were taking me to my death." Now, for the first time, his fear of death acquired another dimension. It was not death so much he feared as a cruel death. In Chinese hands, he was convinced, "I could not even hope for a comfortable death."

On July 31 the train halted at Pogranichny, a border marshaling yard where the Russian tracks terminated parallel to the beginning of the Chinese tracks with their broader gauge bogeys. The Chinese tracks extended from the Manchurian border town of Suifenho.

As the prison train rolled to a stop, the sun settled on the Chinese side of the frontier. This was his last night on Soviet soil. Was it also his last night on earth? The emperor tossed all night, his dreams pressed by visions of an "uncomfortable death." If he thought of suicide, he never said so. His only thought, he later claimed, was whether he would have the courage, in his last agonizing moments, to shout, "Long Live Emperor T'ai Tsung," the reign name of Nurhachu, the Exalted Founder, the first of the imperial Manchu line who died in 1643 just before his armies occupied Peking.

Once the sun rose, P'u Yi felt, he was dead. "My life will last no longer than the morning dew on the windowpanes," he thought poetically. "Once the sun is up, everything will evaporate."

At daybreak the Russians offered him a glass of strong tea and then motioned him to pick up his case and follow them into the adjoining compartment. Numb, his eyes glazed, he trailed behind them. Two Chinese occupied the compartment, one attired in blue civilian clothes of military cut and the other in a khaki uniform without badge of rank but with a breast-patch which read: "Chinese People's Liberation army." They rose as he entered the compartment. P'u Yi might well have uttered Joseph K's chilling line when they came to fetch him in Kafka's *The Trial*, "So you are for me."

Gazing on the last Manchu emperor, the civilian spoke. "I have come to receive you on the orders of Premier Chou En-lai," he said, stiffly. After a momentary pause, in a more relaxed fashion, he added, "Well, now, you have returned to the motherland."

But in P'u Yi's mind he had no motherland, only ancestors.

P'u Yi bowed his head and, as he said later, waited for the handcuffs. Instead, he was led outside and escorted down an aisle formed by two rows of armed troops—one Russian and the other Chinese—and into a waiting Chinese train. Inside the coach, a Chinese soldier relieved him of his case, which still contained his cache of pearls and precious stones and his imperial seal, and placed it in the luggage rack. Although the sun was up, the train was dark. The windows were papered over. At each end of the carriage stood Chinese soldiers armed with submachine guns. The other prisoners were transferred, the coal-burning locomotive grunted, its heavy steel wheels turned, the weight of the engine provided the necessary traction, and the train rolled out of Pogranichny and crossed into China at Suifenho.

As the train rattled along, an unarmed soldier with the bearing of an officer entered the car. "You have returned to your motherland," he said. "*Hun hao,* very good." Bowls and wooden chopsticks appeared at his command, and an astonished P'u Yi was invited to join the soldiers at breakfast—pickled vegetables, salted eggs, and rice porridge. The flavor of this first home-cooked meal in five years whetted his appetite and he ate ravenously. It was like coming home—to mother's apple pie. Well, not quite.

CHAPTER 26

Prisoner 981

For the next nine years, between 1950 and 1959, from the age of forty-two to fifty-one, for many the most creative and productive years of life, P'u Yi languished in a cell undergoing what the Chinese, with linguistic ingenuity, term "brainwashing." Perhaps the most surprising feature of this period is that the Chinese Communist hierarchy troubled to subject him to "thought reform" and "thought control," the official jargon for state indoctrination. After all, given his political record, P'u Yi was pliable, a man without principle whose sole preoccupation, or so it seemed, was survival, a man who lined up with the direction of breeze from any quadrant.

Indeed, why did Peking go to the trouble? To P'u Yi, at first, the answer was not readily apparent. Gradually, he understood that through indoctrination, at a minimum, he would know what was expected of him in the New China. In some way, like the Japanese and Russians before them, the Chinese Communists had special plans for him. Whatever the case, for P'u Yi, the rigors of brainwashing were a surprise. He had expected to be returned to

Peking, tried publicly by a mob and executed forthwith, a fate which had befallen other "enemies of the people."

Instead of Peking, however, his prison train's final destination was Fushun, the site of Manchuria's open-faced coal fields, a mining area situated about 125 miles west of the Yalu River and the Korean frontier. At Fushun, the dominant gold and green colors of Manchuria, the *kaoliang* fields and grasslands, dissolved into black earth. The town was sooty and coal dust hung in the air. Miners in blue uniforms and braided straw helmets, their hands and faces lined with coal dust, strolled everywhere. On the outskirts of the town, where the houses of the workers were located, the drab monotony was broken only occasionally by the red scarves of the children at play in courtyards.

The camp for political prisoners was located several miles from Fushun and was conspicuous—rows of barbed wire, soldiers with fixed bayonets, and a machine gun battery. P'u Yi made the drive in a truck from the railroad station, the vehicle kicking up a wake of black dust. In the center of the concentric rings of barbed wire were high walls. Behind the walls was a cluster of low-lying buildings. In the receiving room there was a large portrait on the wall, surprisingly not of Mao, but of Stalin.

As the iron bolt slammed shut on his cell, his eyes adapted to the poor lighting and he surveyed his place of confinement: It contained several long wooden beds, a wooden table, two benches, and several familiar faces, including his brother P'u Chieh, his three nephews, and his father-in-law, Yuan Jung, Elizabeth's father. In his depressed state of mind, he was momentarily relieved when a guard slipped to him, through the dirty grating of the barred cell door, a toothbrush and towel. At least, "they"—that terrifying pronoun of the political prisoner—planned to keep him for a while before putting him up against a wall, or worse.

At Fushun, his Russian-made garments were taken from him, and he was given a set of coarse work clothes, including a set of white underwear, a pair of blue coolie pants, and a padded cotton quilt jacket bearing the numbers *nien pa i,* 981. And, to his pleasant astonishment, he was given a pack of cigarettes. Although this is speculation, it was probably at this outfitting that he was relieved of his traveling case and its contents of precious stones. Officially, the treasures were not confiscated. Legalistic by nature, as if to justify their actions, the Communists usually give a "receipt" for confiscated property. However, he was permitted to retain a few personal belongings, including a tarnished silver frame which contained photographs of Jade Lute, a small bag of her nail cuttings, and his personal seal, the chop fashioned from those wondrous interlocking pieces of jade, the seal of the Manchu emperors.

He was also provided with approved reading matter, that is, approved by the governor of the War Prisoner Thought Control Center, as the Fushun prison was formally called. For that matter, as in every Marxist-Leninist state, inside *and* outside the political prisons, all publications (books, magazines, and newspapers), all films, all libraries, all literature and art (painting, music, and sculpture) had to be approved by the party. There were no exceptions to prove a rule.

Even so, there were periods when the camp governor was compelled to halt delivery of newspapers to the prisoners, for example, early in 1951 as the Chinese offensive in Korea was turned back over the 38th Parallel and Seoul was retaken by United Nations forces. It was not the course of the war which troubled the governor so much as concern that his wards may be alarmed to read in *People's Daily*, the official party paper, of new "regulations for the punishment of counterrevolutionaries," one of a series of purges in the Stalin mold which swept China in the early years as Mao consolidated his control. In this period, according to Peking's own figures, more than 2 million persons perished.

The books he received principally consisted of the works of Mao Tse-tung with their pledges that in the New China representative government and civil liberties would flourish. Indeed, basic freedoms were incorporated into the new constitution of the People's Republic in 1954—freedom of speech, freedom of press and so on. But Liu Shao-chi, then Mao's successor, hastened to explain to the appointed "constituent assembly" that this "does not mean that once the constitution is introduced all its articles will automatically go into operation."

Mao's *On New Democracy* was one of the first works P'u Yi read. The essay ended with a challenge to the P'u Yis of China. "The New China stands before every one of us," Mao wrote. "We should be ready to receive it. The mast of the ship of New China is appearing on the horizon. We should clap our hands to welcome it. Raise both your hands!" Reading these lines in his cell, P'u Yi probably interpreted the ringing phrase, "Raise your hands!" not as an invitation to applaud but as an invitation to put up his hands in surrender.

After a few weeks, he was separated from the other members of his "family." His new cellmates included former officials of his Manchukuo regime and of the Japanese puppet government in China which had been headed by Wang Ching-wei, who had died in a plane crash shortly before the war ended. Subtly, out of deference to P'u Yi's past authority, his new companions assigned him the wooden bed next to the wall. Later he realized that it was the best location in the cell, adjoining the heating plant, which gave warmth in the cold Manchurian winter.

For some forty years, the Lord of Ten Thousand Years had never once made a bed, folded a quilted blanket, tied shoelaces, handled a needle and thread, put toothpaste on a toothbrush. Housekeeping was a new experience. For the first time, at the age of forty-two, like a Cub Scout on his first overnight camping trip, he faced the challenge of being on his own.

But even the prison authorities treated him with tacit deference in small but significant matters. Among the housekeeping chores was the task of emptying the honey buckets, a distasteful job which was rotated among the prisoners. P'u Yi was horrified. This was a crushing humiliation. "Was I to empty the chamber pot for others?" he asked. "I would humiliate my ancestors." The prison staff intervened and circuitously suggested to the other prisoners that because of his frailty—"illness"—he should miss his turn. The governor acted not out of compassion for his torment, but rather to exploit an opportunity to win his gratitude. He succeeded admirably. "I was as happy as if I had been saved from execution," P'u Yi wrote later, "and I felt grateful for the first time in my life."

In essence, brainwashing is a cut beyond what modern psychologists term "behavioral modification," the systematic manipulation of behavior through psychological processes. In brainwashing, the right of privacy is abrogated, privacy as currently defined in Western law to mean the freedom of the individual to control the time, the circumstances, and the extent to which his attitudes, beliefs, behavior, and opinions are to be shared with or kept from others. P'u Yi was stripped of this privacy with the ruthlessness of a flenser stripping a whale. The state invaded P'u Yi's soul. The regime's supporters viewed the process differently. Fung Yu-lan, presently the leading philosopher at the University of Peking, innocently asked, "What is wrong with brainwashing?" People regularly wash their faces and their clothes, he argued, so "why not their brains?"

As applied in the New China, thought reform involves seemingly endless group discussion, criticism, and self-criticism. The subject maintains a diary in which his thoughts and thought processes are revealed. The diary may be elaborate, tracing an entire lifetime, in substance, an autobiography. (Incidentally this sort of diary formed the basis for P'u Yi's memoirs.) Edward Hunter, who popularized the phrase "brainwashing" in the West in the early 1950s in a book based on interviews with refugees in Hong Kong, concluded that behind the process was the fundamental realization that in such circumstances a prisoner cannot indefinitely mask his true opinions. Moreover, the prisoner's diary is not treated as an intimate journal. It is read aloud in prison, dissected, and discussed.

Eleutherius Winance, a French priest, underwent the process for eighteen months and in *The Communist Persuasion* provided insight into the method. Three times a week he attended group discussions, each of which lasted four hours. Literally, their purpose was to wear him down. He was never threatened with death. He was allowed to live but only in the milieu of his interlocutors. With reason, it is frequently said, an individual in a Marxist-Leninist state can adopt one of three attitudes: leave the milieu, accept the doctrine, or go mad. Political prisoners have only two choices: acceptance or madness.

Marxism possesses, of course, a logic of its own and through a materialist interpretation of human existence, leads the victim to his own negation, to the negation of his very personality, under the fallacious pretext that whenever he says "I" or "mine" he is guilty of the most sordid selfishness. Thus, the individual is quietly led to forget that the goodness of an act derives from the nature of the act. Many, if not most people, are, like Billy Budd, inarticulate. Confined to a prison cell, isolated in a controlled milieu, ceaselessly battered by incessant, intimate questions, compelled to keep a record of thoughts, the average captive succumbs, and accepts the dogma of his captors.

"Who likes to seem to resist logic?" asks Father Winance. "Man is a reasonable animal. He likes to reason. But his animal nature also makes him follow those who know how to shout loudly and who give him something to eat."

With the passage of time, the climate of heroic resistance makes the subject disgusted with his own "egoism." His willpower erodes. He changes his ideas for theirs. "Why not?" Father Winance continued. "Some individuals struggled for a year or more, but in the end the milieu was stronger than they were, and the Communists knew it. They waited patiently for their method to produce results—and it did."

Remolded, the individual is released into the larger prison of society where the milieu is as tightly controlled as the atmosphere in a hothouse. "They have invented a method of making each man the keeper of his brother's thoughts," an informant told Hunter at Hong Kong. "They are doing this through what they call democratic discussion and self-criticism, with the threat of purges hanging over the heads of nonconformists."

That P'u Yi should submit to brainwashing is touched with

irony since, in his name as the Emperor K'ang Teh, Manchukuo submitted to such a humiliation on a massive scale. In 1939, T. Ralph Morton, in his *Today in Manchuria*, painted a portrait of Manchukuo under Japanese rule which paralleled the situation P'u Yi encountered on his return to the New China.

In Manchukuo, all information, from private mail to newspapers, had been censored. No one could travel without providing the police with particulars about the journey. Meetings could not be held without a police permit. The authorities spent much of their time tracking down "dangerous thoughts." An anonymous letter accusing someone of "dangerous thoughts" could result in long imprisonment. The thought control law was not uniformly enforced, but the fear of it put a curb on all unauthorized political activities and ended all individual freedoms. Although the term brainwashing was yet to be minted, Morton wrote eloquently on the subject. "It was a new and strange doctrine, for however much a Chinese had been bound by tradition and had accepted the authority of his rulers, he had always maintained inviolate the small citadel of his own soul," Morton observed. "It may have been a very small place that he could call his own. But in it he was free and he accepted no domination. The artist in China, be he a poet or painter or craftsman, always had his world in which he thought rebellious thoughts and lived his own life. . . . Whatever disaster overtook him, however autocratic was the rule of the government in the distant capital, he never conceived that this private world of his would be taken away from him."

Against this sort of background, P'u Yi was suddenly transferred in October, 1950, from the Fushun thought control center to another prison camp, this one at Harbin, 150 miles closer to the Soviet border and 100 miles further west from the Korean border along the Yalu. There he shared a prison cell with four others, all former officers in his Imperial Manchukuo army. Built by the Japanese, the cells contained no beds; in Japanese-style, the prisoners slept on *tatami*, woven straw floor mats. In this fashion, P'u Yi spent the Korean War years; for, unknown to him as he boarded the prison train for the trip from Fushun to Harbin, Peking had just completed massing nine field armies, composed of thirty-eight divisions, in the Manchurian hills along the Korean frontier. The People's Liberation army was poised to unleash a "human wave," under Lin Piao's command, against the United Nations forces who had all but completed the occupation of North Korea four months after the North invaded the South. Just as the United States to maintain a cold war balance could not stand idly by while the Communists sought forcibly to reunify a territory cut in half by agreement, the Communists had to do the same when the Americans pushed the North Koreans back and began to invade the North. By November 21, the Americans were astride the Yalu, peering across the river and into the Forbidden Palisades Country, Manchuria, P'u Yi's ancestral domain. The Korean War was over, or so it seemed, when, on American Thanksgiving Day, to the sound of bugles, the Chinese crossed the Yalu en masse.

China's intervention in Korea elated P'u Yi. In the air, he sniffed "liberation." Like his fellow prisoners, he thought this way: Japan beat China, America beat Japan; ipso facto, America would beat China. But it did not work quite that simply in Korea. Japan's war against China was total war; so was America's war against Japan. In Korea, the United States, under a United Nations flag, fought a limited war and had no interest in Manchuria. America was prepared to settle for a restoration of the *status quo ante,* with the 38th Parallel marking the border between North and South Korea. P'u Yi, of course, had visions of the Americans brandishing their nuclear arsenal and driving into Manchuria, as the Russians had in 1945. But as he developed this line of reasoning, P'u Yi suddenly entertained second thoughts. So did the other prisoners. If the victorious Americans entered Harbin, the Communists would probably kill the prisoners rather than have them fall into American hands. Doubtlessly, at this juncture, P'u Yi longed for those secure days in a Soviet sanatorium, the only respite from politics he had enjoyed during his maturity.

In early 1951, when the Americans drove the Chinese back

over the 38th Parallel, the prisoners were in a state of panic, a condition hardly conducive to brainwashing.

With the situation almost out of hand, the prison governor addressed them by loudspeaker and chided them about their fears. "Some of you think . . . the Americans are bound to invade the Northeast [Manchuria] and you are worried that we will kill you first," he said frankly. "Why don't you ask yourselves this: Why is the people's government making you study if it plans to kill you?" Reading their reaction, he continued, "If we are not going to kill you, perhaps you will say that it would be a good idea to let you go. No, it wouldn't. If we were to release you before you had been remolded, you might commit other crimes."

In mid-1951 the Communists proposed truce negotiations and the United States, anxious to disengage, readily agreed. News of the Kaesong talks disappointed P'u Yi. If the Americans were prepared to talk cease-fire, he reasoned, then they were not invincible. The turn in events "mystified" him and his cellmates.

The prison years dragged, apparently on without end.

The government-approved third volume of P'u Yi's autobiography deals largely with this period. Unlike the other volumes, this one dealing with the years 1950 through 1956, in particular, cannot be verified or assessed against the background of other sources. Yet this volume is still laced with subtle double entendre, P'u Yi's familiar self-protective gambit.

Thus, squirreled away within P'u Yi's prison testament are flashes which illuminated his predicament. For example, in a discussion group he recalled the Japanese slaughter of Chinese workers on a construction site. The prison governor asked him why he did not protest to the Japanese, especially since he was the emperor. "I . . . I did not dare," he stammered.

"Because you were frightened?" his interrogator asked. P'u Yi nodded. This prompted the governor to mutter under his breath, "What disgusting things fear can do to a man."

Insinuated into paragraphs extolling his prison existence, therefore, was the question: What disgusting thing was fear doing to him at the Communist prisons of Fushun and Harbin? The incident recalls P'u Yi's sinuous performance at Tokyo when he explained that he was not free to express his thoughts to Lord Lytton in 1932 because Itagaki was present; and he inferred he was not able to express his thoughts freely in Tokyo in 1946 because he was a Soviet prisoner in the presence of Russian and Chinese judges and prosecutors.

Thus, the third volume, as editors are wont to say, often does not read. That is, many of the statements are out of character. "I have been thinking about some events of the past," P'u Yi wrote in a typical sentence. "Previously I did not see their true nature, but now I see they were crimes." The merit of this sentence is that it is written in plain language. Not so for other sentences. "The feudalists and compradors were indispensable to imperialism in its aggression against China," he wrote, "and I was a typical example." The style was patently not that of P'u Yi. Here is another example: "For the sake of their dreams of a restoration, the feudal forces used me as their front and collaborated with the Japanese imperialists, while the Japanese had used me as a front when they turned the Northeast [Manchuria] into their colony."

And yet, there is a chance that these commentaries also may be genuine, as P'u Yi succumbed to the brainwashing of his captors.

Whatever the case, studying his statements, the prison authorities concluded that he had made "great progress" in remolding his thought. But his captors were not content to settle for a political conversion. Like the Japanese militarists before them, they sought to destroy his spiritual sanctuary, his faith in Lord Buddha to whose teachings he clung like a man in a storm at sea.

Before Mao occupied the Forbidden City, and established his neo-dynasty, he pledged religious freedom in the New China and observed repeatedly that the People's Republic guaranteed citizens "freedom of religious belief." So much for talk. But in reality, as Shanghai's *Liberation Daily* observed, "Some Buddhist practices . . . must be reformed." P'u Yi must have recoiled, remembering the desecration of his ancestors' tombs when he read the nature of these "reforms" in *People's Daily,* the official party organ which was circulated at the Fushun and Harbin prisons. "Ancestral tombs, long regarded as sacred, have been removed by the masses themselves," the newspaper reported. "In many localities, family altars . . . grave stones, coffins, etc., are used by collective farms for . . . pig sties, latrines . . . manure buckets." And the paper exulted, "Many temples which formerly housed images have been turned into pig sties or processing plants [slaughter houses], thus saving large amounts of expenditure for the collective."

But this was only the outward manifestation of the drive against religion.

In a far more subtle and sophisticated manner, the régime moved against spiritual ideas. The campaign against flies is an example.

Peking's denunciation of the United Nations for allegedly using "germ warfare" in Korea is widely known; actually the campaign was a cover for the lack of public hygiene in the People's Liberation army which gave rise to epidemics behind the Chinese lines. Less known is the campaign against flies. At the same time as the "germ warfare" drive, Peking launched a nationwide patriotic hygiene movement and the campaign was carried inside the prisons and "rectification" camps. Though Buddhism abjures the taking of life, P'u Yi was provided with a fly swatter. "This was the first time I had ever handled a fly-swatter," he wrote, "and I felt rather awkward as I had, to tell the truth, never killed a single fly in my life."

Half-heartedly, he joined the other prisoners in a fly hunt. "When at last I found one on the sill of an open window," confessed the last emperor of China "I waved my swatter to drive it out."

"What do you think you are doing?" a voice shouted harshly from behind him. "Are you killing pests or saving life?"

"I knew what he was getting at," P'u Yi said. "I blushed and in a forced voice said, 'Of course, I am not saving life.'"

"You won't kill because you're afraid of retribution," his accuser said. "Isn't that it?"

"The fly got away," P'u Yi protested lamely. "That is all."

Among Westerners, such a bizarre episode would be dismissed as a put-on. But it was no joking matter. As a Buddhist, P'u Yi had sought to save the fly's life to earn merit in the afterlife just as, in the Manchukuo palace, he once ordered his staff to rescue a mouse from the jaws of a cat.

But in the end, abandoning his religion, P'u Yi forced himself to kill a fly.

Psychologically terrifying, the episode was on a par with his forced acceptance of Shintoism. But if he was to win his release from prison, if he was to survive, he had to conform; that was the message of the thought control center.

No sooner had he slain his first fly than his warders escalated the killing. Now he was urged to kill rats and mice.

Asked one day how many mice he had killed, P'u Yi replied that in time he would kill "at least one."

"So you are still against killing," a Communist official said. "How is it, then, that you are concerned about the fate of flies and mice but not men? Why didn't you protest the murder of coolie laborers to the Japanese?" P'u Yi felt trapped. The Communists had trapped him. So had Lord Buddha.

"I'll do my best to kill at least two," he said meekly, after an embarrassingly long pause. Two? "Even the children in primary schools plan to destroy more than one mouse each," the official said.

P'u Yi reports that he returned to his cell with a heavy heart. Later he captured and killed six mice. Thus, layer by layer, he was stripped of his beliefs and convictions, shorn of his privacy, a punishment as chilling as the death by a thousand cuts which his forebears had practiced.

During these prison years he asked himself repeatedly, as he had in the Soviet Union, why the Communists did not simply do away with him as they had so many other prisoners of war, wartime collaborators, and political prisoners. When Mao occupied Peking, for example, the widow of Wang Ching-wei, Japan's puppet ruler in occupied China, was imprisoned, and her prison key was thrown away. No known effort was made to "remold" her and she died in her cell eleven years later. Clearly, P'u Yi was a special prisoner. Why the magnanimity? Indeed, one chapter heading in his memoirs reads: "Why so Magnanimous?" He provided no answer, other than the propagandistic suggestion that the Communists sought to "remold" him as they intended to remold China and the world in their own image.

But, inwardly, P'u Yi must have suspected that politics was behind the magnanimity. Like Stalin and the Japanese, Mao recognized P'u Yi's uniqueness. P'u Yi must have had an inkling of this, especially since he had access to *People's Daily* and, through it, learned of the first major leadership crisis in the People's Republic, a crisis which involved his old stamping ground, Manchuria.

Vice Premier Kao Kang, a member of the Politburo and party boss in Manchuria, was denounced and expelled from the party in 1953 on Mao's orders for developing Manchuria into "an independent kingdom." The implication was that the Russians were behind Kao Kang and that Stalin had not abandoned the grand design of the Czars to pry Manchuria loose from China. Indeed, Kao Kang had become so independent that he negotiated separate agreements with Moscow, very much the way Marshal Chang Tso-lin had in the twenties. Gradually, between 1950 and 1953 Manchuria acquired the characteristics of a state-within-a-state. For his attempts at independence Kao Kang paid the highest price. In 1955 Peking announced that he had "committed suicide as an ultimate expression of his betrayal of the party." Kao Kang's death was, if nothing else, politically convenient.

The incident doubtlessly impressed on P'u Yi that even under the Communists, Manchuria, his ancestral domain, was a special problem; if this was true, perforce, he had to be a special prisoner.

In the aftermath of the Korean War and Kao Kang's bid to establish an independent-minded, Soviet-backed Manchuria, Mao was determined to drive the Russians once and for all from their Manchurian foothold. Stalin was dead, and this made the situation easier for him to handle; indeed, with Stalin's death in 1953, Mao sought to pick up the late dictator's mantle as first among equals in the Communist world, generating a struggle for primacy which has yet to be resolved. With the first Sino-Soviet fissures developing, in 1955 Mao forced the Russians to withdraw from Port Arthur and to dissolve the Sino-Soviet joint stock companies in Manchuria. That year, for the first time since the days of Manchu glory a century before, Manchuria was again under Peking's complete authority.

P'u Yi recognized the implications and reconciled himself to the new order in China. As a demonstration of newly acquired political consciousness, he acted decisively, as dramatically as when he summarily drove the eunuchs from the Forbidden City in his teens and when he severed with his own hand his queue, the symbol of Manchu strength and power.

During an inspection visit to the Fushun thought control center, to which P'u Yi was returned after the Korean War, a high official from Peking approached P'u Yi's cell. The emperor bowed low.

"I beg to announce, sir," P'u Yi said, "that I wish to present this object of mine to the people's government." In his hand he held his most treasured possession, the seal of the Great Ch'ing Empire, the interlocking pieces of jade, with their magical properties, that had been made in the eighteenth century during the reign of Ch'ien Lung. He was given a "receipt" for the object.

By this solemn act, P'u Yi was transferring the legitimate power held by the Manchu Dynasty to the People's Republic.

As if it were a signal for which Peking had patiently waited, events moved rapidly thereafter. His captors began to allow the former emperor some contact with his relatives in the outside world.

With the collapse of Manchukuo, and the ensuing confusion of the Chinese civil war, P'u Yi's brothers and sisters and other relatives in Hsinking, had miraculously drifted back to Peking where they took up residence with Prince Ch'un. The prince, apolitical and in his dotage, had lived quietly on a monthly government stipend which he received from the Japanese puppet government in occupied China. When the Communists came to power in Peking, they treated him as a stuttering, senile old man who might be useful politically in rallying the support of the Manchu for the new People's Republic, particularly those in the Manchurian borderlands. Thus, one of P'u Yi's sisters, on returning to Peking, found a job in a nursery, another joined the Communists' archivists in the Forbidden City, still another became an illustrator for propaganda posters. One of his brothers became a teacher. Under the circumstances, they had fared incredibly well considering P'u Yi's fate and the Chinese concept of collective responsibility. In 1951 Prince Ch'un died in his sleep in Peking, and the family continued to maintain the old Northern Mansion as a Manchu communal home. There was now only one survivor of the previous generation—Prince Tsai T'ao, P'u Yi's uncle, who also lived in the Northern Mansion. His life under the Communists was fairly typical of that of the Manchu nobility. An expert horseman from the old bannerman school, he served as an adviser to the Horse Administration of the Military Affairs Commission of the People's Consultative Council. With P'u Yi in jail, and Prince Ch'un dead, he also served as titular leader of the Manchu, whom the Communists, like the Nationalists before them, regarded as one of the five peoples making up modern China.

China's new constitution described the People's Republic as "a family of fraternity and cooperation of all nationalities." As window dressing, representatives of the various nationalities—Manchu, Mongol, etc.—were "elected" to the National People's Congress which, under the constitution, was termed the "highest organ of state authority." This, of course, was nonsense; there was only one authority in the New China, Mao Tse-tung. The Congress, which was "elected" to a four-year term, was a rubber stamp which was supposed to meet once every four years but actually rarely met.

In 1954 the first Congress was organized. Prince Tsai was "elected" a representative of the Manchu people. He was also "elected" to the national committee of the Political Consultative Conference, a sort of congressional steering committee. Two years later the aging Prince Tsai attended the committee's second meeting. At the conference Premier Chou En-lai, in whose name P'u Yi had been extradited from the Soviet Union, introduced him to the chairman. "This is Mr. Tsai T'ao," Chou said, "the uncle of P'u Yi."

Mao shook his hand firmly. "I have heard that P'u Yi's studies are going quite well," Mao said, to the prince's surprise and elation. "Why don't you go and visit him?"

At last, after his six long years in prison, the Forbidden City recognized the existence of Prisoner 981. The signal was loud and clear: Mao had personally set P'u Yi on the road back. And in China all roads led to Peking.

To "Mr." Tsai, the chairman's suggestion was tantamount to the old imperial command, "Hear and obey!" Dutifully, the prince rushed off for Fushun to bring his nephew, Prisoner 981, the glad tidings.

CHAPTER 27

The Road Back

P'u Yi's emergence from the shadows in 1956 coincided with a period of "liberalism" in China after seven years of harsh police state rule. With de-Stalinization gaining momentum in the Soviet Union, and ferment spreading among the East European satellites, Mao focused attention on the bubbling cauldron at home, lifting the lid to relieve the pressure. "Let a hundred flowers blossom," he proclaimed in May of that year, "let a hundred thoughts contend." And blossom and contend they did as intellectuals and others surged forward in China to voice openly their first criticisms of the new order. Peking encouraged this liberal outpouring and described the new campaign as a movement "to promote freedom of independent thinking, freedom of debate, freedom of criticism, freedom to express one's own views."

Against this political background, the reins on P'u Yi were loosened. For the first time he received visits from relatives at his prison; he made his first trip outside the prison wall, a Potemkin tour of Manchuria; he appeared in public for the first time in a decade again in the familiar role of witness at a Japanese war crimes trial; and he was interviewed by Western correspondents.

When Prince Tsai visited him, as Mao had suggested, his uncle's voice shook so with emotion that P'u Yi could hardly hear him. P'u Yi tried to control his own emotions, but he ended up bursting into tears. After the Communists had occupied Peking, his uncle told him, many Manchu had worried about the future and were alarmed at the emperor's imprisonment. But, the uncle continued, for the Manchu life under the Communists was surprisingly bearable. The New China wanted their allegiance.

Letters and visits from other relatives, including his two sisters, confirmed Prince Tsai's assessment. According to his autobiography, under the Nationalists, few Manchu had the courage to register their nationality with the government. But after the Communist takeover, large numbers came forward in the Sino-Soviet borderlands to do so. After the adoption of the 1954 constitution, the census reported that the Manchu minority totaled 2.4 million, a figure, P'u Yi claimed, that "surprised" the Manchu themselves. But this is abject nonsense; in 1940 a Japanese-Manchukuo census reported 2.6 million Manchu. Whatever the case, according to P'u Yi's sisters, the future of the Manchu in the New China was "bright and happy."

This latter phrase should also be treated with skepticism. The 1954 constitution, for example, promised "regional autonomy in areas entirely or largely inhabited by national minorities." This precluded regional autonomy for Manchuria where the Chinese population outnumbered the Manchu by better than a dozen to one. But neither the Manchu nor other minorities expected anything other than direct Peking rule. The 1931 Communist constitution notwithstanding, Peking quickly disabused the Manchu and others from thinking about independence. "Any national movement which seeks separation from the Chinese People's Republic for independence will be considered reactionary," *People's Daily* warned in 1951 as the Chinese Communists overran Tibet. The journal explained that independence in the borderlands "would work to the advantage of imperialism." Was "imperialism" in this context an early code word for the Soviet Union, China's principal neighbor?

Yet there is little doubt that Peking sought to win the confidence of the Manchu and secure China's restive northern frontier with Russia. After the Communists came to power, P'u Yi's second cousin, an outstanding player of the *ku chin,* a classical Chinese stringed instrument, and an expert calligrapher, was appointed vice president of the Ku Chin Research Association and president of the Calligraphy Research Association. Another of P'u Yi's cousins emerged as a member of the Institute for Classical and Historical Studies. Others were given visible posts in the New China. At no time since the 1911 revolution were the Manchu treated so well.

In addition to his blood relatives out of the past, Jade Lute appeared, whom he had abandoned with the deranged Elizabeth in the foothills of the Korean border at the close of the war. She looked well, indeed pleasingly plump, like Wen Hsiu, his first love. They spent an hour together, and she passed along the news of Elizabeth's death and Hiro Saga's repatriation to her native Japan.

Abandoned by P'u Yi at Talitzu, Elizabeth, Hiro and her five-year-old daughter, and the remainder of the party, found themselves in political limbo. The Russians occupied the town shortly after P'u Yi's flight and, as elsewhere in Manchuria, ran riot, terrorizing the townspeople. But they conspicuously avoided defiling the house where the imperial family had taken refuge, an indication that they were aware of who its occupants were. With the end of the war, the Russians blockaded Manchuria's ports and airfields to bar the reentry of Chinese Nationalist troops and pave the way for the Chinese Communists' takeover. Fortunately for the imperial family, the commanding officer of the Communists' irregular forces had formerly been in P'u Yi's imperial Manchukuo cavalry where he had been befriended by P'u Chieh, who was nominally in command of the horse troops. He assured P'u Chieh's wife, Hiro Saga, and other members of the group that they would be treated properly. In January of the new year—it was now

311

1946—they were removed to the police barracks at Tunghua. Here, to their surprise, they were joined by Jade Lute, who had been picked up wandering in the mountains. That spring, the party was transferred to Hsinking, which had reverted to its pre-Manchukuo name of Changch'un.

Hiro and her children were permitted to return to Japan with other Japanese repatriates. Jade Lute was released and permitted to return to her Manchurian family. As for the forty-year-old Elizabeth, she deteriorated beyond medical assistance in the absence of drugs. Confined to a cell in the former capital's municipal prison, she increasingly refused to take food and toward the end of her life lost all sense of control and direction. On the ides of June, rolling in her own excrement and urine, the last empress of China joined her ancestors.

Jade Lute reported to her imperial husband that she was living modestly with her family and that she had taken a job at a children's nursery. There, perhaps, she hoped to compensate for her own lack of children.

Although Elizabeth was dead, her death did not automatically elevate Jade Lute to the status of "empress." She remained, as she had been, a concubine, a secondary consort and Peking recognized her in that role.

In law, concubinage was abolished by the republic shortly after the 1911 revolution, but it continued in practice. A new marriage law, promulgated by the Communists in 1950, also banned concubinage but approved relationships that had been entered into before the founding of the People's Republic, providing both parties consented. Apparently Jade Lute preferred to dissolve her tenuous relationship with the emperor, and she asked for a divorce. P'u Yi was agreeable. In late 1956 she obtained a final decree. Once again, the misogynic Lord of Ten Thousand Years found himself truly liberated from the women in his life, from the Empress Dowager Tzu Hsi, the Old Buddha, through the last of his four wives. Incongruously, in prison he acquired a measure of personal freedom he had not known before.

The visits of relatives were interspersed with trips into the countryside so that he could learn first hand that "things have changed, society has changed, all Chinese have changed."

He visited the Fushun collieries, for example, spoke with the workers and noted in a miner's home that instead of the family snapshots on the wall, a Chinese custom, there was "only a picture of Chairman Mao, who was clearly dearer to him than his relations." Later, in the house of a farmer, an old woman showed him a large crock of rice in the corner of the room. "How often did you see that in the time of the Emperor K'ang Teh?" she asked. The remark shook him. Ever since he embarked on the stage-managed tour he was afraid he would be recognized, perhaps in a crowd, and that unforeseen complications might arise. "The K'ang Teh of whom you spoke is P'u Yi, the traitorous puppet emperor of Manchukuo," he is supposed to have said. "I am he."

The old woman was dumbfounded although, according to P'u Yi's memoirs, she suspected he was a political prisoner. How did she know? The ground for this suspicion is never explained. Was this another example of P'u Yi's subtle way of hinting at the true nature of his situation?

Instead of denouncing him for his role in the oppressive Japanese era, the old woman spread her hands and sighed, "it's all over now." And then, as if according to script, she declaimed this line: "As long as you're willing to study, to do what Chairman Mao says, and become a decent person, you'll be all right."

P'u Yi and the old woman both broke into sobs just as P'u Yi had done when his Uncle Tsai told him of his conversation with Chairman Mao, and just as he had done when he extended his felicitations to Hirohito at the end of his first sojourn in Japan. The scene with the old woman is perhaps too pat, even for propaganda. Cecil B. De Mille would probably have rejected it as too maudlin. But in P'u Yi's life story no scene was too far-fetched to be unbelievable.

P'u Yi no sooner returned to the Fushun jail than on July 21, 1956, for the first time in a decade, he made a public appearance. He turned up in Mukden as the star witness before a special military tribunal at the trial of twenty-eight prominent Japanese officials of the Manchukuo regime. The trial lasted almost three weeks. Among the defendants was his old associate, Takebe Rokuzo, the former head of the General Affairs Board whom P'u Yi cited in court as the "real authority" in Manchukuo. "I had no actual power," the former Emperor K'ang Teh truthfully testified. "All policies, all laws and all decrees were determined at meetings presided over by Rokuzo."

Wily as ever, P'u Yi seized on the occasion to declare as a witness that "in all my fifty years this has been my most glorious experience . . . . This is the first time in my life I have served the interests of the people." What about his testimony at Tokyo? "Criminal as I am," he continued, "today even I can feel pride at being a Chinese in the New China." The New China News Agency covered the trial extensively, reporting his every statement, but the official news agency did not report whether the gallery and defendants broke into applause following this declaration. Nor did the agency give any indication of whether the last Manchu emperor would also stand trial. Indeed, nothing was said about his future, if he had any. This was, clearly, a decision reserved for Chairman Mao.

The defendants pleaded guilty and were sentenced to prison terms of twelve to twenty years (they had already been in custody eleven years awaiting trial). Rokuzo was given the longest sentence, but he was terminally ill; as a political gesture toward Tokyo, his sentence was suspended and he was repatriated to Japan together with 662 other Japanese who had been detained as prisoners of war since 1945. On their arrival, a *New York Times* dispatch from Tokyo reported that the prisoners showed the effects of "brainwashing." Their release, however, was interpreted as additional evidence of the new spirit of liberalism epitomized by Chairman Mao's hundred flowers slogan.

After his pleasing Mukden performance—which may be likened to an opening in New Haven before a Broadway run—P'u Yi was now ready to be presented to the outside world. The following month Reuter's Peking correspondent, David Chip, visited Fushun and interviewed him, the first Englishman to talk to him in twenty years.

Chip found him a forlorn figure in his drab blue jacket and matching worn trousers. But there was no doubt about his authenticity; he was betrayed by the ever-present horn-rimmed spectacles. The prison, Chip observed, was encircled by a high wall with an electric fence; and in the exercise yard, in the Manchurian summer sun, forty elderly prisoners, their hair streaked with gray, sat playing cards. To Chip, they played "with the studied, yet aimless, determination of those who have an eternity to spare." P'u Yi's brother, P'u Chieh was among them.

Interestingly, as at the Tojo Trial, although Chip was not aware of it, P'u Yi spoke "haltingly but gradually gained confidence."

"I should not be regarded as a former head of state as I was a traitor to China and helped the Japanese to carry out their aggressive policy," he said, as if by rote. Thereupon he devoted the rest of the interview to a confession of his crimes, real and otherwise. "I was surprised by the lenient treatment I received on returning to China," he said. As for the future, like a man who has had an eternity to spare, P'u Yi said he did not know whether or not he would be tried for treason. Chip then observed that he had already been locked up eleven years, without charge, without trial. P'u Yi interrupted him. "I do not feel it unjust," he said quickly.

Chip's interview brought to mind P'u Yi's conversation with Lord Lytton twenty-five years earlier which was carried on in the presence of the late Itagaki. "As he rose to leave," Chip reported, "he bowed to me and to the three officers who had sat silently through the interview and whose grandfathers would have prostrated themselves in his presence."

P'u Yi had performed magnificently. If Itagaki were alive to witness the scene, he would probably say, "Your Excellency's manner was perfect; you spoke beautifully." One of the three officers may have said as much after Chip departed.

Indeed, P'u Yi performed so beautifully that he was soon placed on display like an antique in a curio shop before another Westerner, Lucien Bodard, the French journalist and author. Bodard described P'u Yi's appearance in terms strikingly similar to those employed by Chip, that is, as a "thin, sad-eyed man dressed in worker's clothes, who talked of nothing but of his guilt." Incessantly, he told Bodard, "I am a traitor who wronged the people and deserve punishment." As a result of his imprisonment, P'u Yi claimed, he had undergone a "complete reeducation" and that he had emerged a new man. The performance, Bodard felt, was pitiful.

A year later, in 1957, in the book *La Chine de la Douceur,* published in Paris, Bodard expanded on the interview, and more than any other writer of this period he captured the pathos of the Celestial Emperor behind bars.

Peking granted Bodard permission to visit Fushun for a ninety-minute interview. But even at Fushun, he discovered, P'u Yi was not easily accessible. In spite of Peking's authorization, Bodard spent seemingly limitless hours visiting offices and making telephone calls "to put in motion the invisible machinery of the Communist authorities," he wrote. Finally, he was escorted outside the town to the thought control center with its barbed wire and soldiers with fixed bayonets. After a new series of delays, he was led to the prison lounge with its enormous portrait of Stalin hanging from the wall. The lounge was tawdry, furnished with chipped vases, stained sofas, torn screens. Bodard's escort, a youthful colonel whose uniform was adorned with epaulettes as big as wings, notified him that the prisoner may speak only in Chinese. After a thirty-minute delay, P'u Yi entered the lounge. He was dressed in a new blue uniform, a worker's blue linen cap and shiny, coarse black shoes.

"I hardly asked the first question, when, without listening more, automatically, he started," Bodard said. "He sounded like a record that keeps going for some minutes."

"In the past," P'u Yi said, "I was a feudal enemy of the people. I was the lackey of the Japanese imperialists, a traitor to the fatherland, to the people. I never considered the life of the people. I thought only of myself and exploited the masses . . . . [Now] I know the truth."

Bodard observed that "he did not utter a sentence without using the word 'people,' " and he added, "His anguish is evident."

As the record played on, a heavyset man in civilian clothes entered the room. "He sits down in an armchair at the back of P'u Yi, some meters from me," Bodard observed. "He is truly powerful: a thickset individual, massive, the head square, the eyes hard, the grayish hair cut short, the expression intelligent and rough. He was not introduced to me." Bodard suspected that he was P'u Yi's warden.

The Frenchman interrupted the former emperor's soliloquy and interposed a question: "Are you the only prisoner or do you have other companions?"

"In my dormitory," P'u Yi replied, "there are other traitors like myself."

As he went on to describe the former Manchukuo officials interned with him, the colonel leaped to his feet. "You don't have the right to interrogate P'u Yi except about himself," he shouted at Bodard. "You are not to put questions to him about other affairs and other people. Don't do this again or I will call a halt to the interview."

Bodard was stunned. "It was the first time in China that I suffered such an outburst," he said. "It is not the manner of the régime."

During the outburst, P'u Yi paled. Quickly, the record player was turned on. "I hate my crimes, I repent," P'u Yi repeated expressionlessly.

Apparently in an effort to ease his embarrassment, Bodard asked him whether he was surprised he had not been shot as a traitor on his return to China. "I was astonished," he replied. "Think back in the history of the world. Have you ever heard of such an example of generosity? . . . Instead of killing me, the Communists have given me true life. My life in this prison is better than it ever was amidst my family."

317

As the time allotted for the interview ebbed, P'u Yi suddenly began to talk about the past and, as he drifted backward in time, Bodard noticed that his expression changed appreciably. P'u Yi spoke of how his heart was filled with rage and revenge after he was driven from the Forbidden City and that in his misery the Japanese were good to him.

"The Japanese gave me asylum and money," he said. "I accepted because it was my only chance. In that way, it all started. . . . Starting in Manchuria, I wanted to retake all of China and reestablish my throne in Peking. But this did not enter the plans of the Japanese. It resulted in a constant confrontation, a secret, everyday struggle between the Japanese and myself."

As P'u Yi spoke, Bodard gathered "the impression that, in the midst of his memories, he was swept away and spoke sincerely. But on a signal from the colonel, P'u Yi's voice lost its tone," Bodard continued, "and he returned to his role. It was like the settling of a dense fog." Once again, the record resumed its familiar themes—feudalism, the people, imperialism.

The colonel halted the monologue. The hour and a half had expired. P'u Yi rose mechanically from his chair—and without offering to shake hands with his interviewer—rapidly turned and left the dilapidated surroundings of the lounge. "I saw him disappear with his drooping shoulders, his long neck, his body slight," Bodard recalled. "The colonel explained to me that it is time for his bridge game, so I left, too, amid polite expressions from the colonel and other officers: The small incident of a while back is forgotten."

Perplexed, Bodard returned first to Fushun and then Peking. Why didn't the Communists execute P'u Yi? Why did they keep him penned up? For propaganda purposes to edify journalists like himself? Bodard doubted it. "There must be another reason," he wrote, "but I don't know it." For some unknown, ulterior purpose, he concluded, Mao had placed P'u Yi on a shelf in his stockroom. "Mao never neglects anything," Bodard observed.

As he mulled over the interview during his return journey, he raised the pregnant question: Was death preferable to the exhibition he had just witnessed? "In this matter," he sagely wrote, "I am no judge."

Just as P'u Yi was periodically interviewed by Japanese correspondents sympathetic to the régime during the Manchukuo period—K. K. Kawakami, the Washington correspondent of *Hochi Shimbun,* for example—Chinese correspondents wearing rose-tinted glasses, also descended on Fushun, among them P'an Chi-chung. In a book published in Peking in 1957, the same year as Bodard's, and based on lengthy interviews with P'u Yi, P'an concluded, "We can believe most of what he says," and he added: "He is frank, and, although a criminal, he has adopted a positive attitude to life."

Embellishing on his new P'u Yi, P'an continued, "From what I have seen, it is only recently that this last of our emperors has begun to understand that which is life and that which is love, and his understanding is becoming deeper every year."

Bodard did a better job assessing P'u Yi's story. "The world's glory is meaningless," he wrote. "This sums up his life . . . ."

CHAPTER 28

Return to Peking

After the heady events of 1956–1957, P'u Yi's hope for early release soared. The visits of his relatives, the interviews with foreign correspondents, the tours beyond the prison walls, his public appearance as a witness at a war crimes trial, above all, the chairman's observation that he was doing "quite well"—all pointed toward his rehabilitation. "I began 1958 full of hope," he said.

But instead of being released, the years in prison lengthened through 1958 and into 1959. Once again, he was the victim of historical forces over which he exercised no control. This time it was the aftermath of the hundred flowers campaign.

The campaign had collapsed into confusion. In the belief that Mao was sincerely motivated in proposing a freer climate of opinion, intellectuals, academicians, students, writers, and others responded openly with a growing storm of criticism against the régime. The concept of thought reform was openly assailed. Critic after critic rose to denounce "brainwashing" as an assault on the person. "I find thought reform repulsive," a philosopher declared publicly." I am not aware that there is anything wrong with my thoughts." A

Peking professor addressed a personal letter to Mao, cited the constitution's guarantee of "freedom of the person" and other civil rights and charged that "the articles of the constitution on human rights have become a sort of window dressing to deceive the people." Popular demonstrations against the régime erupted in many cities. Mao was stunned—although as one with pretensions to intellectualism himself who had rebelled against conformity in his youth and had demanded greater personal freedom, even cutting off his queue in defiance of P'u Yi, it is hard to understand what he expected. If nothing else, Mao's surprised reaction to the hundred flowers campaign illustrated the physical and intellectual isolation of the Forbidden City. No one was immune from the pernicious and debilitating atmosphere of the Violet Enclosure. Just as the milieu of the prison conditioned those undergoing thought reform, so did the atmosphere of the Forbidden City corrupt its occupant, whether an emperor attired in a brocaded gown or a chairman in a quasi-military jacket with mandarin collar.

As the disturbances in China spread, Mao rose to meet the challenge, forcibly. Overnight the hundred flowers campaign was abandoned. The garden was weeded. A "rectification" campaign was initiated, in essence, a drive to terrorize the régime's critics into submission. By June 26, 1957, a buoyant Chou En-lai was able to report to the National People's Congress, while Uncle Tsai probably made notes for his imperial nephew, that 16.8 percent of the "counterrevolutionaries" who sprouted during the hundred flowers campaign were sentenced to death; 43.3 percent, sentenced to "reform through labor"; 32 percent placed under "surveillance"; and 8.9 percent "reeducated" and given clemency. Six months later, on January 6, Marshal Lo Jui-ch'ing, the minister for public security who later became chief of the general staff and disappeared in 1966 in the Cultural Revolution, reported to the Congress that more than 100,000 "counterrevolutionaries" had been unmasked, including three cabinet ministers; "more than 370,000 counterrevolutionaries and other criminals in society throughout the country surrendered voluntarily to the authorities"; and that "more than 2 million reports were submitted throughout the country exposing counterrevolutionaries."

In this atmosphere P'u Yi's hope for release waned. At Fushun there were new rounds of intensified self-criticism and group discussion. The series were painful for him as he was forced to go over the old ground and review his collaboration with the Japanese. He was also accused of continuing to covet "private thoughts and feelings." "At the time when the great leap forward was taking place throughout the country," P'u Yi explained, "the prison governor put it to us that we needed to review our thoughts in order to clear away ideological obstructions to our progress."

A new element was also introduced, reform through labor. P'u Yi worked briefly in a pencil factory and, with winter's approach, carried baskets of coal suspended from a long pole braced across his shoulders, the traditional method of transporting goods in the Far East. The pole bit into the shoulder of the graying, fifty-two-year-old former emperor just as the bamboo cane used for punishment had once bit into the buttocks of his servants. With a smile, the prison governor inquired about his shoulder. "It does not hurt, and it is not swollen," P'u Yi replied. "It is a bit red, that is all." The spirit of "joy through labor," a term first developed by P'u Yi's former ally, Hitler, pervades this portion of his autobiography.

By 1958 the rectification campaign melted into still another campaign, "the great leap forward," a utopian Maoist concept in which the commune was introduced and such absurdities as the construction of backyard blast furnaces were seriously encouraged. According to letters from his relatives in Peking, "everywhere was work and enthusiasm." Typically, with his subtle tongue in cheek, he wrote that from the letters "I learned of many amazing new things"; doubtlessly, including steelmaking in backyards.

As a measure of his rehabilitation, however, he was assigned to work at the prison clinic as a medical orderly. He scrubbed floors, swept up, and did odd chores. Two hours daily were spent in studying medicine, with emphasis on Chinese traditional medicine, acupuncture, and moxibustion. Meanwhile, the group discussions continued.

As his hopes for early release eroded, he again grew despondent. And once again, as on rare occasions in the past, the man of the dramatic decision emerged. For him, he made the ultimate sacrifice.

In mid-1959 he requested an interview with the prison governor and declared that he wanted formally to surrender his Great Ch'ing seal, the symbol of his dynastic power, to the New China. Of course, he had actually done so earlier and received a "receipt" for it. But now, in effect, he made the grand gesture of figuratively tearing up the receipt (he confided to the governor that, "I lost the receipt for it ages ago"). Although we can only speculate, it appears that P'u Yi deliberately "lost" the receipt or, at least, claimed to have lost it. By voluntarily surrendering the seal and then handing over the receipt for it, the emperor who had mounted the Dragon Throne a half century earlier, died. A new P'u Yi emerged as a commoner in the People's Republic. By this act, Mao's Dynasty won its legitimacy from the dynasty which preceded it, just as the Manchu won their legitimacy from the Ming.

In Peking, the grand gesture had an impact, as P'u Yi intended. Mao sprang him. In the summer of 1959, shortly after he had made his sacrifice, the prison governor summoned him for a private talk.

"I've been looking at the record of your cell," he said. "How are things? Have you been having any ideological problems recently?"

P'u Yi sensed that the moment of truth was at hand. Enthusiastically, he spoke of his past wrongs and confirmed his new outlook on life. "If you speak the truth you have nothing to fear," the governor replied, adding: "You still don't really understand that to be a real man you need courage."

"You must have the courage to speak the truth," the governor emphasized.

Of all the attributes of manliness, the most prominent one that P'u Yi never possessed was perhaps the courage to speak the truth.

In this sense, to employ the governor's phrase, he was never "a real man."

On September 14, as the New China prepared to observe the tenth anniversary of the founding of the People's Republic, Mao declared that "it would be fitting to announce and put into effect a special pardon for a number of war criminals, counterrevolutionaries and common criminals who have genuinely reformed." In the chairman's view, "the policy of combining reform through labor with ideological education has achieved great success." Three days later, on cue, Liu Shao-chi, Mao's heir-apparent, proclaimed a special pardon.

At Fushun, as P'u Yi and his inmates listened to the news over the state radio, they burst into cheers, and applause, shouting slogans of "Long live the People's Republic!" "It was as if ten thousand strings of firecrackers had exploded at once," P'u Yi recalled.

But the régime kept the prisoners dangling in expectation. Two months passed and nobody was released. Then one evening the deputy governor of the prison visited him. "What would you think if you were included in the special pardon?"

"It is out of the question," P'u Yi replied, laughing uncontrollably.

The very next day the prisoners were ordered to assemble in the auditorium. A broad strip of crimson cloth stretched across the stage, emblazoned with extra large characters, and reading: "Fushun War Criminal Prison—Special Pardon Meeting." P'u Yi trembled.

After a few words from the governor of the prison, a representative of the Supreme People's Court mounted the stage and read the following proclamation:

Notice of a Special Pardon from
the Supreme People's Court
of the People's Republic of China

In accordance with the Special Pardon Order issued by the Chairman of the People's Republic of China on September 17, 1959, this Court has investigated the case of the "Manchukuo" war criminal Aisin-Gioro P'u Yi.

The war criminal Aisin-Gioro P'u Yi, male, 54 years old [Chinese-style] of the Manchu nationality, and from Peking, has now served ten years' [sic] detention.

As a result of remolding through labor and ideological education during his captivity, he has shown he has genuinely reformed. In accordance with the stipulations of Clause I of the Special Pardon Order, he is therefore to be released.

[Seal]   Supreme People's Court
of the People's Republic
of China.

December 4, 1959

P'u Yi wept.

That night, over Radio Peking, China learned that the former Celestial Emperor was returning to Peking. P'u Yi's release made the papers around the world, in Tokyo, London, Cairo and Hong Kong. In New York it was played on the front page.

Among those released with him were thirty former high-ranking Nationalist officials, including field-grade officers, an ex-cabinet minister, and several Manchukuo generals. Also freed was a prominent Mongolian leader, General Siono-donbob, who was briefly groomed by the Japanese in the 1930s to rule Mongolia if they had succeeded in wresting Inner Mongolia from China and Outer Mongolia from the Soviet Union.

From Peking, the New China News Agency (NCNA) circulated a dispatch which reported that the group received clemency because "they had repented, acknowledged their crimes and showed they are turning over a new leaf." In a joint resolution, the report continued, the newly released prisoners expressed their determination "to continue to remold themselves so as to contribute to the building of the New China." The new citizens also expressed their unbounded gratitude to the state.

P'u Yi was presented with a new suit, a quilted jacket, and a train ticket to Peking. *Peiching*. He stared at the characters, overcome with emotion.

Like a departing ambassador, he made a round of hearty farewells at the prison. Just before he left, the governor gave him a gift, the French gold watch found among the treasures confiscated earlier, a watch he had purchased in 1924 during the German Hospital caper.

From Fushun he took the local to Mukden, gazed on the tomb of Nurhachu and boarded the express to Peking, which lay some 500 miles to the southwest and at times had seemed like 500 light years away. As the fortunes of destiny would have it, he had both left Peking in 1925 and returned in 1959 in anonymity.

As the train sped through Shan Hai Kwan, the gate at the eastern-most tip of the Great Wall through whose portal the Manchu bannermen streamed in triumph in 1644, his heartbeat quickened and seemed to keep pace with the clicking of the train's wheels. The train then turned westward and headed for Peking over tracks first laid in 1897 during the reign of his great-aunt, the Old Buddha.

On December 9, as he peered through the window, which was blotched by patches of frost, he made out the approaches to Peking, the broad and lofty crenellated battlements of the Manchu-Tartar city. As he stepped from the train, the golden roofs of the Imperial City which enclosed the Forbidden City, sparkled in the sunlight in the distance.

As he had promised himself, and his ancestors, P'u Yi had returned to the city of his birth, of his fame, and of his misfortune. But he had returned in a fashion utterly inconceivable when he left thirty-four years earlier.

CHAPTER 29

Ascent of the Dragon

At the Peking station platform, not far from the Hata-men, or Gate of Sublime Learning, Uncle Tsai, P'u Yi's brothers and sisters, their spouses and their children, formed a large anxious party to welcome him to the city of his destiny. Some he had not seen in more than a generation; some he had never seen. He was at a loss to know how to act. Should he throw himself into their embrace? That struck him as unseemly for an emperor, even an ex-emperor. Reserved, but with a face wreathed in cloudless happiness, he extended his right arm and shook hands firmly with each and every one of them, permitting himself a public display of emotion by patting the children on the shoulders. How should they respond to him? Uncle Tsai and P'u Yi's brothers and sisters were also at a loss to know how to act. Then, as P'u Yi began to shake their hands, with ease, spontaneously, they referred to him as "elder brother," a common familial form of Chinese address they never dared utter in the old days. If the secret police witnessed the homecoming scene, they gave no indication of their presence. Glancing at the large station clock, P'u Yi took out his gold pocket watch and adjusted it to mark,

327

he said, "the beginning of my new life." He set the watch at Peking time.

In the warmth of his family's company, he was driven to the northern part of the city and to his father's old house. There he was besieged by well-wishers, old friends, Manchu bannermen and former eunuchs from the days of glory in the Forbidden City. All of them were aged.

Settling down after a few days, yet still awash with excitement, he longed to gaze once again on T'ien An Men, the Gate of Heavenly Peace, a portal once reserved for emperors. Now it was open to the public. The great archway led to the Forbidden City and was flanked by two carved marble columns built by the Perfect Emperor "in order that anyone might write upon them an opinion as to the acts of the ruler, or suggestions for improvements in the government"—the origin of China's wall posters or newspapers. Of course, what P'u Yi truly wanted to see again was not the majestic Heavenly Gate itself but the Forbidden City which lay beyond it, the city of his reality in childhood and of his dreams in adulthood.

As he left for the Forbidden City with its walls of familiar violet-colored mortar, he took in the sights of modern Peking. The city was still as spacious as ever. It appeared cleaner than in the old days; the rickshaws were missing, and so were the beggars. The mixed, clashing colors, noises, and smells of the old Peking were also gone, replaced by a quiet uniformity dominated by a drab gray punctuated by the great blue coats and smart looking hats of hares' furs worn by party functionaries and government officials. As in 1924, when he last saw Peking, there were few cars in the main thoroughfares and those that were there were not Fords, Austins, and Bugattis but the new models he recognized from his days of Soviet internment: Zims and Moskovas. But the street lamps along Chang-tien Avenue, once Peking's most fashionable shopping boulevard, heartened him; they were the same queer, globular lamps of the past. Above all, he was surprised by the city's growth beyond its ancient walls. Incredibly to him, the urban sprawl stretched to the Summer Palace. And on the southern approaches to the city was an industrial suburb beyond his recognition, marked by clusters of machine tool plants, an enormous steel mill and a printing plant.

Then, in the course of his perigrination, he suddenly set a true course and headed for the Great Within. Slowly he walked across T'ien An Meng, Heavenly Peace Square, savoring the view with each step. Enveloped in his dreams, he walked alone under the red tunnel of the T'ien An Men and down the path of dragon flagstones leading directly into the Forbidden City. His heartbeat quickened, his head felt light. It was all there, just as he remembered, the Palace for the Cultivation of Happiness, his "little red school house," where he had spent his adolescent years with Johnston; the Altar of Heaven where, as a boy, he knelt and spoke directly to heaven; the Palace of Tranquil Earth where, in panic, he had spent his wedding night with Elizabeth; the Palace of Treasured Beauty, Elizabeth's private residence; and the Palace of Long Springtime where the pudgy, dimpled Wen Hsiu, his secondary consort, dwelt.

Under the republic, large areas of the Violet Enclosure had been opened to the public since the twenties as a living museum. Nostalgia seized P'u Yi as he entered the imperial gardens and saw children frolicking in the winter sun and old men sipping hot tea. It was January thaw and, although there were patches of snow on the ground and along the peaked roofs, the Forbidden City, protected from the winds by its high walls, radiated the warmth of false spring. In the distance he saw the Hall of the Blending of the Great Creative Forces in which the celestial and terrestrial powers of the universe intermingled and interacted in perfect harmony. In that building were housed the imperial seals. He wondered whether Mao personally kept in the great hall the seal that he, P'u Yi, had turned over to the state for safekeeping.

With strange emotions he glanced upward at the golden, serpentine roof of the Hall of Supreme Harmony where it all had begun for him in 1908. He may have recalled the comment he made in 1932 when China was torn by civil war and the Japanese banged at the gates: "If someone else would undertake the responsibility for the country and bring disaster to an end with the True Way, I would be happy to remain a commoner." This sentiment may have flashed through his mind as he peered deeper into the recesses of the Forbidden City, off limits to commoners and heavily guarded, where the founder of the new dynasty, Mao Tse-tung, guided the destinies of three-quarters of a billion people. Mao not only possessed the shadow of authority, the seal and the Forbidden City, but also the substance. His authority within China was as complete, and awesome, as that of past emperors; national obeisance to him was absolute. In his state of mind, P'u Yi probably would have been content to find a weathered bench and spend each of his remaining days in the imperial garden, inwardly keeping alive the image of the past. But once again, as he was drawn inexorably into the vortex of power politics, he was fated never to enjoy a placid day.

At home and abroad, throughout his life, for better or worse, he was a celebrity, a curiosity. It had always been that way and it would always be. Peking had gone to great lengths to "remold" him. If he were drawn into the régime, he would be a glittering illustration of the New China's benevolence toward old adversaries, a living broadside beckoning others, notably the Chinese on Taiwan, to return to the bountiful earth of the Middle Flowery country. Accordingly, Peking placed P'u Yi on open display as a showpiece of the régime's good will and humanity, and as the acknowledged liege of the Manchu people inhabiting the border regions abutting on the Soviet Union.

A fortnight after his return to the center of the world, P'u Yi spoke to the nation over Radio Peking. Interviewed by a radio correspondent, he played the familiar role of the ventriloquist's dummy. As a result of his experiences at Fushun, he claimed, he came to realize that as emperor he was "but a leader of criminal warlords." Surprisingly for so late in the game, he confessed that he had prayed for an American victory over China in the Korean War. Automaton-like, as if under a spell, he lavishly praised the New China.

In March of the new year, 1960, expressing an interest in horticulture, an interest which he had developed at Khabarovsk, he was assigned to work in the Peking botanical gardens of the Chinese Academy of Sciences' Institute of Botany. As evidence of his newly acquired loyalty, he joined a local militia for the overaged and partook in his first public demonstration in Heavenly Peace Square. And so, incredibly, the former Celestial Emperor paraded in front of the Forbidden City with the multitudes, carrying a placard and shouting political slogans. The occasion was the Communist campaign against ratification of the Japanese-American Security Treaty which eventually culminated in massive leftist demonstrations in Tokyo and the cancellation of a visit to Japan by President Eisenhower.

Unavoidably, step by step, P'u Yi was guided back into the political maelstrom. On April 10, Hsieh Chueh-tsai, chairman of the Supreme People's Court, reported to the Congress on the decision to release "reformed" prisoners and singled out P'u Yi as a classic illustration. " 'The P'u Yi who was once emperor is now dead,' " he said, quoting the former emperor. " 'The present one is the P'u Yi of the new life given to me by the Communist Party.' " Seven months later, on November 22, P'u Yi was accorded full rights as a citizen of the People's Republic. His reemergence into prominence moved relatively rapidly thereafter.

An uninterrupted flow of visitors (sightseers, really) crowded his compound. The Japanese, their consciences seared by the "China Incident," were particularly fascinated by him and there was scarcely a Japanese correspondent assigned to Peking who did not consider an interview with the former emperor of China and Manchukuo de rigueur. P'u Yi also turned up at diplomatic dinners and state functions, for example, at the formal banquet for Viscount Montgomery of Alamein, the controversial British field marshal who toured the People's Republic in June, 1960. "Everywhere," Montgomery subsequently wrote in the London *Sunday Times,* "I saw a happy, laughing people—cheerful, friendly and seemingly contented with their lot." However, the discipline was marked, he noted, and he concluded that as long as an individual accepted the discipline and obeyed the rules, he had nothing to fear.

At the government's behest, P'u Yi also devoted less and less time to the botanical gardens and more and more time to working on his autobiography. As he researched the book, the figure of the tall, gracious, aging Manchu gentleman in the immaculately tailored tunic affected by the régime's leadership, his eyes wreathed by a pair of spectacles, became an increasingly familiar sight at the National Archives, the History Museum, the Capital Library and the Peking Library. He read the memoirs of Chen Pao-shen and Johnston, the official histories of the Great Ch'ing Dynasty, and other documents of the period.

As his activity intensified, he was "elected" to the National Committee of the People's Political Consultative Conference and partook in the rubber-stamping reports of the National People's Congress, which last convened in 1964. He also became a commissioner of the Political Consultative Conference's arts and history research section. In 1963 the minister of culture announced that approval had been granted for the publication of his autobiography. The following year the government printing office brought out the three volumes. They caused a sensation inside China and among overseas Chinese. Their publication in English later that year by Peking's Foreign Language Press, an official government agency, propelled P'u Yi back into the view of foreigners.

Significantly, P'u Yi's return to prominence kept pace with the devolution of Sino-Soviet relations. The alliance between the two great Communist powers disintegrated amid explosive ideological, territorial, racial, economic, nuclear, and diplomatic tensions. Indeed, only a few months after P'u Yi's release from the Fushun prison, the schism surfaced—when Moscow formally notified Peking of the Kremlin's decision to suspend economic and technical assistance to China, and confirmed the Kremlin's earlier abrogation of the Sino-Soviet nuclear-sharing agreement. Two years later, in the autumn of 1962, the Soviet Union conspicuously failed to support China, a "fraternal country," to employ Marxist-Leninist phraseology, in China's masterfully directed border war with India.

Ominously, the following year, on September 20, 1963, Tass, the official Soviet news agency, reported that "since 1960, Chinese servicemen and civilians have been systematically violating the Soviet border." This was a development reminiscent of the Russo-Japanese border tension in Manchuria in the 1930s. "In the single year of 1962," Tass claimed, "more than 5,000 violations of the Soviet border from the Chinese side were registered." In rebuttal, Peking accused Moscow of instigating the border disputes along the Sino-Soviet frontier.

As the tension deepened, the Red army reinforced its borders with China, and on July 10, 1964, the year P'u Yi's autobiography appeared, with its lengthy chapter on his internment at Khabarovsk, Mao publicly accused the Soviet Union of deploying the Red army along the Manchurian frontier. "About a hundred years ago, the area to the east of Lake Baikal became Russian territory, and since then Vladivostok, Khabarovsk, Kamchatka, and other areas have become Soviet territory," Mao said. "We have yet to present our account for this list."

In another salvo, Mao observed the following month that the Soviet Union's 220 million people occupied 8.6 million square miles of territory. "It is about time," the chairman said, "to put an end to this allotment." In turn, China reinforced its forces in Manchuria heavily, prompting *Pravda,* the official Soviet Communist Party daily, to warn, "We are faced with an openly expansionist program with far-reaching pretensions."

In a showdown between Moscow and Peking, the border peoples would serve as cat's paws, a valuable asset for such clandestine activity as intelligence gathering and guerrilla operations. Along the Amur and Ussuri rivers separating Manchuria and the Soviet maritime province, no people knew both sides of the river better than the Manchu, bred and raised along their banks. Thus, the deterioration in relations between Russia and China immeasurably strengthened P'u Yi's political value. In the rivalry between Russia and China for the allegiance of the Manchu and Mongols,

Mao held P'u Yi, their hereditary liege, as a trump. This, then, explained why he survived in the prison camps first of Moscow and then of Peking.

Remolded outwardly if not inwardly, close to the Forbidden City, emerging once more as the spokesman for the Manchu, P'u Yi's role in the New China secured his future. There was nothing more that Peking could conceivably demand of him. Or was there?

For 368 years dynastic law had forbidden a Manchu emperor from marrying a Chinese. The purity of the Aisin-Gioro line, therefore, was never diluted. In the person of even P'u Yi the former ruling Manchu house remained as ethnically pure and separate from its former subjects as ever. Like the Japanese before him, however, Mao moved to "rectify" the situation. But while the Japanese succeeded only in having the emperor's brother P'u Chieh marry a Japanese to infuse Japanese blood into the imperial line, Mao went further. P'u Yi's demurrers notwithstanding, the chairman arranged another marriage for him, this one to a Chinese woman. The wedding was held, appropriately, on May Day, 1962, a day set aside in New China as a tribute to the glory of labor.

Thus, in this manner, the homoerotic P'u Yi acquired his fifth and last wife, Li Shu-hsien, an attractive, forty-year-old nurse from Hangchow, a city famed for its lovely women. As with Hiro Saga, P'u Chieh's wife, in Manchukuo a generation earlier, the ruling power had insinuated a permanent observer into the emperor's immediate circle.

There was, of course, no need to arrange a marriage for this purpose. If nothing else, the People's Republic was a modern police state. As early as 1954 Peking adopted the Organic Regulations of Urban Street Offices, which set up a nationwide surveillance system patterned after the old *pao chia* system which had existed in Manchu China. Resident Committees were established on the basis of one for every 100 to 600 households, and then divided into Resident Teams for each 15 to 40 households within the group. Cooperating closely with the secret police, their function was to maintain public order and security by keeping every individual under constant surveillance.

After spending 1945–59 in prison, P'u Yi was hardly likely to oppose the régime actively. Thus, his marriage was not arranged to put him under police surveillance. Far more important, from a Chinese perspective, was the fact that he was marrying outside the Manchu nationality. Even if the new union produced no offspring, indeed, if it were never consummated, the dynastic law of almost four centuries would be broken, and broken irrevocably. Thus, in a symbolic political sense, on May 1, for the first time in their stormy relationship, Manchuria and China were united, the union of the Manchu dragon and a Chinese woman, an alliance brought about, astonishingly, by a Communist dynasty.

Their friends gave the couple a gala dinner party the night before the nuptials, and the next day P'u Yi said, "I and my bride, Li Shu-hsien, started our own little home." As a wedding gift, Mao had provided P'u Yi with a stately brick Peking-style mansion. As compared with the lavish surroundings of the Forbidden City, of course, he subconsciously characterized the impressive residence as a "little home."

Not unexpectedly, the marriage raised eyebrows at home and abroad. From Hong Kong, the London *Times* correspondent pondered the "riddle of Peking's hospitality to the last Manchu emperor. . . . There is the suspicion, however, that they [the Manchu] may be of use to Peking in a possible claim to the whole of Mongolia," the paper speculated. The reference, of course, was to Outer Mongolia, long a Chinese province, which the Soviet Union had wrested away. "No doubt Peking would not be put out if the new Chinese wife of the ex-emperor produced a Chinese male heir," the *Times* dispatch continued. "Even in a republic, it is possible that a place would be found for him in Ulan Bator, the Mongolian capital, or if not there . . . perhaps in Mukden."

Photographs of the attractive couple appeared in China. P'u Yi, with a touch of gray at the temples but otherwise hardly showing

335

either his age or the strain of an extraordinarily eventful life, was a picture of good health. Indeed, he often boasted to relatives and friends that after his rigorous, ascetic prison life, his appetite was better than ever and that he no longer suffered from insomnia. Visitors reported that when they shook hands with him, his grip was firm and hard. As for his bride, she appeared in the photographs as a smart looking upper-class woman, the sort who might, under other circumstances, set off for a shopping spree.

P'u Chieh, the emperor's brother, joined their household and so did his Japanese wife who had voluntarily returned to Peking and his side in 1961. They all shared the old Ch'un property together with its high walls, screened windows and doors, and walk-around porch. For P'u Yi these were the quietest years since his days of idleness at Khabarovsk. Three years passed in this pleasant fashion, with his brother, sister-in-law, two sisters, and his new wife at his side. Most of the time he spent in the library, researching and reliving the Manchu past.

Then there was tension along the Amur River which separates Russia and Manchuria, and China proper was caught up in another of those here-today-gone-tomorrow campaigns. This one was known as The Great Proletarian Cultural Revolution. All schools were closed. The children were massed into units known as Red Guards, and turned loose on the streets to parade, demonstrate and riot as the evolving Cultural Revolution warranted.

Early in the campaign, in 1966, the Red Guards demonstrated along the Amur River and called for the return of China's "lost territories." Peking also promulgated "new regulations" which ignored the joint Sino-Soviet Navigation Treaty governing shipping on the Amur and Ussuri. The new rules made it almost impossible for a Russian flagship to sail the rivers without infringing on Chinese regulations. On one occasion that year, Red Guards became so incensed at the sight of Russian vessels that they fired shots at Soviet shipping. Three years later, in 1969, the Russian and Chinese armies were openly skirmishing along the Ussuri.

Given this background, P'u Yi's position appeared stronger

than ever on February 7, 1967, as he celebrated his sixty-first birthday. Indeed, his uniqueness held out a flicker of hope for greater things to come, although among China's 208 verifiable emperors, only 4 lived to be eighty or more, the oldest, the greatest of all Manchu emperors, Ch'ien Lung, attaining the age of eighty-eight.

The Cultural Revolution, as it is popularly known in the West, crested that year, and at times, like a swollen river, ran out of control and flooded its banks. The upheaval is ascribed to many causes—to an internal power struggle (Mao's designated successor, Liu Shao-chi, was purged at the outset and his successor's successor, Lin Piao, was purged in the aftermath); to a reaction to a disastrous foreign policy, notably the failure of Peking's efforts to achieve paramount influence in the Afro-Asian world on a wide belt from Algeria to Indonesia; an ideological struggle between dogmatists and pragmatists within the party; to frustration arising out of the presence of a million Soviet troops along China's northern and western borders; the massive American intervention in Vietnam and the presence of the United States Seventh Fleet on China's eastern flank; to the corrupting influence of absolute power, especially within the isolated precincts of the Forbidden City where the political atmosphere has traditionally been marked by intrigue and conspiracy; and, lastly, to irrationality, in part growing out of Mao's recognition that he was mortal and that there was no way to ensure the future as he saw it. None of these factors are mutually exclusive and the Cultural Revolution was probably motivated by a combination of them.

In 1967 the turmoil was in full heat. As violence broke out in major cities as many as 2 million people were detained, arrested, dispatched to thought control centers and labor camps, and executed or killed in street clashes. The acts of destruction during the Cultural Revolution took on many forms: the persecution of Chinese intellectuals; the denunciation of the "four olds," old culture, old thinking, old customs and old habits; the compulsory study of the Little Red Book, a reader composed of the "thoughts of

Mao Tse-tung; the "rectification" of "renegade," "undesirable elements," and, inevitably in a Marxist-Leninist state of mind, "class enemies."

At the outset, the tone of the Cultural Revolution was signalled in an editorial in *Hung Chi* (Red Flag), the theoretical organ of the Chinese Communist Party. "In dealing with the enemy of revolution, we cannot rely on persuasion [brainwashing] but we must rely on struggle," the journal said. "If you don't struggle against him, he will struggle against you. If you don't hit him, he will hit you. Without destruction there will be no construction."

Wall newspapers, called big character posters, appeared all over Peking. Feudalism and imperialism were denounced enthusiastically, and in the process, once again, P'u Yi found himself enmeshed in uncontrollable historical forces. On August 24 of that year, for example, he learned with trepidation that the Red Guards, gathered in Peking, brandishing hammers and shouting slogans, attacked the Central Institute of Arts, smashed statues of Lord Buddha, and slashed portraits of China's emperors and empresses as "relics of feudalism and imperialism."

As the nihilist movement intensified, the Red Guards ridiculed ancestor worship and denounced as a devil Confucius, who preached the idea that heaven gave a mandate to earthly rulers and that therefore no régime and no dynasty was interminable, not even Mao's. As in 1928, the crypts of the dead were broken into and desecrated. Incidents were reported at the tombs of the seventy-two martyrs of the 1911 revolution who had sacrificed their lives to bring down P'u Yi, and also at cemeteries in Shanghai, the hotbed of the Communist Party's radical wing. These macabre events must have distressed P'u Yi who was, if nothing else, a living reminder of "feudalism" and "imperialism."

As the Cultural Revolution spread, like an oil slick, the Peking correspondent of Kyodo, the Japanese news agency, sent a report on October 18, 1967, that P'u Yi had suddenly died the day before. The Peking correspondent of Tokyo's *Nihon Keizai* filed a similar story. But there was no immediate official confirmation.

After a lapse of another twenty-four hours, the New China News Agency confirmed the reports in a two-sentence dispatch:

> Peking—(NCNA)—Mr. Aisin Gioro P'u Yi, member of the National Committee of the Chinese People's Political Consultative Conference, died here of cancer of the kidney, uremia, and anemic heart disease at 0230 on 17 October after he failed to respond to a long period of medical treatment. He was 60 [sic] years old.

But another version of his death soon filtered out of China. At this writing, it still cannot be corroborated.* In some future definitive study of the Great Proletarian Cultural Revolution, the truth may emerge. The late Kao Pai-shih, an author and columnist, averred based on Peking sources that P'u Yi was a victim of the Cultural Revolution. On six different occasions, he wrote, the former Lord of Ten Thousand Years was denounced in wall newspapers. Red Guards marched into his mansion in mid-October and dragged him out. He was tormented with burning cigarettes and with the Japanese water treatment—in which water is forced down the victim's throat with his nostrils pinched tight. Finally, he was paraded in the streets, "his eyes plucked out with a knife." As a result of the pain, he lost consciousness. The following day, with two lines of blood tears streaming down his cheeks, he was racked by convulsions and died.

Similar stories circulated in Japan. The first reaction is to treat such tales with considerable skepticism, at least until an eyewitness or participant in the alleged atrocity comes forward. At present, given the nature of the Chinese régime, which even during the Cultural Revolution was essentially a tightly controlled closed society, such a development is unlikely. Nor is P'u Yi's case unique. Many case files are unresolved in contemporary Peking—the 1953 "suicide" of Kao Kang, the Soviet Union's Manchurian candidate, the recent demise of Liu Shao-chi and Lin Piao, Mao's heirs apparent, the 1972 death from "cancer" of the minister for public

* For a fuller discussion see page 346 ff.

security, the notorious Hsieh Fu-chieh, and a host of other unsolved mysteries.

Be that as it may, as the life of the last Manchu emperor of China ebbed, two questions arose. Did he die as a result of natural causes or was he, perhaps unintentionally, a victim of the Cultural Revolution? And at his death, whether from one cause or the other, did he muster the courage, as he once expressed the hope that he would, to cry out before his dragon spirit ascended to heaven, "Long live the Emperor T'ai Tsung!"?

Author's Note

Talleyrand, it is said, conducted his own biography and, in a manner of speaking, so did P'u Yi, but not without assistance. P'u Yi's memoirs appeared in three volumes as *Wo-ti ch'ien pan-sheng* (Peking, 1964) and, interestingly, he wrote under his reign name and that of his dynasty. Thus, the Peking edition credits the authorship to him as Ch'ing Hsüan Tung.

There are three foreign-language editions, one in Japanese and two in English. In the authorized Japanese edition, the emperor signed his name as Ch'ing Hsüan Tung Aisin-Gioro P'u Yi, which touches all the bases; Aisin-Gioro is, of course, his Manchu clan name. In the two-volume authorized English translation by W. J. F. Fenner, *From Emperor to Citizen*, Vol. I (Peking, 1964) and Vol. II (Peking, 1965), the author is identified as Aisin-Gioro Pu (sic) Yi. Whatever the case, as Jerome Ch'en observed in an article, "The Last Emperor of China," which appeared in the *School of Oriental & African Studies Bulletin*, Vol. 28 (London, 1965), on the basis of literary style, historical content and ideological tone, P'u Yi's autobiography is the work of "at least one professional [writer]

341

breathing down his neck . . . [plus] a trained historian and an English-speaking assistant at his elbow . . . [and] the hand of a party cadre with an extremely alert mind." Since P'u Yi was then a commissioner of the arts and history research section of the People's Political Consultative Conference, Ch'en suggested that his colleagues assisted him in researching and organizing his material, polishing his literary style and eliminating ideological flaws. "It is safe to say that this is teamwork," he concluded, "not the product of a solitary pen."

An unofficial translation of the P'u Yi memoirs appeared in the West as *The Last Manchu* (New York: Putnam, 1967), edited by Paul Kramer, who formerly worked for the Central Intelligence Agency (CIA), and translated by Kuo Ying Paul Tsai, whose father was among the first hundred Chinese sent by the Manchu to the United States in 1872 for a Western education. A prominent official in the Ch'ing dynasty, Professor Tsai's father retired when P'u Yi abdicated in 1912. In a private communication, Professor Tsai recalled how his father took him to visit the former emperor at Chang Gardens during P'u Yi's Tientsin interregnum.

The great difficulty with P'u Yi's autobiography is that it is understandable only by foreign students of Chinese affairs, or, of course, by the Chinese themselves. But the story is bigger than that. While drawing to the fullest on the autobiography, I have attempted to provide the background for historic events which are either taken for granted or omitted from the autobiography for political reasons. All the quotations ascribed to P'u Yi in this book, unless otherwise noted, are taken directly from his autobiography. Quotations of others come from other memoirs, official documents and the like. All quotations are factual; assiduously, I have made no attempt to concoct dialogue.

Like Professor Tsai, I have also had the opportunity of personally observing the last Manchu emperor, but not only fleetingly; rather, I did so daily over a two-week period in 1946 in Tokyo when P'u Yi was a prisoner of the Russians and under the jurisdiction of the Americans. As a result of this first-hand experience, I realized that the popular and often scholarly appraisal of P'u Yi as shallow-minded and slow-witted was largely armchair and ivory-tower stuff in need of refutation.

Covering P'u Yi (and the Tojo Trial), as a young United Press (UP) correspondent, left an indelible imprint on me. I had the opportunity to observe personally Doihara and Itagaki for almost a year during their trial. I also traveled as part of Hirohito's entourage for about two weeks on the first tour the emperor ever took through Japan. I retained my original notes over the years. At the time I was already thoroughly familiar with P'u Yi; at the age of eight I had started to compile a scrapbook on the Mukden Incident and its aftermath and, before joining the UP, I studied Chinese.

I returned to the United States in 1956 and three years later, as a staff writer for the defunct "News of the Week in Review" of *The New York Times,* I again came into contact with P'u Yi, albeit indirectly, writing a short piece on Peking's announcement of his reformation and resurrection from the obscurity of prison. When his memoirs appeared in 1964, I was excited about the possibility of working on a readable Western biography of P'u Yi. This is the result.

Surprisingly little, I discovered, had been written about P'u Yi given the length of time during which he had been appearing, like a fisherman's bobber, on the surface, as a focus of international attention and speculation. Indeed, the only first-hand material extant on his childhood and boyhood was Sir Reginald F. Johnston's classic, *Twilight in the Forbidden City* (New York: Appleton-Century, 1934), which contained a preface by P'u Yi and a photograph of the fan (p. 448) which later became a source of controversy among handwriting experts at the Tojo Trial, and, doubtlessly, chiromancers too. Appropriately, Johnston dedicated his book "To His Majesty the Emperor P'u Yi, in memory of a happy relationship begun fifteen years ago in the Forbidden City, and in the earnest hope that, after the passing of the twilight and the long night, the dawn of a new and happier day for himself, and also for his people on both sides of the Great Wall, is now breaking, this book is dedicated by his faithful and affectionate servant and tutor."

Glimpses of, and other references to, P'u Yi also turned up in other memoirs and accounts of the period: for example, in *With the Empress Dowager* by Katherine A. Carl (New York: Century, 1905); *Old Buddha* by Princess Der Ling (New York: Dodd, Mead, 1928); *Manchukuo: Child of Conflict* by Kiyoshi K. Kawakami (New York: Macmillan, 1933); *A Visit to Manchukuo* by Henry G. Woodhead (Shanghai: Mercury Press, 1932); *The House of Exile* by Nora Waln (Boston: Little, Brown, 1933); *The Last Empress* by Danielle Vare (New York: Sun Dial, 1936); *Tides from the West* by Chiang Monlin (New Haven, Conn.: Yale University Press, 1947); *La Chine de la Douceur* by Lucien Bodard (Paris: Gallimard, 1957); *Mo-tai Hwang-ti Ch'uan-ch'i* by P'an Chi-chiung (Peking: 1957); *The Passing of the Manchus* by P. H. B. Kent (London: 1912); *Ruten No Ohi* by Hiro Aishinkakura [Hiro Saga] (Tokyo: 1959); and *Kotei Fugi* by Seiichiro Yamada (Tokyo: 1960).

I have made extensive use of these sources and also of references to P'u Yi in official diplomatic dispatches of the period, notably those of the Department of State; various newspapers and periodicals, published in China, Japan, Britain, and the United States; League of Nations documents; and in the documents captured by the Allies at the end of World War II and introduced as evidence at the Tojo Trial (International Military Tribunal for the Far East). Other documentation has run the gamut from the magnificent translations of Chinese and Manchu chronicles by such authorities as J. O. P. Bland and E. Backhouse to the *United States Senate: The Deportation of Gregorii Semenov* (Hong Kong: Beamur, 1972), a reprint of the 1922 hearings.

Only one previous attempt at a biography of P'u Yi has appeared (for only an attempt can be made at one, given his inaccessibility at critical turns in his life) *A Dream of Tartary* by Henry McAleavy (London: Allen & Unwin, 1963). McAleavy, who passed away in 1968, relied heavily on Japanese source material. His romanticized book was published while P'u Yi was still alive, and McAleavy did not enjoy the advantage of having access to the P'u Yi memoirs. In a private communication, his widow, a Japanese, observed, "He could have written many more useful and informative books on China had he lived."

A complete bibliography, covering other sources, would fill a dozen pages and largely duplicate the bibliographies found in *The Chinese: Their History and Culture* by Kenneth Scott Latourette (New Haven, Conn.: Yale University Press, 1934); *Manchuria: An Annotated Bibliography* by Peter A. Berton (Washington: Library of Congress, 1951); *Contemporary China* by Peter Berton and Eugene Wu, edited by Howard Koch, Jr. (Stanford: Stanford University Press, 1967); and *Area Handbook for Communist China* (Washington: Government Printing Office, 1967).

Several works should be singled out for special acknowledgment, notably, *Peking* by Juliet Bredon (Shanghai: Kelly and Walsh, 1919); *Manchuria since 1931* by F. C. Jones (London: Oxford University Press, 1949); *China and Japan at War, 1937–1945* by John Hunter Boyle (Stanford: Stanford University Press, 1972); *Defiance in Manchuria* by Sadako N. Ogata (Berkeley: University of California Press, 1964); *The Manchu Abdication and the Powers, 1908–1912* by J. G. Reid (Berkeley: University of California Press, 1935); *The Origin of Manchu Rule in China* by Franz Michael (Baltimore: Johns Hopkins, 1941); *The Reform Movement in China, 1898–1912* by Meribeth E. Cameron (Stanford: Stanford University Press, 1931); *The Rising Sun* by John Toland (New York: Random House, 1970); *The Puppet State of Manchukuo* by T'ang Leong Li (Shanghai, 1935); and *Soviet Policy in the Far East* by Max Beloff (London: Oxford University Press, 1953). In recent years, two scholarly accounts of the nature of Manchu rule have appeared, *Local Government in China under the Ch'ing* by T'ung-tsu Ch'u (Cambridge, Mass.: Harvard University Press, 1970) and *The Manchurian Frontier in Ch'ing History* by

Robert H. G. Lee (Cambridge, Mass.: Harvard University Press, 1970). Others are mentioned and quoted directly in the course of the narrative.

In addition to acknowledging the debt the author owes to so many before him, I should like to acknowledge the professional assistance I received from Mary Kohn, reference librarian, Western Connecticut State College, where I am a member of the adjunct graduate faculty, and Emily Chang, a co-librarian at WesConn, who ably assisted me in Chinese translations and in brushing up my long unused Chinese. A word of gratitude also goes to my editor, Norman Kotker, and my typist, Isabelle Bates.

As for the controversy surrounding P'u Yi's death, the first published report that he was a victim of the Cultural Revolution was attributed to Japanese sources in Peking by the late Kao Pai-shih in his *Ku Ch'un-feng-lou so-chi*, published in Hong Kong, 1968. It reappeared in Wang Chia-yu's *Ti-huang Sheng-huo* (Taipei: Hsueh-sheng Shu-chu, 1968). An English version of Wang's work, translated by T. C. T'ang, appeared under the title *Loves and Lives of Chinese Emperors* (Taipei: Mei Ya, 1972). Wang, a vice president of the Central News Agency (CNA), in a private communication, said that "all details of my story about P'u Yi's death were based on newspaper reports" and that he no longer had the clippings at hand.

In an effort to track down the reports, I discovered, surprisingly, that the principal China "listening posts" in Hong Kong—the Union Research Institute, the Chiluen Research Institute, Chow Ching-wen's Continental Research Institute and *Ming Pao*—did not even keep a file on P'u Yi, much less have firm knowledge of the circumstances surrounding his death.

Many China-watchers adhere to the official version of P'u Yi's passing as belatedly reported by NCNA, among them, Paul Kramer, who edited the unauthorized English translation of his memoirs. "I have every reason to believe that P'u Yi's death in 1967 was a natural one," the former CIA man said. "He had cancer." Chang Kuo-sin, a former UP correspondent and bureau manager in China when I served in a similar capacity in Southeast Asia, who formerly published from Hong Kong the informed weekly, *Chinese Viewpoint*, also discounts Kao's version.

In search of hard information, I have been in contact with a senior diplomat stationed in Peking. He reported "no evidence whatsoever that P'u Yi died of other than natural causes." But, he continued, since P'u Yi was a controversial figure, the Peking diplomatic community was reluctant to raise the matter directly with Chinese officials. "If the report that he suffered at the hands of the Red Guard is true," the diplomat wrote, "it would be enough to guarantee their silence." Professor Jurgen Domes, the director of the Research Unit on Chinese and East Asian Politics at the Otto-Suhr Institute of the Free University of Berlin, however, was able to shed indirect light on the question. Acknowledging, like many others, that "unfortunately, I have not particularly followed the fate of Henry P'u Yi during the Cultural Revolution," he recalled that in 1972 a former Red Guard refugee whom he interviewed at Hong Kong told him that he saw *ta tzu pao*, big character newspapers (wall posters), attacking P'u Yi while he was in Peking. As for himself, Domes said, "I can only say for sure that in the more than 750 Red Guard newspapers which I went through for other purposes, there has been no reference to him."

Another authority, W. J. F. Fenner, the translator of Peking's authorized English language version of the P'u Yi autobiographies, who is presently a member of the Department of Chinese Studies at the University of Leeds, confirmed that P'u Yi was criticized during the Cultural Revolution. "I know," he wrote, "that the publication of his ghosted autobiography both in Chinese and foreign languages was criticized during the Cultural Revolution." But on the question whether P'u Yi was killed by the Red Guards, Fenner said, "I am not aware of any evidence that he may have been a victim of the Cultural Revolution." In conclusion, it is noteworthy that Peking has often used Hong Kong to transmit news. Thus, for example, the "physical death" of the purged Liu Shao-chi, once Mao's successor, was first disclosed November 1, 1974, by a Communist newspaper there, and then denied. Prior to that, for three years, the rumor was

347

that Liu, like P'u Yi, had died of "medical complications," ostensibly cancer. To date, the manner of Liu's death, if he is dead, has not been officially disclosed in Peking, nor is this especially surprising; the Peking press has yet to report man's landing on the moon.

In looking back on P'u Yi's troubled life, the opinions of two Chinese academicians, with different perspectives on contemporary China, provide an overview. "Many men of less resilience or adaptability would certainly have broken down or committed suicide in the monotonous process of periodical metamorphosis, but not he," wrote Jerome Ch'en. "By virtue of his ability to survive them all, he is thus a species by himself, a phenomenon in the incongruity of Twentieth Century politics . . . ." And Kuo Ying Paul Tsai, who remembered his visit with P'u Yi as a child, wrote, "I am in sympathy with him as a man who, like a puppet, was manipulated all his life, from childhood through adulthood to old age." He must have suffered a good deal, Tsai continued, and "I am surprised that he could have lasted till even 60."

A final footnote. At this writing, the struggle for Manchuria and the Manchu is not yet over. On November 8, 1973, the Soviet weekly, *Literaturnaya Gazeta,* charged Peking with forcibly suppressing minority rebellions during the Cultural Revolution and since 1967—significantly, the year P'u Yi died—of practicing genocide among China's minorities, including the Manchu, either through annihilation or assimilation. In a curious commentary the following year, on February 4, 1974, Radio Moscow observed that the Red army had occupied Manchuria in 1945 and turned the region into "a strategic base from which the Chinese [Communists] launched an extensive struggle for national liberation." Therefore, the broadcast said, the Red army should be judged as the "liberators of Dairen and Shenyang [Mukden], of Harbin and Changch'un"— that is, the liberators of Manchuria. Adding to the tension in the present period, a London *Economist* correspondent reported recently that a Soviet source of repute offered him a solution to the current Sino-Soviet dispute. History, the Russian said, showed that buffer states are necessary to keep the peace between great powers.

Luckily, he went on, the material for such new countries lay at hand along the Sino-Soviet border. "You could start off with Manchuria, on the eastern part of the frontier, where two or three million Manchus would be happy to be independent of China," he said. The correspondent of the *Economist* was aghast. "This project was offered neither entirely seriously nor completely as a joke," he wrote. Even allowing for the most devious motives, the fact that a Russian should even mention such an idea to an inquisitive Westerner was the most disturbing sign of the appalling state of Russian-Chinese relations that appeared in the correspondent's whole journey. Such as the case may be, the Chinese did not consider it a joke. On February 2, 1975, the New China News Agency reported that "along with militia men and women of Han [Chinese] nationality, those of Manchu . . . and other minority nationalities in Heilungkiang province are playing an ever more important role in defending and building up the motherland's frontier areas." Heilungkiang or Black Dragon River province abuts on the Amur or Black Dragon River.

With P'u Yi's death, his brother P'u Chieh—William—assumed the reins as titular leader of the Manchu. With the official ending of the Cultural Revolution at the end of 1974, P'u Chieh, now sixty-eight, suddenly surfaced in public. While this author was in the Far East in early 1975, P'u Chieh turned up in Tokyo accompanied by his faithful wife, Hiro. It was his first trip outside China since his release, with P'u Yi, from prision in 1959. The ostensible reason for the visit was a reunion with his second daughter, Mrs. Kosei Fukunaga, and four grandchildren. In Hong Kong, the consensus among professional China-watchers was that P'u Chieh's visit, with a wife distantly related to Hirohito, was part of Peking's renewed drive to woo the sentimental Japanese. Shortly before P'u Chieh's arrival, leftists staged a December 8 rally in Tokyo to campaign for "conclusion of a Japan-China peace and friendship treaty at the earliest possible date," reflecting Peking's mounting alarm over deepening ties between Tokyo and Moscow, China's traditional adversaries.

Quite astonishingly, and coincidentally, P'u Chieh's first wife, Princess Tang Shih-hsia, also bobbed up at this time. In a memoir, "Manchu Princess: Memories of the Forbidden City," published in Hong Kong's *Arts of Asia*, November-December 1974, she recalled P'u Yi as an intelligent young man whose secluded existence in the Great Within, she said, "was abnormal."

Early in 1975, at Hong Kong, I had the opportunity of meeting her. At a breakfast with two companions, Princess Tang talked about P'u Yi, Elizabeth, Reginald Johnston, and the other figures of that bygone era in the *ta nei,* the Great Within. "I read P'u Yi's autobiography," she said. "Some of the things he wrote about did not happen. Other things he wrote about were distorted."

As an example of the latter, she cited the circumstances surrounding his mother's suicide. "Indeed," she said, "his mother committed suicide but not because of a dispute with the then empress dowager. There was something P'u Yi wanted to do. The empress dowager approved. But when P'u Yi's mother heard about it, she protested and the empress dowager reconsidered and reversed her decision. Both mothers, real and 'adopted,' sought to dissuade him from such a thing. But P'u Yi was adamant. I remember the day his mother committed suicide. P'u Yi saw her fingering a ball of medicine. 'What is that for?' he asked. 'Just medicine,' she replied. Actually, it was a ball of opium and she used it to kill herself."

The mother's protest apparently worked because P'u Yi did not carry out his plan. Intrigued, I asked the princess what he had planned to do. Although I pressed her several times, she replied, obviously still horrified herself at the thought of the whole affair, "Even now the real reason she committed suicide cannot be revealed."

"The circumstances in which he was reared would have spoiled any man," she said. "He was surrounded by people who catered to his *every* wish and desire."

Was he sexually abnormal? "I do not know if he was a homosexual," she said laughingly. "I was hardly in a position to know." But, she recalled, at the time of his marriage to Elizabeth the court thought he acted oddly. "He did not select Elizabeth but instead chose the ugliest girl from the collection of photographs [Wen Hsiu]," she said. "We all thought that was very strange." Clearly, the Manchu court did not hold to the view that beauty is in the eye of the beholder

Was Elizabeth a drug addict? "I heard rumors that Wan Jung had turned to drugs, but I for one do not believe it," Princess Tang said, adding, however, "If it happened, it probably occurred during their Manchukuo period."

"As for Reginald Johnston," she continued, "he was an exceedingly intelligent man, a gentleman, a farsighted person." She then confirmed what had long been rumored. "Johnston advised P'u Yi to go to England and P'u Yi wanted to do so, but the advisers around the emperor blocked it."

Looking back on P'u Yi's life and times, she empathized with him. "His whole life was a life of tragedy and trouble. He was genuinely a very intelligent, strong-willed person who was brought up in a thoroughly pampered manner. Yet, I think, he sought to maintain a balance although sometimes he exceeded the bounds of decency. But such behavior was expected of him."

How did he die? "I do not know," she said. "But it was said it was the result of illness. I do not know what kind of illness caused his death. A political illness? I do not know."

"If he had gone to England, as Johnston suggested," she concluded, "many of the things that happened would not have happened."

In any event, P'u Yi is not forgotten. In the course of the campaign against Confucius and Lin Piao, *Ta Kung Pao*, once the most prestigious Chinese-language newspaper, now reduced to replaying the Peking line, on June 30, 1974, dredged up the 1917 restoration of P'u Yi. The paper claimed that the "restoration movement received support from Russian, German, and Japanese imperialists," sought to revive "Confucius and his reactionary ideas," and reverted "openly to armed force to enthrone the deposed P'u Yi."

The restoration's failure, *Ta Kung Pao* held, taught this lesson: "The overthrown reactionaries will never be reconciled to their own defeat and will dream of restoration all the time." Clearly, this implied that P'u Yi had never abandoned the hope of regaining the Forbidden City, not even after his "brainwashing." The paper then went on to vilify Lin Piao and accuse him of trying to "establish a feudal fascist dynasty of the Lin family." Still further, on the eve of what may be another here-today-gone-tomorrow campaign, Mao's supporters on March 1–2, 1975, in an article and Radio Peking broadcasts, quoted a letter Mao wrote in 1966 which held, "In China, since the emperor [P'u Yi] was overthrown in 1911, no reactionary has been able to stay long in power." Once again, thought control techniques and P'u Yi's pawn value in Manchurian strategy notwithstanding, Mao apparently continued to regard P'u Yi as a "reactionary."

And so, clearly, if he had lived, P'u Yi probably would never have escaped those historical forces which continue to swirl around Manchuria, as in his days in the Forbidden City and as a prisoner of the Japanese, Russians, and Chinese.

Index

INDEX